Maths Progress

international 11–14

Contributing editors: Dr Naomi Norman and Katherine Pate

9

Pearson

Published by Pearson Education Limited, 80 Strand, London, WC2R 0RL.

www.pearsonschoolsandfecolleges.co.uk

Text © Pearson Education Limited 2020
Project managed and edited by Just Content Ltd
Typeset by PDQ Digital Media Solutions Ltd
Original illustrations © Pearson Education Limited 2020
Cover illustration by Robert Samuel Hanson

The rights of Nick Asker, Jack Barraclough, Sharon Bolger, Greg Byrd, Lynn Byrd, Andrew Edmondson, Keith Gallick, Sophie Goldie, Catherine Murphy, Su Nicholson, Mary Pardoe, Katherine Pate, Harry Smith and Angela Wheeler to be identified as authors of this work have been asserted by them in accordance with the Copyright, Designs and Patents Act 1988.

First published 2020

24

10

British Library Cataloguing in Publication Data
A catalogue record for this book is available from the British Library.

ISBN 978 1 292 32719 8

Printed in Great Britain by Bell and Bain Ltd, Glasgow

Acknowledgements
The publisher would like to thank the following for their kind permission to reproduce their photographs:

123RF: Alexander Raths 27, david clifton harding 92, Rainer Plendl 95, HONGQI ZHANG 129, 219, Danil Chepko 146, William Perugini 156, roger ashford 174, Nataliya Hora 178, Lisa Young 201; **Alamy Images:** Ian Canham 54, Steppenwolf 98, incamerastock 213; **Getty Images:** IngaNielsen 1, Stocktrek Images 9, RudyBalasko 29, chabybucko 32, SAEED KHAN 58, picturegarden 60, FRANCK FIFE 100, chris-mueller 102, Eyematrix 124, Cottonfioc 172, Lonely Planet 173, 177, 187, 190, 194, Maksymka 176, kavram 198, Getty images276; **Pearson Education:** Gareth Boden 77, Jörg Carstensen 153, Martin Sookias 196; **Science Photo library:** JAMES KING-HOLMES 7, GARY HINCKS 37, BRIAN BELL 149; **Shutterstock:** Geoffrey Robinson 4, imredesiuk 11, KK Tan 25, yuyangc 35, Natalia van D 52, Ververidis Vasilis 56, Bayanova Svetlana 68, Kitch Bain 74, FERNANDO BLANCO CALZADA 80, Zeljko Radojko 105, RyFlip 121, ollirg 127, mikeledray 144, Marcio Jose Bastos Silva 212, Mark Herreid 216, Photographee.eu 222, Boris Rabtsevich 225, konstantinks 245, haveseen 248, Noel Powell 251, CharlotteRaboff 254, Galyna Andrushko 257, 123dartist 271, Parilov 273, ESB Professional 279

All other images © Pearson Education

The publisher would like to thank Diane Oliver for her input and advice.

Note from the publisher
Pearson has robust editorial processes, including answer and fact checks, to ensure the accuracy of the content in this publication, and every effort is made to ensure this publication is free of errors. We are, however, only human, and occasionally errors do occur. Pearson is not liable for any misunderstandings that arise as a result of errors in this publication, but it is our priority to ensure that the content is accurate. If you spot an error, please do contact us at resourcescorrections@pearson.com so we can make sure it is corrected.

Contents

Maths Progress International

Confidence • Fluency • Problem-solving • Progression

Confidence at the heart

Maths Progress International is built around a unique pedagogy that has been created by leading educational researchers and teachers. The result is an innovative learning structure based around 10 key principles designed to nurture confidence and raise achievement.

Pedagogy – our 10 key principles

- Fluency
- Problem-solving
- Reflection
- Mathematical reasoning
- Progression
- Linking
- Multiplicative reasoning
- Modelling
- Concrete - Pictorial - Abstract (CPA)
- Relevance

This edition of Maths Progress has been designed specifically for international students and provides seamless progression into Pearson Edexcel International GCSE Mathematics (9–1), as well as complete coverage of the Pearson Edexcel iLowerSecondary Award and the UK National Curriculum.

Student books

The **Student books** are based on a single well-paced curriculum with built-in differentiation, fluency, problem-solving and reasoning so you can use them with your whole class. They follow the unique unit structure that has been shown to boost confidence and support every student's progress.

Workbooks

The **Workbooks** offer extra practice of key content. They provide additional support via guided questions with partially-worked solutions, hints and QR codes linking to worked example videos. Confidence checkers encourage students to take ownership of their learning, and allow them to track their progress.

Progress with confidence

This innovative 11–14 course builds on the first edition KS3 Maths Progress (2014) course, and is tailored to the needs of international students.

Take a look at the other parts of the series

*Active*Learn Service

The *Active*Learn service enhances the course by bringing together your planning, teaching and assessment tools, as well as giving students access to additional resources to support their learning. Use the interactive Scheme of Work, linked to all the teacher and student resources, to create a personalised learning experience both in and outside the classroom.

What's in *Active*Learn for Maths Progress International?

 Front-of-class Student books with links to PowerPoints, videos and animations

 Over 40 assessments and online markbooks, including end-of-unit, end-of-term and end-of-year tests

 Online, automarked homework activities

 Interactive Scheme of Work makes re-ordering the course easy by bringing everything together into one curriculum for all students with links to resources and teacher guidance

 Lesson plans for every Student book lesson

 Answers to the Student books and Workbooks

 Printable glossaries for each Student book contain all the key terms in one place

 Student access to glossaries, videos, homework and online textbooks

*Active*Learn Progress & Assess

The Progress & Assess service is part of the full *Active*Learn service, or can be bought as a separate subscription. This service includes:

* assessments that have been designed to ensure that all students have the opportunity to show what they have learned
* editable tests that mimic the style of Pearson Edexcel International GCSE exams
* online markbooks for tracking and reporting
* baseline assessments for Year 7 and both tiers of International GCSE.

Welcome to Maths Progress International
Student books

Starting a new course is exciting! We believe you will have fun with maths, while at the same time nurturing yo confidence and raising your achievement. Here's how.

Learn fundamental knowledge and skills over a series of *Master* lessons.

Some questions are tagged as *Finance* or *STEM*. These questions show how the real world relies on maths.

Literacy hints (explain unfamiliar terms) and *Strategy hints* (help with working out).

You can improve your ability to use maths in everyday situations by tackling *Modelling*, *Reasoning*, *Problem-solving*, and *Real* questions. *Discussions* prompt you to explain your reasoning or explore new ideas with a partner.

Clear objectives show what you will cover in each lesson.

Why learn this? shows you how maths is useful in everyday life.

Improve your *Fluency* – practise answering questions using maths you already know.

The first questions are *Warm up*. Here you can show what you already know about this topic or related ones...

...before moving on to further questions, with *Worked examples* and *Hints* for help when you need it.

Key points explain key concepts and definitions where you need them.

Your teacher has online access to *Answers*.

A printable *Glossary* containing all the key mathematical terms is available online.

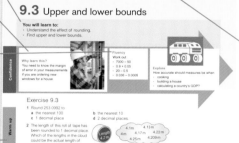

Topic links and *Subject links* show you how the maths in a lesson is connected to other mathematical topics and other subjects.

Explore a real-life problem by discussing and having a go. By the end of the lesson you'll have gained the skills you need to start finding a solution to the question using maths.

At the end of each lesson, you get a chance to *Reflect* on how confident you feel about the topic.

At the end of the Master lessons, take a **Check up** test to help you decide whether to Strengthen or Extend your learning. You may be able to mark this test yourself.

Choose only the topics in **Strengthen** that you need a bit more practice with. You'll find more hints here to lead you through specific questions. Then move on to *Extend*.

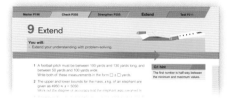

Extend helps you to apply the maths you know to some different situations. Strengthen and Extend both include Enrichment or Investigations.

When you have finished the whole unit, a **Unit test** helps you to see how much progress you are making.

STEM lessons

These lessons focus on STEM maths. STEM stands for Science, Technology, Engineering and Maths. You can find out how charities use maths in their fundraising, how engineers monitor water flow in rivers, and why diamonds sparkle (among other things!).

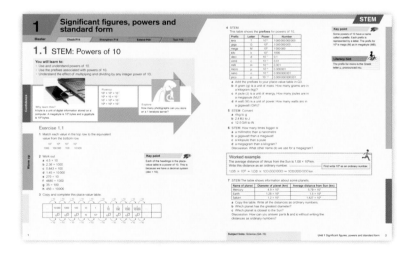

Further support

You can easily access extra resources that tie into each lesson by logging into *Active*Learn. Here you will find online homework clearly mapped to the units, providing fun, interactive exercises linked to helpful worked examples and videos.

The workbooks, full of extra practice of key questions, will help you to reinforce your learning and track your own progress.

1.1 STEM: Powers of 10

You will learn to:
- Use and understand powers of 10.
- Use the prefixes associated with powers of 10.
- Understand the effect of multiplying and dividing by any integer power of 10.

Confidence

Why learn this?
A byte is a unit of digital information stored on a computer. A megabyte is 10^6 bytes and a gigabyte is 10^9 bytes.

Fluency
$10^2 \times 10^3 = 10^{\square}$
$10^4 \times 10 = 10^{\square}$
$10^7 \div 10^5 = 10^{\square}$
$10^8 \div 10^2 = 10^{\square}$

Explore
How many photographs can you store on a 1 terabyte server?

Exercise 1.1

1 Match each value in the top row to the equivalent value from the bottom row.

$10^2 \quad 10^4 \quad 10^3 \quad 10^5$
$1000 \quad 100\,000 \quad 100 \quad 10\,000$

Warm up

2 Work out
a 4.5×10
b 2.36×1000
c 0.843×100
d $1.45 \times 10\,000$
e $270 \div 10$
f $4685 \div 1000$
g $35 \div 100$
h $450 \div 10\,000$

Key point

Each of the headings in the place-value table is a power of 10. This is because we have a *dec*imal system (*dec* = 10).

3 Copy and complete this place-value table.

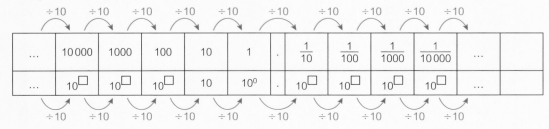

	$\div 10$	$\div 10$	$\div 10$	$\div 10$	$\div 10$	$\div 10$	$\div 10$	$\div 10$	$\div 10$	$\div 10$	
...	10 000	1000	100	10	1	.	$\frac{1}{10}$	$\frac{1}{100}$	$\frac{1}{1000}$	$\frac{1}{10\,000}$	...
...	$10^{\square}$	$10^{\square}$	$10^{\square}$	10	10^0	.	$10^{\square}$	$10^{\square}$	$10^{\square}$	$10^{\square}$	...

$\div 10 \quad \div 10 \quad \div 10 \quad \div 10 \quad \div 10 \quad \div 10 \quad \div 10 \quad \div 10 \quad \div 10 \quad \div 10$

4 STEM

This table shows the **prefixes** for powers of 10.

Prefix	Letter	Power	Number
tera	T	10^{12}	1 000 000 000 000
giga	G	10^{9}	1 000 000 000
mega	M	10^{6}	1 000 000
kilo	k	10^{3}	1000
deci	d	10^{-1}	0.1
centi	c	10^{-2}	0.01
milli	m	10^{-3}	0.001
micro	μ	10^{-6}	0.000 001
nano	n	10^{-9}	0.000 000 001
pico	p	10^{-12}	0.000 000 000 001

  a Add the prefixes to your place-value table in Q3.

  b A gram (g) is a unit of mass. How many grams are in a kilogram (kg)?

  c A joule (J) is a unit of energy. How many joules are in a megajoule (MJ)?

  d A watt (W) is a unit of power. How many watts are in a gigawatt (GW)?

5 STEM Convert

  a 4 kg to g

  b 2.4 MJ to J

  c 12.5 GW to W.

6 STEM How many times bigger is

  a a millimetre than a nanometre

  b a gigawatt than a megawatt

  c a kilojoule than a joule

  d a megagram than a kilogram?

  Discussion What other name do we use for a megagram?

> ### Key point
>
> Some powers of 10 have a name called a **prefix**. Each prefix is represented by a letter. The prefix for 10^{6} is mega (M) as in megabyte (MB).

> ### Literacy hint
>
> The prefix for micro is the Greek letter μ, pronounced mu.

Worked example

The average distance of Venus from the Sun is 1.08×10^{8} km.

Write this distance as an ordinary number. ——— First write 10^{8} as an ordinary number.

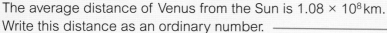

$1.08 \times 10^{8} = 1.08 \times 100\,000\,000 = 108\,000\,000$ km

7 STEM The table shows information about some planets.

Name of planet	Diameter of planet (km)	Average distance from Sun (km)
Mercury	4.9×10^{3}	5.79×10^{7}
Earth	1.28×10^{4}	1.5×10^{8}
Saturn	1.2×10^{5}	1.427×10^{9}

  a Copy the table. Write all the distances as ordinary numbers.

  b Which planet has the greatest diameter?

  c Which planet is closest to the Sun?

  Discussion How can you answer parts **b** and **c** without writing the distances as ordinary numbers?

8 STEM / Problem-solving The Space Shuttle had a lift-off mass of 1.1×10^5 kg. How many tonnes is this?

9 STEM The table shows the dimensions of some small organisms.

Name of organism	Length	Width
dust mite	0.42 millimetres	0.25 millimetres
bacteria	2 micrometres	0.5 micrometres
virus	0.3 micrometres	15 nanometres

a Write all the **dimensions** in metres.

b Which organism has the greatest length?

c Which organism has the smallest width?

Discussion How can you answer parts **b** and **c** without writing the dimensions as ordinary numbers?

10 STEM / Reasoning An atom is the smallest object that you can see with an electron microscope. The width of an atom is about 0.1 nanometres.

What is this distance in millimetres?

11 Explore How many photographs can you store on a 1 terabyte server?

What have you learned in this lesson to help you to answer this question?

What other information do you need?

12 Reflect After this lesson Jaina says, 'I understood this lesson well because it's all about place value.' Look back at the work you have done in this lesson.

How has place value helped you?

What other maths skills have you used in this lesson?

Q8 hint

1 tonne = 1000 kg

Q9 Literacy hint

The **dimensions** of an object are its measurements.

1.2 Calculating and estimating

You will learn to:
- Calculate with powers.
- Round to a number of significant figures.

Why learn this?
The organisers of sporting events often round the number of spectators to estimate the income from ticket sales.

Fluency
What is
2^3
2^4
2^5
2^6?

Explore
When is it a good idea to round numbers? When is it not a good idea?

Exercise 1.2

1 Simplify
  a $5^2 \times 5^4$
  b $\dfrac{8^5}{8^3}$
  c $\dfrac{7^4 \times 7^6}{7^7}$

2 Work out
  a -4×-4
  b -7×-7
  c $(-3)^2$
  d $(-10)^2$

3 Use rounding to estimate the answers.
  a $97 \div 4$
  b 12.3×10.2
  c $18.6 \div 5$

4 Evaluate $\dfrac{2 \times 3^9}{3^7}$

$$\dfrac{2 \times 3^9}{3^7} = 2 \times 3^{\square}$$
$$= 2 \times \square$$
$$= \square$$

5 Work out
  a $\dfrac{5 \times 2^{12}}{2^9}$
  b $\dfrac{3^2 \times 4^4}{4^3}$
  c $\dfrac{2 \times 5^3 \times 5^5}{5^4}$
  d $\dfrac{6^{15} \times 10}{6^7 \times 6^6}$

6 Problem-solving Work out $\dfrac{2^8 \times 16 \times 32 \times 7}{8 \times 2^{10}}$

7 Reasoning Sarka and Rashid both work out the same calculation. Here is what they write.

Sarka
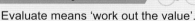
$32 - (-5)^2 = 32 - -25$
$= 32 + 25$
$= 57$

Rashid
$32 - (-5)^2 = 32 - +25$
$= 32 - 25$
$= 7$

Who is correct? Explain the mistake that the other one has made.

Key point
You can simplify expressions containing powers to make calculations easier.

Q4 Literacy hint
Evaluate means 'work out the value'.

Q4 hint
Simplify the powers of 3, $\dfrac{3^9}{3^7} = 3^{\square}$, then multiply by 2.

Q6 Strategy hint

Write as many numbers as possible as powers of 2.

Warm up

8 Sort these cards into matching pairs.

$14 + 4^2$ $14 - 4^2$ $14 + (-4)^2$ $14 - (-4)^2$

$25 - 2^2 - 6^2$ $25 - (-2)^2 + 6^2$ $25 - 2^2 + (-6)^2$ $25 - 2^2 - (-6)^2$

Discussion What method did you use?

1 a Work out   **i** $(2 \times 5)^2$ **ii** $2^2 \times 5^2$
   b Work out   **i** $(2 \times 5)^3$ **ii** $2^3 \times 5^3$
2 What do you notice about your answers to Q1?
3 a Write a rule for calculating the power of the product of two numbers.
      Check that this rule works using two numbers of your own.
   b Will this same rule work for three or more numbers?
4 a Work out   **i** $(10 \div 2)^2$ **ii** $10^2 \div 2^2$
   b What do you notice about your answers to part **a**?
5 Write a rule for calculating the power of the quotient of two numbers.
   Check this rule works using two numbers of your own.
6 a Work out   **i** $(3 + 4)^2$ **ii** $3^2 + 4^2$
   b What do you notice about your answers to part **a**?
Discussion Is there a rule for calculating the power of the sum or difference of two numbers?

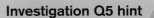

Investigation Q5 hint

Make sure that the second number divides exactly into the first, and that the power is greater than 2.

9 Work out

   a $\dfrac{(3 \times 4)^2}{2^2 \times 3}$

   b $\dfrac{(3 \times 4)^3}{2^2 \times 9}$

   c $\dfrac{3^2 \times 5^3}{(5 \times 4)^2}$

   d $\dfrac{(6 \times 2 \times 8)^2}{4^3 \times 3}$

Q9 hint

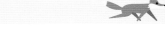

$$\frac{(3 \times 4)^2}{2^2 \times 3} = \frac{3^2 \times 4^2}{2^2 \times 3} = \frac{3 \times \cancel{3} \times \cancel{4}^2 \times \cancel{4}^2}{\cancel{2}^1 \times \cancel{2}^1 \times \cancel{3}^1} = \ldots$$

Worked example

Round these numbers to the given number of **significant figures**.

a 42.038 (4 s.f.)
b 0.05713 (3 s.f.)
c 21561 (2 s.f.)

> When the next digit is 5 or above, round the previous digit up. Here the fifth significant figure is an 8, so round the 3 up to a 4.

a 42.04

> The fourth significant figure is 3, so leave the third digit as 1.

b 0.0571

c 22000

> 2 and 1 are the first 2 significant figures. The third is 5, so round the 1 up to 2.

Key point

You can round numbers to a given number of **significant figures (s.f.)**. The first significant figure is the one with the highest place value. It is the first non-zero digit in the number, counting from the left.

10 Round these numbers to the given number of significant figures.
   a 47.368 (4 s.f.)
   b 0.00662 (1 s.f.)
   c 579452 (2 s.f.)

Topic links: Negative numbers, Volume, Range, Order of operations

Subject links: Science (Q15)

11 Estimate the answer to each calculation by rounding each number to 1 significant figure.

   a 37×492

   b 6230×26

   c $897 \div 28$

   d $45\,239 \div 183$

Q11a hint

$37 \times 492 \approx 40 \times 500 = \square$

Q11 Literacy hint

$\approx$ means approximately equal to.

Q12a hint

$\dfrac{(1.2 + 3.5)^2}{1.8^3} \approx \dfrac{5^2}{8}$

What number is a multiple of 8 and close to 5^2? Use this to estimate the final answer.

12 Estimate the answer to each calculation by rounding each number to 1 significant figure.

   a $\dfrac{(1.2 + 3.5)^2}{1.8^3}$

   b $\dfrac{(27 - 14)^3}{7.3^2}$

   c $\dfrac{(3.3^2 \times 2)}{(2.3 + 4.2)^2}$

   d $\dfrac{(786 - 529)^2}{7.4^2}$

13 The diagram shows a cuboid.

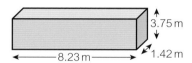

   3.75 m   8.23 m   1.42 m

   Work out the volume of the cuboid.

   Give your answer in m³ correct to 3 significant figures.

14 **Problem-solving** Sarita starts with a whole number.

   She rounds it to 2 significant figures.

   Her answer is 670.

   a Write down two different numbers she could have started with.

   b What is the largest number she could have started with?

   c What is the smallest number she could have started with?

15 **STEM** The table shows the diameters of five planets.

Planet	Mercury	Venus	Earth	Mars	Uranus
Diameter (km)	4878	12 104	12 756	6794	51 118

   a Round each diameter correct to 1 significant figure.

   b Work out an estimate of the range in diameters.

16 **Real** A football stadium seats 42 785.

   The average price of a ticket is £32.

   Estimate the total money taken from ticket sales for one match.

17 **Explore** When is it a good idea to round numbers?

   When is it not a good idea?

   Look back at the maths you have learned in this lesson.

   How can you use it to answer this question?

18 **Reflect** Look back at Q12.

   Use a calculator to work out the exact answer to each part.

   How can your estimate help you to check your calculator answer?

Explore

Reflect

1.3 Indices

You will learn to:
- Use negative indices.
- Work out powers of fractions.

Why learn this?
Carbon dating uses negative indices to describe the decay of carbon-14.

Confidence

Fluency
- Work out $3^3 - 4^2$
- Which is larger: $\frac{1}{2} \times \frac{1}{2}$ or $\frac{1}{3} \times \frac{1}{3}$?
- Work out -15×-3

Explore
Does raising a number to a power always make the number bigger?

Exercise 1.3

Warm up

1 Write as a single power.
  a $3^4 \times 3^5$
  b $7^9 \div 7^5$
  c $4^{13} \div 4^{10}$
  d $(2^4)^3$
  e $(11^7)^3$
  f $(5^5)^5$
  g 8×2^6
  h $3^5 \times 81$
  i $5^{10} \div 125$

Q1 hint

To multiply powers, add the indices.
To divide powers, subtract the indices.
To work out the power of a power, multiply the indices.

Investigation

Reasoning

1 Copy and complete the sequence of powers. Write your numbers as integers or fractions of 10.
2 Repeat part **1** for powers of 2.
3 Copy and complete.

  a $10^{-2} = \dfrac{1}{10^\square}$
  b $2^{-3} = \dfrac{1}{2^\square}$

  c $2^{-5} = \dfrac{1}{2^\square}$
  d The reciprocal of 10^4 is $\square$

4 Copy and complete the rules.

  $2^{-n} = \dfrac{1}{2^\square}$

  $10^{-n} = \dfrac{1}{10^\square}$

5 Write down the value of 5^{-2} as a decimal. Check your answer with a calculator.
Discussion What is the value of any number raised to the power 0?

$$10^5 = 100\,000$$
$$10^4 = 10\,000 \;\Big\}\,\div 10$$
$$10^3 =$$
$$10^2 =$$
$$10^1 =$$
$$10^0 =$$
$$10^{-1} =$$
$$10^{-2} =$$
$$10^{-3} =$$
$$10^{-4} =$$
$$10^{-5} =$$

2 Copy and complete.
  a $3^{-2} = \square$
  b $\dfrac{1}{3} = 3^\square$

  c $6^\square = \dfrac{1}{36}$
  d $\square^{-2} = \dfrac{1}{169}$

  e $4^{-3} = \square$
  f $\dfrac{1}{81} = 3^\square = 9^\square$

  g $\dfrac{1}{64} = 8^\square = 4^\square = 2^\square$
  h $5^{-1} = \square$

Key point

A number raised to a negative power is the same as the reciprocal of that number to the power.

Topic links: Calculations with fractions, Laws of indices

3 Write each calculation as a single power.

   a $10^5 \times 10^{-2}$ **b** $4^3 \times 4^{-1}$

   c $11^{-2} \times 11^{-5}$ **d** $7^2 \div 7^{-5}$

   e $6^{-2} \div 6^4$ **f** $8^{-7} \div 8^{-3}$

   g $(9^{-2})^5$ **h** $(12^{-4})^{-2}$

Q3 hint

The laws of indices still apply with negative numbers.

4 Write each calculation as
   i a single power
   ii an integer or a fraction.

   a $3^2 \times 3^{-1} \times 3^{-4}$ **b** $4^2 \times 4^{-1} \div 4^{-2}$

   c $5^{-3} \div 5 \div 5^{-2}$ **d** $\dfrac{2^{-3} \times 2^{-5}}{2^{-4}}$

5 Write each calculation as a fraction.

   a $\dfrac{1}{3} \times \dfrac{1}{3}$ **b** $\left(\dfrac{3}{4}\right)^2$

   c $\left(\dfrac{3}{5}\right)^3$ **d** $\left(\dfrac{2}{3}\right)^4$

Q5 hint

The brackets show that the whole fraction (the numerator and denominator) is squared.

6 Write each number as a fraction raised to a power.

   a $\dfrac{16}{100}$ **b** $\dfrac{9}{49}$

   c $\dfrac{25}{64}$ **d** $\dfrac{8}{64}$

   e $\dfrac{16}{625}$ **f** $\dfrac{1}{27}$

7 Problem-solving Jamal eats half a cheesecake, his brother eats half of what is left and his sister eats half of what is then left. How much cheesecake remains?

Write your answer
   a as a fraction
   b as a fraction raised to a power.

8 Explore Does raising a number to a power always make the number bigger?

Choose some sensible numbers to help you explore this situation.
Then use what you've learned in this lesson to help you to answer the question.

9 Reflect Rhiannon says, 'Mathematics is often about spotting patterns'. Do you agree? Explain.
When else have you used pattern spotting in maths?

Q9 hint

Look back at this lesson and the previous lesson. Can you find any questions where you were spotting a pattern?

Explore

Reflect

1.4 Standard form

Confidence

You will learn to:
- Write numbers using standard form.
- Order numbers written in standard form.

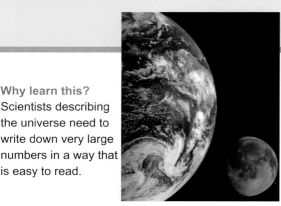

Why learn this?
Scientists describing the universe need to write down very large numbers in a way that is easy to read.

Fluency
Multiply 3.05 by
- 10
- 1000
- 0.1

Work out $10^3 × 0.15$

Explore
What units are used to measure distances in the Universe?

Warm up

Exercise 1.4

1 Work out

  a $2.5 × 100$ **b** $7.3 × 0.01$

  c $4.06 × 10^{-1}$ **d** $9.55 × 10^{-3}$

2 Copy and complete.

  a $23.4 × 10^3 = \square$ **b** $2.35 × 10^{\square} = 235$

  c $34 × 10^{\square} = 34\,000$ **d** $0.067 × 10^2 = \square$

3 Which of these numbers are written in **standard form**?

  a $2.8 × 10^3$ **b** $7 × 10^5$

  c $0.2 × 10^2$ **d** $27 × 10^{-5}$

  e $3.3 × 10$ **f** $5.022 × 10^{-6}$

4 These numbers are written in standard form.
Write them as ordinary numbers.

  a $7 × 10^2$ **b** $2.5 × 10^{-5}$

  c $5.4 × 10^6$ **d** $3.04 × 10^{-3}$

Key point

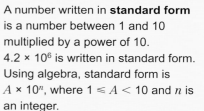

A number written in **standard form** is a number between 1 and 10 multiplied by a power of 10.
$4.2 × 10^6$ is written in standard form.
Using algebra, standard form is $A × 10^n$, where $1 \leqslant A < 10$ and n is an integer.

Q4 hint

$7 × 10^2 = 7 × 100 = \square$

Worked example

Write each number using standard form.

a $41\,000$

b $0.003\,94$

$41\,000 = 4.1 × 10^4$

$0.003\,94 = 3.94 × 10^{-3}$

> 4.1 lies between 1 and 10. Multiply by the power of 10 needed to give the original number: $4.\overset{\frown}{1000}$

> 3.94 lies between 1 and 10.
> Multiply by the power of 10 needed to give the original number.
> The number is less than 1 so the power of 10 is negative.
> This is the same as dividing by a power of 10: $0.\overset{\frown}{003}94$

Topic links: Powers, Laws of indices, Priority of operations   **Subject links:** Science (Explore, Q6, Q8–10)

5 Write each number in standard form.

   a 23500   **b** 315   **c** 12000000

   d 0.04   **e** 0.00035   **f** 0.0000000901

Q5 Literacy hint

Standard form is sometimes called **standard index form**.

6 **STEM** The distance light travels in a year is called a light-year.

   a Write each of the distances in the table in standard form.

Object	Distance from Earth (light-years)
Centre of our galaxy	26000
Andromeda (a neighbouring galaxy)	2500000
Betelgeuse (a star of Orion)	600

   b The Triangulum Galaxy is the furthest galaxy you can see without a telescope.
      It is 3×10^6 light-years away. Is it closer to Earth than Betelgeuse?

7 Put these sets of numbers in order, from smallest to largest.

   a 9.87×10^2 8.65×10^4 1.9×10^3 3.59×10^2 1.95×10^4

   b 5.3×10^{-3} 4.8×10^{-2} 3.99×10^{-5} 8.05×10^{-6} 8.76×10^{-3}

   c 3.22×10^{-2} 3.02×10^2 3.2×10^{-3} 3.22×10^2 3.22×10^{-3}

Q7 hint

Write each number in full to help you to order them.

8 **STEM / Problem-solving** The table shows the masses of the planets in our Solar System.

   a Rewrite each mass in standard form (some already are).

Planet	Mass (kg)
Earth	5.97×10^{24} kg
Jupiter	1899×10^{24} kg
Mars	0.642×10^{24} kg
Mercury	0.33×10^{24} kg
Neptune	102×10^{24} kg
Saturn	568.5×10^{24} kg
Uranus	86.8×10^{24} kg
Venus	4.87×10^{24} kg

   b Approximately how many times heavier is Earth than Mars?

   c Which planet is approximately 1000 times heavier than Mars?

9 **STEM** Write these atoms in order of the size of their nucleus, largest first.

Atom	Size of nucleus (m)
gold	1.4×10^{-14}
helium	3.8×10^{-15}
aluminum	7.2×10^{-15}

10 **STEM** Write the following measurements as ordinary numbers

      i in metres   **ii** in millimetres.

   a The diameter of the core in an optical fibre: 6.25×10^{-5} m

   b The line width on a microprocessor: 1.8×10^{-7} m

Q10 hint

There are 1000 mm in 1 metre, so multiply by $10^{\square}$.

11 **Explore** What units are used to measure distances in the Universe?
     Is it easier to explore this question now that you have completed the lesson?
     What further information do you need to be able to answer this?

12 **Reflect** Look back at your answer to Q7. You could answer this using ordinary numbers or standard form. Which method did you choose? Explain your choice.

Explore

Reflect

1.5 STEM: Calculating with standard form

You will learn to:
- Calculate with numbers written in standard form.

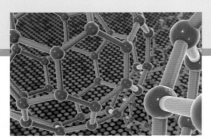

Why learn this?
Scientists exploring nanotechnology need to describe very small numbers in a way that is easy to read.

Fluency
Write as a single power of 10
- $10^4 \times 10^3$
- 10×10^{-5}
- $(10^2)^{-3}$
- $10^2 \times 10^3 \times 10^3$

Explore
What is the smallest organism you can see?

Exercise 1.5: Orders of magnitude

1 Write each number in standard form.
  a 59 000
  b 0.0601
  c 0.000 000 072
  d 5323

2 Write as a single power of 10
  a $10^{-3} \times 10^2$
  b $10^{-3} \times 10^{-2}$
  c $10^3 \div 10^{-1}$
  d $10^{-1} \div 10^2$

Worked example

Write $(2.7 \times 10^3) \times (4 \times 10^2)$ in standard form.

$(2.7 \times 10^3) \times (4 \times 10^2) = 2.7 \times 4 \times 10^3 \times 10^2$ — Rearrange so that the numbers are together and the powers of 10 are together.

$= 10.8 \times 10^5$ — Calculate the product of the numbers and use laws of indices to simplify the powers of 10.

$= 1.08 \times 10 \times 10^5$

$= 1.08 \times 10^6$ — Rewrite the answer in standard form, if necessary: $10.8 = 1.08 \times 10^1$

3 Work out each calculation. Give your answers in standard form.
  a $(1.2 \times 10^2) \times (3 \times 10^3)$
  b $(1.5 \times 10^5) \times (5 \times 10^3)$
  c $(4 \times 10^4) \times (6.25 \times 10)$
  d $(1.2 \times 10^3)^2$

4 Work out each calculation. Give your answers in standard form.
  a $\dfrac{6 \times 10^8}{3 \times 10^2}$
  b $\dfrac{8 \times 10^5}{2 \times 10^3}$
  c $\dfrac{1.2 \times 10^6}{3 \times 10}$
  d $\dfrac{2 \times 10^5}{1.25 \times 10^4}$

Q4 hint

Divide the number parts. Use the laws of indices to divide the powers of 10.

Topic links: Ratio, Enlargement

Subject links: Science (Q6–15, Q18)

5 Use a calculator to work out

a $(9.6 \times 10^7) \times (6.41 \times 10^3)$ **b** $\dfrac{1.342 \times 10^{11}}{6.1 \times 10^5}$

Discussion Which buttons do you use on your calculator? Is the answer in standard form?

 6 STEM Light travels at 299 792 458 metres per second (m/s).

a Write down the speed of light in km/s, correct to 1 significant figure

   i as an ordinary number   **ii** using standard form.

The distance from the Sun to the Earth is 1.496×10^8 km.

b Use your answer to part **a** to work out how long it takes light to travel from the Sun to the Earth. Give your answer to the nearest minute.

 7 STEM / Problem-solving Sound travels at 3.4×10^2 m/s.

What is the ratio of the speed of light to the speed of sound?

Give your answer in the form $n : 1$, to 2 decimal places.

Q7 hint

Use the speed of light given in Q6.

8 STEM / Reasoning A human hair has a diameter of approximately 1×10^{-1} mm. The human eye cannot easily see anything smaller than a human hair without a microscope.

An optical microscope can enlarge an image to 1000 times the size of the object. Is it possible to see these organisms with a microscope?

a polio virus 2×10^{-5} mm

b human red blood cell 1×10^{-2} mm

c staphylococcus 5×10^{-4} mm

Q8c Literacy hint

Staphylococcus is a bacteria that causes food poisoning.

 9 STEM / Modelling The table gives the sizes of eggs from different animals.

Object	Approximate diameter (m)
Extinct elephant bird	2.5×10^{-1}
Ostrich	1.5×10^{-1}
Hummingbird	1×10^{-2}
Sea star	9×10^{-4}
Human	1.2×10^{-4}

A model of an ostrich egg is built for an exhibition. Its diameter is 10 m. The same scale is used to build models of the other objects.

a Work out the length of each model. Choose an appropriate unit of length for each answer.

b Is this a good scale to use? Would you be able to hold each model in your hand?

10 STEM A 3D electron microscope magnifies objects 1 000 000 times. A water molecule has a diameter of 2×10^{-10} m.

How large will it appear in the microscope?

Give your answer in millimetres.

 11 STEM Graphite is made up of layers of graphene sheets. Each sheet of graphene is one atom thick. There are 3×10^6 layers of graphene in 1 mm thickness of graphite. If you ignore the thickness of the layers, what is the gap between the layers? Give your answer in standard form.

Q11 hint

Layers of graphene are so thin, about 1.4×10^{-10} m thick, that they can be ignored in this calculation.

12 STEM Here are some wavelengths in the electromagnetic spectrum.

Gamma ray 1×10^{-12} m
Red light 6.8×10^{-7} m
Microwave 1.22×10^{-1} m
VHF radio wave   3 m
Low frequency radio wave   10 km

   a How many gamma ray wavelengths fit into the length of one red light wave?

   b How many times larger are low frequency radio waves than microwaves?

   c Which is longer: 10^2 VHF radio waves or 3×10^{10} red light rays?

13 STEM / Problem-solving The mass of a proton is about 2000 times larger than the mass of an electron.
Copy and complete this sentence, using standard form.
The mass of an electron = the mass of a proton $\times \square \times 10^{\square}$

14 Real / STEM Sunglasses are coated with very thin layers to cut out ultraviolet radiation. These layers are about 4×10^2 nm thick. Give the thickness in metres.

15 Real Your fingernail grows about 1 nm per second. How much could your fingernail grow in 4 weeks? Give your answer in millimetres.

16 Work out each calculation. Give your answers in standard form.

   a $5.1 \times 10^8 + 1.45 \times 10^8$ **b** $9.05 \times 10^5 + 7.8 \times 10^5$
   c $6.75 \times 10^{-4} + 4.25 \times 10^{-4}$ **d** $3.9 \times 10^7 + 4.2 \times 10^6$
   e $5.6 \times 10^{-4} + 2.07 \times 10^{-3}$

17 Work out

   a $9.6 \times 10^{-7} - 6.3 \times 10^{-7}$ **b** $8.88 \times 10^4 - 8.37 \times 10^4$
   c $5.33 \times 10^6 - 2.8 \times 10^5$ **d** $7.02 \times 10^{-3} - 6.1 \times 10^{-4}$

18 STEM The wavelengths in the visible light spectrum extend from 3.8×10^{-7} m to 7.5×10^{-7} m.
What is the range of wavelengths in the visible light spectrum?

19 Explore What is the smallest organism you can see?
Is it easier to explore this question now that you have completed the lesson?
What further information do you need to be able to answer this?

20 Reflect The title of this lesson is 'Orders of magnitude'. Why do you think scientists find it useful to know about orders of magnitude?

Literacy hint

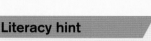

1 nm = 1 nanometre = 10^{-9} m

Q16d hint

Both numbers need to have the same power of 10 before you add them.
$4.2 \times 10^6 = \square \times 10^7$

Explore

Reflect

1 Check up

Powers of 10

1 a Copy and complete this table of prefixes.

Prefix	Power of 10	Number
giga	$10^{\square}$	
mega	$10^{\square}$	
kilo	$10^{\square}$	1000
deci	$10^{\square}$	
centi	$10^{\square}$	
milli	$10^{\square}$	0.001
micro	$10^{\square}$	

b Match the cards that show the same value.

50 000 milligrams

5000 kilograms

5 grams

5 megagrams

500 decigrams

0.005 kilograms

2 Write these numbers in order of size, starting with the smallest.

4.6×10^4 $8.9 \div 10^5$ 2.1×10^5 $2.4 \div 10^7$

Calculating and estimating

3 Use rounding to estimate the answers to
  a 13.3×12.8
  b $24.8 \div 5.2$

4 Evaluate
  a $\dfrac{3^3 \times 5}{2}$
  b $\dfrac{4^2 \times 3}{2^3}$

5 Work out the area of this triangle.
Give your answer in m² correct to 3 significant figures.

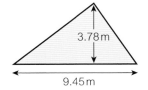

3.78 m

9.45 m

Indices

6 Write each of these numbers as a fraction.
  a 5^{-3}
  b 6^{-1}
  c 2^{-4}

7 Write as a single power.
   a $10^3 \times 10^{-4}$
   b $3^{-2} \div 3$
   c $(3^{-2})^3$
   d $7^{-5} \div 7^{-2}$

Standard form

8 Write each number in standard form.
   a 345
   c 34.5×10^3
   d 0.005×10^6

9 Write 0.007 231 in standard form.

10 Write these numbers in order, from smallest to largest.

   3.1×10^{-2} 3.2×10^{-3} 3.22×10^3 3.022×10^4 3.2×10^{-5}

Calculating with standard form

11 Work out each calculation. Give your answers in standard form.
   a $(4.1 \times 10^{-6}) \times (2 \times 10^3)$

   b $\dfrac{6 \times 10^3}{1.5 \times 10^2}$

12 Work out each calculation. Give your answers
   i in standard form
   ii as ordinary numbers.

   a $\dfrac{23.31 \times 10^5}{3.7 \times 10^7}$

   b $(7.09 \times 10^2) \times (6.3 \times 10^3)$

13 The mass of iron in planet Earth is 2.090×10^{24} kg.
   Given that the Earth has a mass of 5.972×10^{24} kg, find the
   percentage of the Earth's mass that is iron.

14 How sure are you of your answers? Were you mostly
   ☹ **Just guessing**   😐 **Feeling doubtful**   ☺ **Confident**
   **What next? Use your results to decide whether to strengthen or
   extend your learning.**

Challenge

15 $a = 2.3 \times 10^6$ and $b = 2.3 \times 10^{-3}$
   Calculate
   a a^2 **b** b^3

   c a^3b^4 **d** $\dfrac{a}{b^6}$

   Give your answers in standard form.

1 Strengthen

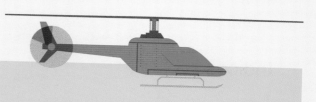

You will:
- Strengthen your understanding with practice.

Powers of 10

1 Copy and complete
  a kilo (k) = 10^3 = 1000
  b mega (M) = 10^6 = ☐
  c giga (G) = 10^9 = ☐

> **Key point**
>
>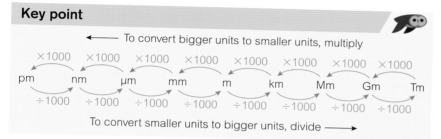
>
> ← To convert bigger units to smaller units, multiply
>
> ×1000　×1000　×1000　×1000　×1000　×1000　×1000　×1000
>
> pm　　nm　　μm　　mm　　m　　km　　Mm　　Gm　　Tm
>
> ÷1000　÷1000　÷1000　÷1000　÷1000　÷1000　÷1000　÷1000
>
> To convert smaller units to bigger units, divide ⟶

> **Literacy hint**
>
> To write an abbreviation, put the letter for the prefix before the letter for the measure. So pm means picometre, nm means nanometre and so on.

2 Convert
  a 6.5 Tm to km
  b 0.014 m to nm
  c 50 000 nm to mm
  d 2200 km to Mm
  e 0.000 000 6 Gm to mm

> **Q2a hint**
>
> 6.5 × 1000 × 1000 × 1000 = ☐

3 Convert
  a 5 kilojoules (kJ) to joules (J)
  b 0.021 megawatts (MW) to watts (W)
  c 270 000 *l* to m*l*
  d 720 μg to mg

4 STEM
  a Safia's computer processor has a speed of 6.1 megahertz (MHz). What is its speed in kilohertz (kHz)?
  b The wavelength of a red light is 690 nm. Convert this length to μm.

Calculating and estimating

1 Copy these numbers. Circle the first significant figure. Write down its value.
  a 32.45　　　**b** 0.64　　　**c** 25 800　　　**d** 0.0782

2 Write the numbers in Q1 to 1 significant figure.

3 Round these numbers to the given number of significant figures.
  a 53 876 (2 s.f.)　　　**b** 0.735 (2 s.f.)
  c 56.554 (3 s.f.)　　　**d** 0.002 410 6 (3 s.f.)

> **Q2a hint**
>
> Circle the first significant figure. It's in the 10s column, so round to the nearest 10.

> **Q3a hint**
>
> Circle the second significant figure. What place-value column is it in?

4 Round each number in these calculations to 1 significant figure. Then estimate the answer to each calculation.

    a 44×273 **b** 67×534 **c** $421 \div 18$ **d** $(585 \div 33)^2$

Q4a hint

$\textcircled{4}4 \rightarrow 40, \textcircled{2}73 \rightarrow 300, 40 \times 300 = \square$

Indices

1 a i $3^2 \div 3^5 = 3^\square$

   ii $3^2 \div 3^5 = \dfrac{\cancel{3} \times \cancel{3}}{\cancel{3} \times \cancel{3} \times 3 \times 3 \times 3} = \dfrac{\square}{\square}$

   iii Use your answers to copy and complete: $3^{-3} = \dfrac{1}{3^\square}$

  b Copy and complete.

    i $7^{-2} = \dfrac{1}{7^\square}$ **ii** $4^{-5} = \dfrac{1}{4^\square}$ **iii** $\dfrac{1}{9^3} = 9^\square$ **iv** $\dfrac{1}{5^7} = 5^\square$

Q1a hint

Which index rule can you use?

2 Write each calculation as a single power.

    a $7^2 \times 7^{-4} = 7^{2 + -4} = 7^\square$

    b $3^{-1} \times 3^5 = 3^{\square + \square} = 3^\square$

    c $5^{-4} \times 5$

    d $8^2 \div 8^6 = 8^{\square - \square} = 8^\square$

    e $4^{-3} \div 4^{-5}$

    f $\dfrac{10^3}{10^7}$

    g $(5^{-2})^3 = 5^{-2 \times \square} = 5^\square$

    h $(6^5)^{-4}$

Q2c hint

$5 = 5^1$

3 Which calculations in Q2 have answers that are less than 1?

Q3 hint

Write each answer as a fraction. Which fractions have a numerator smaller than the denominator?

Standard form

1 Work out

    a 3.7×10^3

    b 2.5×10^4

    c 8.1×10^2

    d 5.4×10^7

2 Work out

    a 9.3×10^{-3}

    b 7.3×10^{-2}

    c 1.5×10^{-4}

    d 4.9×10^{-6}

Q1a hint

3.7

3 7 0 0

3.7×10^3 means multiply 3.7 by 10 three times.

Q2a hint

9.3

0.0 0 9 3

9.3×10^{-3} means divide 9.3 by 10 three times.

3 A number written using standard form looks like this:

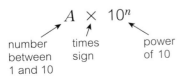

$A \times 10^n$

number between 1 and 10   times sign   power of 10

Write each number using standard form.

    a $3100 = 3.1 \times 10^\square$ **b** $29\,000$

    c $7\,150\,000$ **d** $69\,000\,000\,000$

4 Write each number using standard form.

   a $0.0064 = 6.4 \times 10^{\square}$

   b 0.072

   c 0.000004

   d 0.000000021

Q4a hint

      6.4 How many 10s do you

0.0 0 6 4 divide by to get 0.0064?

6.4 lies between 1 and 10.

5 Write the numbers in each list in order, from smallest to largest.

   a 1.8×10^5 3.7×10^{-2} 9.4×10^2 6.9×10^{-7}

   b 4×10^{-1} 4.2×10^{-2} 4.22×10^2 2.4×10^2 2.44×10^{-1}

Q5 hint

Look at the powers of 10 first.
If numbers have the same power of
10, sort them by the decimal number.

Calculating with standard form

1 Work out each calculation. Give your answers in standard form.

   a $(3 \times 10^4) \times (2.6 \times 10^5) = 3 \times 2.6 \times 10^4 \times 10^5 = \square \times 10^{\square}$

   b $(1.7 \times 10^5) \times (2 \times 10^3)$

   c $(5 \times 10^2) \times (2.5 \times 10^8)$

   d $\dfrac{6.6 \times 10^6}{2.2 \times 10^2} = \dfrac{6.6}{2.2} \times \dfrac{10^6}{10^3} = \square \times 10^{\square}$

   e $\dfrac{7.8 \times 10^3}{3 \times 10^7}$

   f $\dfrac{2 \times 10^9}{8 \times 10^5}$

2 Work out each calculation. Give your answers in standard form.

   a $(6.41 \times 10^5) \times (1.8 \times 10^7)$

   b $(3.7 \times 10^{-3}) \times (9.3 \times 10^{10})$

   c $\dfrac{55.8 \times 10^9}{6.2 \times 10^2}$

   d $\dfrac{2.136 \times 10^3}{3.56 \times 10^8}$

Q2a hint

Use the $\boxed{10^x}$ key on your calculator.

3 The average distance from the Sun to the Earth is approximately 1.5×10^8 km.

   Light travels at $3 \times 10^8 \, \text{m s}^{-1}$.

   Find the time taken for light to travel from the Sun to the Earth.

Q3 hint

Ensure that you use the same units.

 4 Problem-solving How thick is a single page in this book?
Follow these steps to find out.
a Find out how many sheets of paper are in the book.
b Use a ruler to measure the total thickness of the pages in the book (in mm).
c Use your calculator to find the thickness of one sheet in mm. Write the answer in standard form.
d Convert your answer in part **c** to nanometres (nm). Give your answer to 1 decimal place.

Q4d hint

$1\,\text{nm} = 10^{-6}\,\text{mm}$

5 Real Write these countries in order of population size, from smallest to largest.

Country	Population (July 2014)
UK	6.411×10^7
New Zealand	4.540×10^6
Iceland	3.263×10^5
Japan	1.271×10^8
St Lucia	1.8×10^5
Brazil	2.028×10^8

6 Real Use the information in the table in Q5 to answer these questions.
a Write the population of Iceland as an ordinary number.
b Calculate the total population of all the countries in the table.
c How many times bigger is the population of the UK than the population of St Lucia?

7 STEM An electron has a mass of $9.109 \times 10^{-31}\,\text{kg}$.
a How many electrons are there in 1 kg of electrons?
A proton has a mass of $1.673 \times 10^{-27}\,\text{kg}$.
b How many electrons are equivalent to one proton?

Enrichment

8 On Earth, the oceans cover an area of $3.62 \times 10^8\,\text{km}^2$ with a mean depth of $3.68 \times 10^4\,\text{m}$.
Use this information to estimate the volume of water in the oceans of the Earth. Give your answer in standard form in m^3.

9 Reflect Nandini says, 'Working with indices, powers and roots is all about adding, subtracting, multiplying and dividing'.
Look back at the questions you answered in these Strengthen lessons. Describe when you had to:
• add
• subtract
• multiply
• divide.
Do you agree with Nandini's statement? Give some examples to explain why.

1 Extend

You will:
- Extend your understanding with problem-solving.

1 a Match each prefix to its correct power of 10.

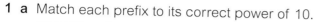

centi　　micro　　giga　　pico　　kilo

10^3　10^{-3}　10^9　10^{-2}　10^{-6}　10^{-1}　10^{-12}

b Write the prefixes for the remaining powers of 10.

2 Work out these conversions.
  a 1 kilogram (kg) = $\square$ g
  b 1 megajoule (MJ) = $\square$ J
  c 1 gigatonne (Gt) = $\square$ t
  d 1 terawatt (TW) = $\square$ W
  e 1 decilitre (dl) = $\square$ l

> **Q2e hint**
> 1 decimetre = 0.1 m

3 The diagram shows a cuboid.

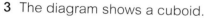
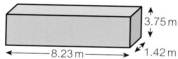

3.75 m
8.23 m
1.42 m

What is the surface area of the cuboid?
Give your answer to 3 significant figures.

4 Write as a single power.

  a $11^7 \times 11^{-3} \div 11^{-2}$
  b $3^{-13} \times 3^4 \div 3^{-5} \div 3^2$
  c $\dfrac{7^{-7} \times 7^{-2}}{7^{-1} \div 7^8}$
  d $\dfrac{5^{-3} \div 5^3}{5^{10} \times 5^{-3}}$

5 Work out

  a $3^{-3} \times 2^{-2} \times 2^{-1} \times 3^4$
  b $\left(\frac{1}{2}\right)^{-3} \times \left(\frac{1}{3}\right)^{-1} \times \left(\frac{1}{2}\right)^2 \times \left(\frac{1}{3}\right)^{-1}$
  c $\left(\frac{1}{2}\right)^{-2} \times \left(\frac{1}{3}\right) \times \left(\frac{1}{2}\right)^3 \times \left(\frac{1}{3}\right)^{-2}$
  d $\left(\frac{1}{2}\right)^{-3} \times \left(\frac{1}{2}\right)^3$

6 Real / STEM Scientists often use units written with negative indices.
  For example, 30 m/s = 30 ms^{-1}.
  Write these units using negative indices.
  a km/h　　**b** m/s^2　　**c** kg/m^3　　**d** miles/h

7 STEM There are 100 trillion microorganisms in the human intestines.
  This is 10 times the number of cells in a human body.
  Write the number of cells in a human body, in standard form.

> **Q7 Literacy hint**
> 1 trillion = 1 000 000 000 000

8 Problem-solving Write these numbers in order, from smallest to largest.

  1.26×10^{-3}　0.12×10^{-2}　0.00124　1205×10^{-6}　$\dfrac{1}{8 \times 10^2}$

> **Q8 Strategy hint**
> Write each number in standard form first.

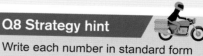

9 Real The table shows how people accessed information about a football tournament.

	Number of people (to 3 s.f.)
Connected with the official site	1.12×10^8
Apps downloaded	2.20×10^7
Facebook users	4.55×10^8
Tweets during the match	3.66×10^7

Use the data to work out the missing number in each sentence.
  a There were roughly .... times more Facebook users than people connected to the official site.
  b There were roughly .... times more Facebook users than tweets in the match.
  c There were roughly .... times more tweets in the match than people who downloaded apps.

10 Put the answers to these calculations in order, from smallest to largest.
  A $(2.3 \times 10^{-3}) \times (7.4 \times 10^{-2})$
  B $(1.3 \times 10^{-2})^2$
  C $(5.3 \times 10^{-2}) \div (3.2 \times 10^2)$
  D $(1.091 \times 10^{-4}) + (6 \times 10^{-5})$
  E $(1.8 \times 10^{-4}) - (1.8 \times 10^{-5})$

11 Work out the reciprocals of these numbers. Give your answers in standard form.
  a 2×10^9
  b 8×10^7
  c 4×10^{-5}
  d 1.6×10^{-4}

12 Real The number of app downloads in July 2008 was 1.0×10^7. There were 10 times as many in September 2008 and 10 times as many again in April 2009.
In June 2014 there were 7.5×10^{10} app downloads.
  a How many downloads were there in April 2009?
  b What was the increase from July 2008 to June 2014?

13 STEM / Reasoning The smallest size the human eye can see is 10^{-4} m. The diameter of a virus particle is 170 nm.
Could you see a group of 1 million virus particles with the naked eye? Explain your answer.

14 STEM The formula for working out the frequency of a wave in the electromagnetic spectrum is
$f = \frac{c}{\lambda}$ where c is the speed of light and λ is the wavelength.
$c = 3 \times 10^8$ m/s
Work out the frequency of
  a red light with wavelength 6.9×10^{-7} m
  b blue light with wavelength 4.65×10^{-7} m.
Give your answers in standard form to 2 significant figures.

Q14 Literacy hint

λ is the Greek letter *lambda*. It is sometimes used instead of a letter from our alphabet.
The unit for frequency is hertz (Hz).

15 Reasoning

a Which of these numbers have the same value?

$(0.5)^3$ 8^{-2} $\left(\frac{1}{4}\right)^2$ $\left(\frac{1}{2}\right)^3$ 2^{-3} $\left(\frac{1}{64}\right)^{\frac{1}{2}}$

b In how many different ways can you write $\frac{1}{9}$?

16 Real The populations of Bangladesh, China, India and Pakistan in 2014 are shown in the table.

Country	Population in 2014
Bangladesh	1.556×10^8
China	1.366×10^9
India	1.247×10^9
Pakistan	1.880×10^8

a Write these countries in order of population size, from smallest to largest.

b What is the difference between the population of India and China?

c How many times larger is the population of India than that of Pakistan?

d What is the total population of these four countries?
The world population is 7.183×10^9.

e What proportion of the world's population lives in China or India?

Challenge

17 Real / STEM / Modelling A science museum wants to make a scale model of the Solar System.

Not drawn to scale

3.84×10^8 m 1.5×10^{11} m

Moon   Earth   Sun

The diagram shows the real distances between the Earth, Moon and Sun.
In the model the Earth and the Moon are 10 cm apart.
How far away from the Earth will the Sun need to be?
Discussion Is this a good scale for the model? Suggest some distances that might work better.

Investigation

Reasoning

The speed of light is 3×10^8 m/s.
a How many kilometres does light travel in one year? (Assume 1 year to be 365 days).
Neptune is approximately 4.5 billion km from the Sun.
b Work out how long it takes light from the Sun to reach Neptune.

18 Reflect In this unit you have learned a lot of new vocabulary.
Write a list of all the new vocabulary you have used.
Write, in your own words, a definition for each one.
Compare your definitions with those of your classmates.
Did you all learn the same thing?

Q18 hint

A light year is the distance travelled by light in one year.

Reflect

1 Unit test

1 Real The stadium that will host the 2020 Superbowl seats 98 025 people.
The average price of a ticket is $120.
Estimate the total money taken from ticket sales for the Superbowl.

2 Work out

  a $\dfrac{4 + 3 \times 6 - 4}{3^2 - 4}$

  b $25\left(3^3 + 2\right) \div 5 \times 3$

3 Use rounding to one significant figure to estimate

  a 1875×5.36

  b $\dfrac{285 \times 3.16}{11.2}$

4 Write each number in standard form.
  a 820
  b 0.000 091 5

5 Put these numbers in order, from smallest to largest.
  1.24×10^{-2}
  1.21×10^{-4}
  1.2×10^{2}
  1.23×10^{3}
  1.24×10

6 Work out each calculation. Give your answers in standard form.
  a $\dfrac{8.8 \times 10^8}{2.2 \times 10^3}$

  b $(2.5 \times 10^4) \times (5 \times 10^{-7})$

7 Work out each calculation. Give your answers in standard form.

  a $(1.505 \times 10^{-9}) \times (8.3 \times 10^4)$

  b $\dfrac{48.96 \times 10^3}{5.1 \times 10^{-3}}$

8 Write as a single power.

  a $6^3 \times 6^{-4}$

  b $3^{-4} \div 3^{-2}$

  c $(7^{-3})^2$

  d $\dfrac{4^{-4} \div 4^{-2}}{4^{-1} \times 4^{-1}}$

9 a Arrange these cards into their correct groups.
Each group must have one card of each colour.

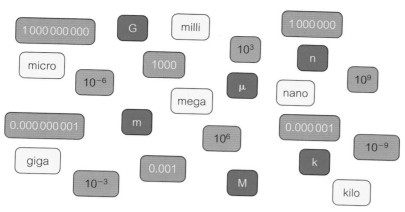

b Convert
   i 9 GJ to joules
   ii 13 kW to watts
   iii 8.5 Ms to seconds.

10 An African elephant weighs about 6 tonnes.
The Earth weighs 5.97×10^{24} kg.
  a How many kg are in a tonne?
  b How many tonnes does the Earth weigh?
  c What is the mass of the Earth, measured in elephants?
    Give your answer in standard form.
  d Look back at the data in Exercise 1.4 Q8.
    How many elephants do you need to make the mass of each planet?

Challenge

11 Problem-solving A publisher prints 1.25×10^7 copies of a newspaper.
Each newspaper consists of 16 sheets of paper.
  a Calculate the number of sheets of paper needed to print all the newspapers. Give your answer in standard form.
To make the newspapers, the sheets of paper are folded in half.
  b The height of a pile of newspapers is 125 cm. The pile contains 420 newspapers.
    Calculate the thickness of one sheet of paper. Give your answer in metres in standard form.

12 Reflect Which of the questions in this unit test:
- took the shortest time to answer? Why?
- took the longest time to answer? Why?
- were the most interesting? Why?

2.1 Surface area of prisms

Confidence

You will learn to:
- Sketch nets of 3D solids.
- Calculate the surface area of prisms.

Why learn this?
Design engineers have to calculate surface area because it affects the speed of a racing car.

Fluency
Describe the faces of this solid.

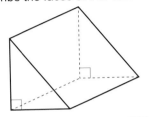

Explore
Why do African elephants have larger ears than Asian elephants?

Exercise 2.1

Warm up

1 Calculate the area of each shape.

a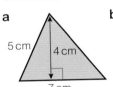
5 cm 4 cm 7 cm

b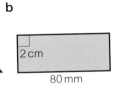
2 cm 80 mm

c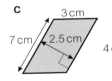
3 cm 7 cm 2.5 cm

d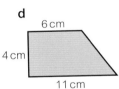
6 cm 4 cm 11 cm

> **Q1 hint**
> First make sure that all measurements are in the same unit. Remember to write units cm² or mm² in your answers.

2 For each solid
   i sketch the net   **ii** calculate the surface area.

a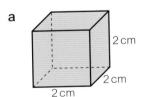
2 cm 2 cm 2 cm

b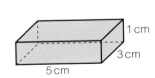
1 cm 3 cm 5 cm

3 The diagram shows a triangular prism and its net.
  a Copy the net. Write the missing lengths.
  b Calculate the area of each shape in the net.
  c Calculate the total surface area of the prism.
  Discussion Are any of the faces congruent? Is there a quicker way of finding the surface area of the prism?

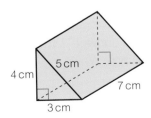
4 cm 5 cm 7 cm 3 cm

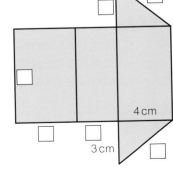
4 cm 3 cm

4 a Which of these solids look like **right prisms**?

A   B   C   D   E   F

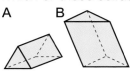   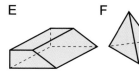

b What shapes are their **cross-sections**?

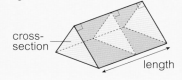
5 For each solid

   i sketch the net

   ii calculate the total surface area.

a

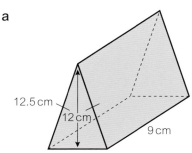

12.5 cm
12 cm
9 cm
7 cm

b

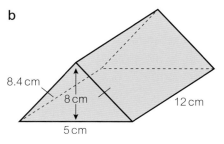

8.4 cm
8 cm
12 cm
5 cm

6 Real Work out the area of canvas needed to make this tent.

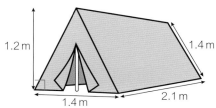

1.2 m
1.4 m
1.4 m
2.1 m

7 Problem-solving The diagram shows a design for a bowl.
It has four sides in the shape of congruent trapezia.
The bottom of the bowl is square.
Work out the total surface area of the outside of the bowl.

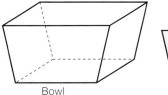
Bowl

12 cm
8 cm
6 cm

8 Problem-solving These two solids have the same surface area.
Work out the value of x.

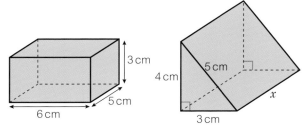

3 cm
5 cm
6 cm
4 cm
5 cm
x
3 cm

9 Explore Why do African elephants have larger ears than Asian elephants?
Look back at the maths you have learned in this lesson.
How can you use it to answer this question?

10 Reflect Sami says, 'A right prism always has two end faces that are exactly the same'.
Katrin says, 'The faces that aren't end faces are always rectangles'.
Omar says, 'It is called a **right** prism because the end faces and other faces are always at **right** angles to each other.'
Jason says, 'The shape of the end faces always give the prism its name'.
Are they all correct?

Q10 hint

Look carefully at the pictures of the right prisms you identified in Q4.

Explore

Reflect

2.2 Volume of prisms

You will learn to:
- Calculate the volume of right prisms.

Why learn this?
Landscape gardeners use volume to work out the amount of soil needed in gardens.

Fluency
- How many cm³ in
  6 m*l*   2 *l*?
- What is the formula for the volume of a cuboid?
- Which of these units are used for volume?
  mm³   cm²   m³   cm³   m²

Explore
What volume of water do you need to fill a swimming pool?

Confidence

Exercise 2.2

Warm up

1 Calculate the area of each shape.

a

3 cm   2.5 cm   6 cm

b

4.5 cm   6 cm   7 cm   7.5 cm   8 cm

c

5 cm   40 mm   2.2 cm

Q1 hint

Make sure that all measurements are in the same unit.
Remember to write units cm² or mm² in your answers.

d

6.5 cm   9 cm   3 cm   4 cm

e

30 mm   55 mm   60 mm   50 mm   30 mm

2 The diagram shows a cuboid.

   a Work out the volume of the cuboid.

   The cuboid is cut along the red lines to make two congruent triangular prisms.

   b Use your answer to part **a** to work out the volume of each triangular prism.

   c Work out the area of the triangular face of each prism.

   Discussion Haru says, 'The volume of a triangular prism is the area of the triangular face times the length.' Is he right?

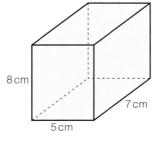

8 cm   7 cm   5 cm

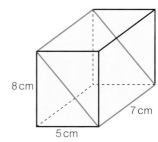

8 cm   7 cm   5 cm

3 For each triangular prism, work out
  i the cross-sectional area   **ii** the volume.

a

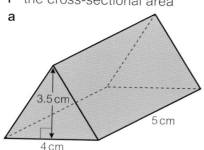

b

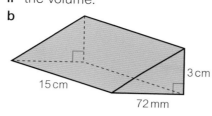

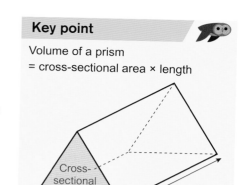
4 Calculate the volume of each prism.

a

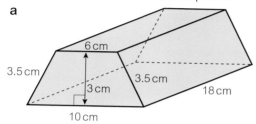

b

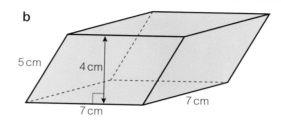

5 The volume of this prism is 84 cm³.
  Calculate the length marked x.

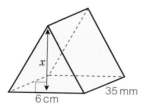

6 **Problem-solving** This glass in the shape of
  a hexagonal prism has a **capacity** of 270 ml.
  The inside of the glass is 8 cm tall.
  a What is the area of the base of the inside
    of the glass?
  The edges of the hexagon are each
  3.5 cm long.
  b What is the surface area of the inside of the glass?

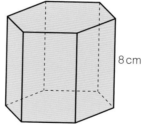

7 **Problem-solving** The volume of a 3D solid is 36 cm³.
  Sketch a possible solid and label its dimensions.
  Discussion How many possible answers are there?

8 This is the vertical cross-section of a diving pool.
  a Work out the area of the cross-section.
  The width of the pool is 15 m.
  b Calculate the volume of the pool in m³.
  c Calculate the capacity of the pool in litres.

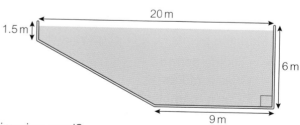

9 **Explore** What volume of water do you need to fill a swimming pool?
  What have you learned in this lesson to help you to answer this question?
  What other information do you need?

10 **Reflect** Maths is not the only subject where you use volume.
  Describe when you have used volume in science.
  In which ways is volume the same or different in science and in this
  maths lesson? Do you think volume means the same in all subjects?
  Explain.

Explore

Reflect

2.3 Circumference of a circle

You will learn to:

- Calculate the circumference of a circle.
- Solve problems involving circles or prisms.
- Use appropriate apparatus (including pairs of compasses) to identify and draw the diameter and radius of a circle.
- Identify the circumference, arc and sector of a circle.

Why learn this?
Stadium designers use circumference when planning the curved portion of a running track.

Fluency
What is the perimeter of this shape?

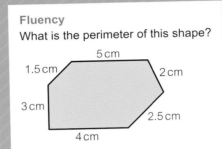

Explore
How long would it take to fly around the world?

Exercise 2.3

1 Write
  a 4.3275
      i to 1 decimal place
      ii to 2 decimal places
  b 9.367 m to the nearest centimetre
  c 7.453 cm to the nearest millimetre.

2 $C = 3d$. Work out the value of
  a C when $d = 6$ cm
  b C when $d = 1.5$ cm
  c d when $C = 33$ cm
  d d when $C = 7.5$ cm.

3 a Draw a circle with a radius of 4 cm.
  b Mark the points O, P, Q, S on your diagram, where

  - O is the **centre**
  - OS is a **radius**
  - PQ is a **diameter**.

  c Write the letters of another line that is also a radius.
  d Colour the **arc** PS.
  e Mark any other point T on the **circumference**.
  f Does the picture show the diameter of a circle?
      Explain your answer.

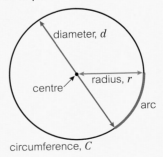

4 a A circle has diameter 12 cm. What is its radius?

b A circle has radius 4.2 cm. What is its diameter?

5 Find the circumference of each circle.
Give your answers in terms of π.

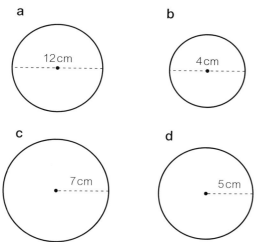

a

12 cm

b

4 cm

c

7 cm

d

5 cm

Key point

The Greek letter π (pronounced 'pi')
is a special number, 3.141 592 653…
To find the circumference, C, of
a circle with diameter d, use the
formula $C = \pi d$.
If you know the radius, r, you can
use the equivalent formula $C = 2\pi r$.
Use the π key on your calculator.

Q5 Strategy hint

Do you know the diameter or radius?
Which formula will you use?

6 STEM Calculate the circumference of each circular object.
Round your answers to 1 decimal place.

a The lens of a mobile phone camera with diameter 3.75 mm.

b A Ferris wheel with diameter 30.7 m.

c A crater on the Moon with radius approximately 173 km.

7 Each diagram shows a whole circle and a sector shaded yellow.
For each diagram, work out

i the circumference of the whole circle

ii the fraction of the whole circle shown by the shaded sector

iii the arc length of the shaded sector.

Round your answers to 1 decimal place.

Key point

A **sector** is the part of a circle
enclosed by two **radii** and an arc.

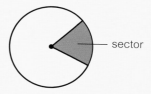

sector

Radii is the plural of radius.

a

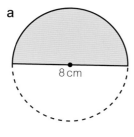

8 cm

b

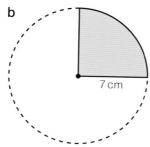

7 cm

8 For each shape, work out

i the length of the arc

ii the perimeter of the whole shape.

Give your answers in terms of π.

Q8 hint

The perimeter of a shape is the
distance around the edge of the
whole shape.

a

2 cm

b

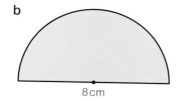

8 cm

Subject links: Science (Q6), Sport (Q9 and Q11)

9 **Real** Work out the length of this race track.
Round your answer to 2 decimal places.

Q9 hint

The two curved ends join together to make one circle.

Discussion What is the length in metres and centimetres?
Would it be sensible to round to 3 decimal places?

10 **Problem-solving** Noah says, 'The circumference of a circle with radius 10 cm is double the circumference of a circle with radius 5 cm.'
Is he right? Explain your answer.

11 **Real / Problem-solving** At the Olympic opening ceremony, there is a large light display of the five Olympic rings.
Each ring has radius 10 m.
Light bulbs are spaced every 50 cm around each ring.
How many light bulbs are there altogether?

12 A circle has circumference 24 cm.
Work out its diameter.
Round your answer to the nearest millimetre.

Q13 Strategy hint

Substitute the values you know into the formula and rearrange.

13 Work out the radius of a circle with circumference 150 millimetre.
Round your answer to the nearest centimetre.

14 **Explore** How long would it take to fly around the world?
What have you learned in this lesson to help you to answer this question?
What other information do you need?

15 **Reflect** Close your book and write down as many facts about circles as you can.
Make sure that you include all the ones you remember from this lesson.
Then open your book again and look back at the lesson.
Did you miss any facts? If so, add them to your list.
Did you make any spelling mistakes?
If so, correct them.

2.4 Area of a circle

You will learn to:
- Calculate the area of a circle.
- Solve problems involving circles.

Why learn this?
Garden designers calculate the area of flower beds to work out how many plants they need.

Fluency
- Work out
  8^2 11^2 $\sqrt{49}$ $\sqrt{25}$
- Which of these units are used for area?
  cm³   cm²   mm
  mm²   mm³   km

Explore
How much would it cost to put carpet down in a circular room?

Exercise 2.4

1 Using the formula $A = 4r^2$, work out the value of
   a A when $r = 2$
   b A when $r = 5$
   c r when $A = 100$
   d r when $A = 9$

2 Substitute into each formula to work out the unknown quantity.
   Round your answers to 1 decimal place.

   a $x = 4\pi$

   b $A = 3.14r^2$ when $r = 9$

   c $p = \sqrt{\dfrac{A}{3}}$ when $A = 60$

> **Q2a hint**
>
> Use the π key on your calculator.

3 Work out the area of each circle.
   Give your answers in terms of π.

a 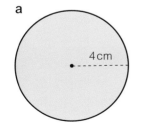 4 cm

b 2 cm

c 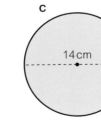 14 cm

d 6 cm

> **Key point**
>
> The formula for the area, A, of a circle with radius r is $A = \pi r^2$

> **Q3c, d hint**
>
> First work out the radius of the circle.

4 Work out the area of each circular object.
   Round your answers to 1 decimal place.
   a A food chopping board with diameter 18 cm.
   b A Frisbee with radius 16.3 cm.
   c A coin with radius 19 mm.
   d A Japanese sumo wrestling ring with diameter 4.55 m.

Warm up

5 This circle has radius 7 cm.
Work out the area of
  a the whole circle
  b the yellow sector
  c the red sector.
Give your answers in terms of π.

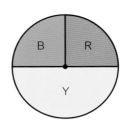

6 Work out the area of each shape.
Round your answers to 1 decimal place.

a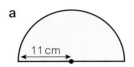
11 cm

b
4.7 cm

c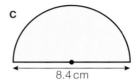
8.4 cm

Q7 hint

Divide each shape up into different parts.

7 Work out the area of each shape.
Round your answers to 1 decimal place.

a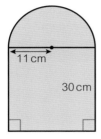
11 cm
30 cm

b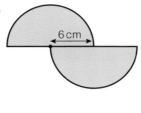
6 cm

c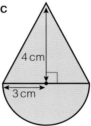
4 cm
3 cm

d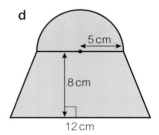
5 cm
8 cm
12 cm

8 **Problem-solving** Anil says, 'The area of a circle with radius 8 cm is double the area of a circle with radius 4 cm.'
Is he right?
Explain your answer.
Discussion What happens to the circumference when you double the radius? Does the same happen for area?

9 **Real** Copy and complete this table showing the cost of different pizzas.

Pizza diameter	Pizza area (1 d.p.)	Cost
8 inch		£5.99
10 inch		£7.99
12 inch		£9.99

Which pizza represents best value for money?
Explain your answer.

Q9 hint

How much of each pizza do you get for £1?

10 Work out the radius of each circle.
Round your answers to the nearest millimetre.

a
Area
83 cm²

b
Area
68.5 cm²

Q10a hint

$A = \pi r^2$
$83 = \pi \times r^2$
$r^2 = \dfrac{83}{\pi}$
$r = \square$

Topic links: Rounding, Fractions of an amount, Formulae   **Subject links:** Sport (Q12–13)

11 Problem-solving These diagrams show the area of part of a circle. For each shape, work out the radius of the circle.

a

Area 16 m²

b

Area 7 cm²

Q11 hint

First work out the area of the whole circle. Round your answers for the radius to a sensible degree of accuracy.

12 Real / Reasoning A circular trampoline has an area of 20 m².
a Calculate the radius of the trampoline to 1 decimal place.
For safety, there must be at least a 1 m-wide free space beyond the edge of the trampoline, around the outside.
b How wide must the total space be for the trampoline to safely fit?
c The trampoline only just fits in a square garden.
What is the area of the garden?

13 Real The diagram shows the dimensions of a running track.
What area of land is available for the field events inside the track?
Round your answer to the nearest square metre.

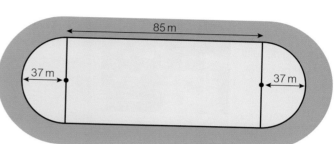

85 m

37 m   37 m

14 Problem-solving Work out the shaded area of each shape.
Round your answers to 1 decimal place.

a
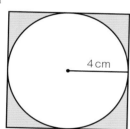
4 cm

b
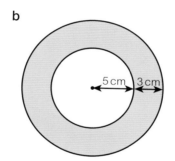
5 cm 3 cm

Q14 Strategy hint

Work out the area of the larger shape and subtract the area of the smaller shape.

15 Real / Problem-solving The top of a test tube rack is made from a piece of metal. Six holes of diameter 15 mm are removed from the metal.
What is the area of the remaining metal?
Give your answers in terms of π.

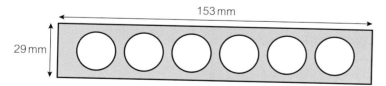

153 mm

29 mm

16 Explore How much would it cost to put carpet down in a circular room?
What have you learned in this lesson to help you to answer this question?
What other information do you need?

17 Reflect Look back at Q11
List the steps you took to work out the answer.
Compare your steps with those of others in the class.

2.5 Cylinders

Confidence

You will learn to:
* Calculate the volume and surface area of a cylinder.

Why learn this?
The volume of the piston cylinders in a car engine tells us how powerful the car is.

Fluency
Work out
* 7^2 5^2 11^2 15^2
* $1\,cm^3 = \square\,ml$
* $1\,litre = \square\,cm^3$

Explore
What is the volume of beans in a tin can?

Exercise 2.5

Warm up

1 For each circle A and B, work out
   i   the circumference
   ii the area.

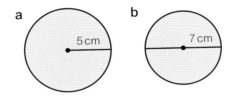

a   5 cm

b   7 cm

2 $V = 3a^2b$. Work out
   a V when $a = 4$ and $b = 2$
   b b when $V = 81$ and $a = 3$
   c a when $V = 96$ and $b = 2$

3 What is the volume of this right prism?

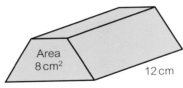

Area 8 cm²   12 cm

4 The diagram shows a cylinder and its net.

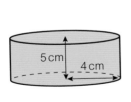

5 cm   4 cm

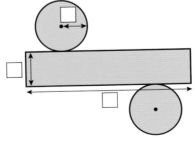

a Copy the net. Work out and write the missing lengths.
b Work out the area of each shape.
c Add the areas together to work out the surface area of the cylinder.

Q4a hint

The rectangle wraps around the circle, so the length of the long side must be the .... of the circle.

5 a Copy this net and write the missing lengths.
   b Write an expression for the area inside each shape.
   c Write an expression for the total area.
      Total surface area of a cylinder = ... + ...

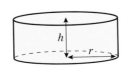

h r

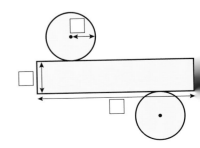

6 Work out the surface area of each cylinder.

a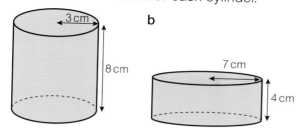
3 cm
8 cm

b
7 cm
4 cm

7 For each cylinder, work out
  i the area of a circular end   **ii** the volume of the cylinder.

a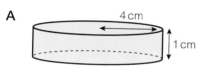
5 cm
9 cm

b
8 cm
3 cm

c
9 cm
3 cm

8 STEM These three cylinders have the same volume.

A
4 cm
1 cm

B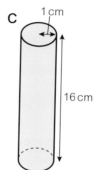
2 cm
4 cm

C
1 cm
16 cm

  a Which cylinder do you think will have the smallest surface area? Explain your answer.

  b Work out the surface area of each cylinder to check your answer to part **a**. Were you correct?

  Discussion The amount of heat energy entering or leaving an object depends on its surface area. Explain why a tall, thin mug of tea will cool more slowly from its surface than a short wide one.

9 Modelling The inside of a saucepan has diameter 20 cm and height 13 cm. The manufacturer claims that the pan has a capacity of 4 litres. Is the claim correct? Explain your answer.

10 Explore What is the volume of beans in a tin can? Is it easier to explore this question now that you have completed the lesson? What further information do you need to be able to answer this?

11 Reflect Obinze says, 'You can't make a perfect net of a cylinder. They are all just approximations.' Explain what he means. Do you agree?

Explore

Reflect

2.6 Pythagoras' theorem

You will learn to:
- Use Pythagoras' theorem in right-angled triangles.

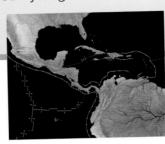

Why learn this?
Geologists use Pythagoras' theorem to help calculate the epicentre of an earthquake.

Fluency
- Work out
  3^2 4^2 5^2 12^2 13^2
- Which is the longest side in this triangle?

Explore
What size of wall space is needed for a 42-inch TV?

Confidence

Warm up

Exercise 2.6

1 Work out
   a $8^2 + 3^2$ **b** $2.7^2 + 9.1^2$ **c** $\sqrt{9^2 + 7^2}$ **d** $\sqrt{3.5^2 - 2.1^2}$

2 **a** Draw this triangle on centimetre squared paper.
   b Measure the lengths of the three sides to the nearest millimetre.
   c What is the length of the **hypotenuse**?

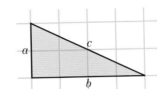

Key point

The longest side of a right-angled triangle is called the **hypotenuse**.

   Discussion Darren says, 'The largest angle in a right-angled triangle will always be the right angle.'
   Lea says, 'The hypotenuse will always be the side opposite the right angle.' Who is right?

3 Which side is the hypotenuse in each triangle?

   a   **b**   **c**   **d**

Investigation

Reasoning

1 Draw these triangles accurately on squared paper.
2 Measure the hypotenuse c.
3 Copy and complete this table.

	a	b	c	$a^2 + b^2$	c^2
X	4	3		$4^2 + 3^2 =$	
Y	12	5			
Z	8	6			

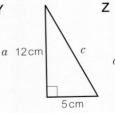
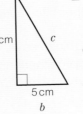
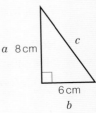

X   **Y**   **Z**

a 4 cm a 12 cm a 8 cm

3 cm   5 cm   6 cm

b b b

c c c

4 What do you notice about your answers in the last two columns?
5 Write a formula linking the shorter sides, a and b, and the hypotenuse, c.

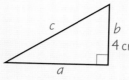

Worked example

Work out the length of the hypotenuse of this right-angled triangle, to the nearest millimetre.

Sketch the triangle. Label the hypotenuse c and the other sides a and b.

$c^2 = a^2 + b^2$

$c^2 = 6.5^2 + 4^2$

Substitute $a = 6.5$ and $b = 4$ into the formula for Pythagoras' theorem, $c^2 = a^2 + b^2$

$c^2 = 42.25 + 16 = 58.25$

$c = \sqrt{58.25} = 7.632\,168\ldots$ — Use a calculator to find the square root.

The length of the hypotenuse is 7.6 cm to the nearest millimetre. — Round to the nearest mm.

Discussion Does it matter which way round you label the sides a and b?

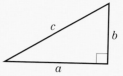

4 Use **Pythagoras' theorem** to work out the missing length of each right-angled triangle.
Round your answers to the nearest mm.

a

7 cm
4 cm

b

3 cm 6 cm

c
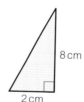
8 cm
2 cm

5 **Real** To meet safety requirements, a wheelchair ramp must rise 1 m over a distance of 12 m.
How long must the ramp be?
Round your answer to the nearest centimetre.

6 **Problem-solving** Work out which of these triangles are right-angled triangles.

a

7 cm
10 cm
7 cm

b
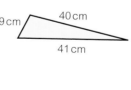
9 cm
40 cm
41 cm

c
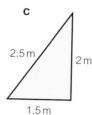
2.5 m
2 m
1.5 m

7 Work out the missing length in each right-angled triangle.
Round your answers to 1 decimal place.
The first one has been started for you.

a

9 cm 10 cm

$c^2 = a^2 + b^2$
$10^2 = 9^2 + b^2$
$100 - 81 = b^2$
$b = \sqrt{\square}$

b
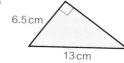
6.5 cm
13 cm

c
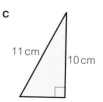
11 cm
10 cm

Topic links: Squares and square roots, Rounding, Formulae

8 Problem-solving
Work out the area of this triangle.

8 cm h

3 cm

Q8 hint

Work out the height, h, first.

9 Problem-solving
Work out the area of this triangle.

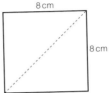

12 cm h

6 cm

Q9 hint

Work out h using Pythagoras' theorem.

10 Real Andy sets the bottom of his ladder 0.8 m away from the base of his house. His ladder is 6.3 m long. How far up the wall will the top of his ladder touch?

Q10 Strategy hint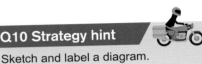

Sketch and label a diagram.

11 Problem-solving The diagram shows a square with side length 8 cm.

8 cm

8 cm

a Work out the area of the square.
b Calculate the length of the diagonal of the square.
c Multiply the lengths of the two diagonals together.
Compare with your answer to part **a**.
What do you notice?
d Use your answer to part **c** to find the area of this square.

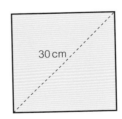

30 cm

12 Problem-solving
  a Use the triangle shown and Pythagoras' theorem to calculate the length AB.
  b Calculate the lengths of
    i CD
    ii EF
    iii GH.

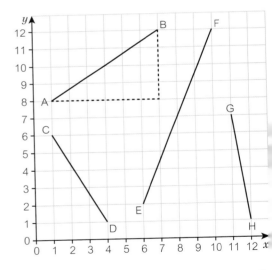

13 Explore What size of wall space is needed for a 42-inch TV? What have you learned in this lesson to help you to answer this question?
What other information do you need?

14 Reflect Look at the worked example.
List the steps to solve the problem in your own words.
Use pencil in case you wish to change them or add more steps later.
Look back at Q5.
Do your steps work to solve this problem? If not, change them.
Look back at Q8 and do the same.
Now compare your steps with those of others in your class.
Have you missed out any steps? If so, change them.

Q14 hint

You could write – Step 1: label the sides of the triangle a, b, c (where c is the hypotenuse)

Explore

Reflect

Active Learn   Homework, Year 9, Unit 2

2 Check up

Surface area and volume of prisms

1 Work out the surface area and volume of this triangular prism.

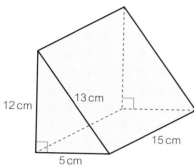

12 cm
13 cm
15 cm
5 cm

2 A triangular prism has a cross-sectional area of 15 cm² and a volume of 225 cm³.
What is the length of the prism?

3 For this prism, work out
   a the volume
   b the surface area.

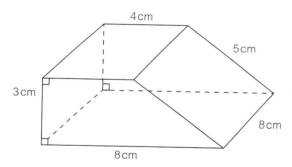

4 cm
5 cm
3 cm
8 cm
8 cm

Circumference and area of a circle

4 For each circle in parts **a** and **b**, calculate
   i the circumference
   ii the area.
   Round your answers to 2 decimal places.

a
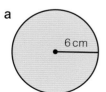
6 cm

b
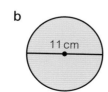
11 cm

5 For this shape, calculate
 a the area
 b the perimeter.
 Round your answers to 2 decimal places.

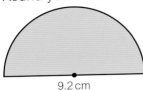

9.2 cm

6 A circle has a diameter of 20 cm. What is the circumference of the circle?
 Give your answer in terms of π.

7 Find the area of the circle with diameter 10 cm.
 Give your answer in terms of π.

8 A large, circular piece of cardboard has a radius of 20 cm.
 It has a smaller circle of radius 10 cm cut from it.
 Calculate the area of the larger piece of cardboard.
 Give your answer in terms of π.

Cylinders

9 For this cylinder, work out
 a the volume
 b the surface area.
 Round your answers to 2 decimal places.

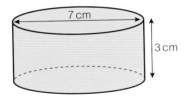

7 cm

3 cm

Pythagoras' theorem

10 Work out the missing length in each right-angled triangle.

 a

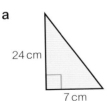

24 cm

7 cm

 b

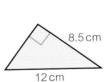

8.5 cm

12 cm

11 How sure are you of your answers? Were you mostly
 ☹ **Just guessing** 😐 **Feeling doubtful** ☺ **Confident**
 What next? Use your results to decide whether to strengthen or extend your learning.

Challenge

12 The perimeter of a semicircle is 5(2 + π) cm.
 What is the length of the straight edge of the semicircle?

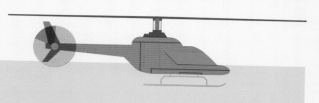

2 Strengthen

You will:
* Strengthen your understanding with practice.

Surface area and volume of prisms

1 a Sketch all the faces of the triangular prism. Label all the lengths. The first one has been started for you.

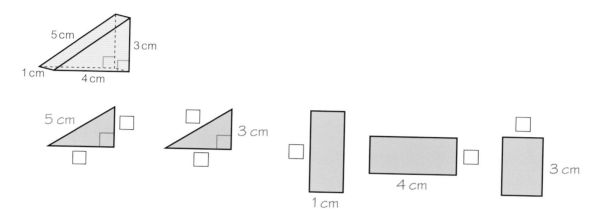

b Work out the surface area of the triangular prism.

2 Work out the surface area of this triangular prism.

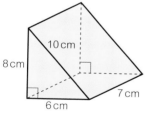

3 Work out the volume of the triangular prism in Q2.

Circumference and area of a circle

1 Write the length of the radius and the diameter of each circle.

a
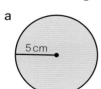

b
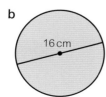

Q1b hint

Work out the area of each face and then add them together.

Q3 hint

Volume = cross-sectional area × length

You worked out this cross-sectional area in Q2.

Q1 hint

r for radius d for diameter

2 Circumference, $C = \pi \times$ diameter

a What is the diameter of this circle?

b Copy and complete $C = \pi \times \square$

c Work out the circumference.
Round your answer to 1 decimal place.

7 cm

3 a Copy and complete these statements.

   i diameter = $\square \times$ radius

   ii $\pi \times$ diameter = $\pi \times \square \times$ radius

   iii $\pi d = \square \pi r$

b Work out the circumference of each circle.

Q3b hint

Circumference = $2\pi r$

Circumference = πd

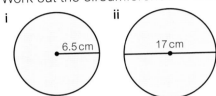

i 6.5 cm   **ii** 17 cm

Give your answer in terms of π.

4 The area of a circle, $A = \pi \times$ radius^2

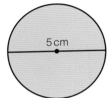

5 cm

a What is the radius of this circle?

b Copy and complete
$A = \pi \times \square^2$

c Work out the area.
Give your answer in terms of π.

5 Work out the area of each circle.
Round your answer to 1 decimal place.

Q5b hint

First work out the radius.
Area = πr^2

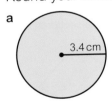

a 3.4 cm

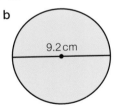

b 9.2 cm

Q6c hint

Use your answers to parts **a** and **b**.

Q6e hint

10 cm

6 a What fraction of a circle is this shape?

b Work out the area of the whole circle.
Round your answer to 1 decimal place.

c Work out the area of the sector shown.

d Work out the circumference of the whole circle.
Round your answer to 1 decimal place.

e Work out the length of the blue arc.

f Work out the perimeter of the sector.

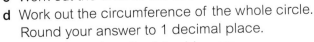

10 cm

Q6f hint

10 cm

7 For this shape, work out
   a the area
   b the perimeter.
   Round your answer to 1 decimal place.

6.2 cm

8 Work out the area of this compound shape.
   Round your answers to 1 decimal place.

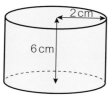

3 cm

20 cm

Q7b hint

Circumference

Q8 hint

Divide the shape into a rectangle and a semicircle.

Cylinders

1 Here is a cylinder.

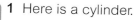

2 cm

6 cm

   a Sketch its faces. Label the lengths you know.
   b Work out the long length of the rectangle and label it.
   c Work out the area of each face.
   d Work out the total surface area of the cylinder.
   e Work out the volume of the cylinder.
   Round your answers to 1 decimal place.

Pythagoras' theorem

1 How long is the hypotenuse in each triangle?

a

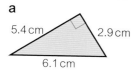

5.4 cm   2.9 cm

6.1 cm

b

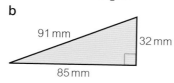

91 mm   32 mm

85 mm

c

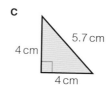

4 cm   5.7 cm

4 cm

Q1 hint

The hypotenuse is the longest side of a right-angled triangle.

2 For each triangle
   i sketch the triangle
   ii label the two shorter sides a and b, and label the hypotenuse c
   iii use the formula $c^2 = a^2 + b^2$ to find the length of the hypotenuse.

Q2a iii hint

$c^2 = a^2 + b^2$
$c^2 = 3^2 + 8^2$

a

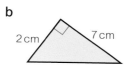

8 cm

3 cm

b

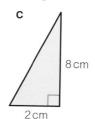

2 cm   7 cm

c

8 cm

2 cm

3 Work out the length of the missing side in each right-angled triangle. The first one has been started for you.

a
8 cm, 11 cm

b
159 mm, 134 mm

c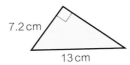
7.2 cm, 13 cm

Q3 hint

Follow the steps in Q2.

a
$$c^2 = a^2 + b^2$$
$$11^2 = a^2 + 8^2$$
$$11^2 - 8^2 = a^2$$

4 Work out the area of each shape.

a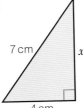
7 cm, x, 4 cm

b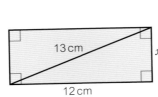
13 cm, x, 12 cm

c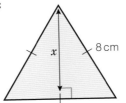
x, 8 cm

Q4 hint

Sketch each right-angled triangle and label the sides.
Use Pythagoras' theorem to first find the length labelled x.
Work out the area of the shape.

Enrichment

1 A cylinder has a height of 10 cm and volume of 40π cm³.
What is the surface area of the cylinder?

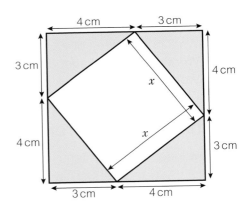

2 The diagram shows a smaller square inside a larger square.
  a Find the area of the smaller square.
    Try the two methods below.
    Method A Work out
    1 the length of one side of the larger square
    2 the area of the larger square
    3 the area of one triangle
    4 the area of the smaller square, using your answers to
       steps **2** and **3**.
    Method B Work out
    1 the length of x, using Pythagoras' theorem
    2 the area of the smaller square, using your answer to step **1**.
  b Which method for working out the area of the smaller square
    did you prefer?
    Explain your answer.

Q2b hint

'Explain' means write a sentence that begins, for example,
'Method ☐, because _____.'

3 **Reflect** In these lessons you used these formulae
- Circumference = $\pi \times$ diameter
- Area of a circle = $\pi \times$ radius²
- Volume of a prism = area of cross-section $\times$ length
- Pythagoras' theorem $c^2 = a^2 + b^2$

Which formula was easiest to use? Explain.
Which formula was most difficult to use? Explain.
Discuss the formula you found most difficult with a classmate.
Ask them to explain to you a question they answered using
this formula.

2 Extend

You will:
- Extend your understanding with problem-solving.

1 Work out the perimeter of each shape.
Round your answers to the nearest millimetre.

a

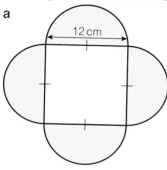

12 cm

b

4 cm

> **Q1 hint**
>
> First work out the circumference of one semicircle.
> Then work out the perimeter of the whole shape.

2 The diagram shows a circle of radius 6 cm inside a square.
   a Calculate the area of the circle.
   b Calculate the area of the square.
   c What percentage of the square is shaded?
   d Repeat parts **a** to **c** for a radius of 4 cm.
   Discussion What do you notice about your answers in parts **c** and **d**?

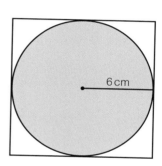

6 cm

3 Here is a circle.
Lana says, 'The circumference is 14π and the area is 49π.'

7 cm

a Explain how she got her answers.
b Now work out the circumference and area of this circle.
Leave your answer in terms of π, as in part **a**.

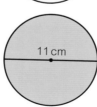

11 cm

> **Q3a hint**
>
> Write the calculations
> $C = 2 \times \pi \times \square = \square\pi$
> $A =$

> **Q3b hint**
>
> To write an answer in terms of π (pi), your answer should be $\square\pi$.
> This gives an exact figure for area and circumference.

4 **Problem-solving**
   a Mark a dot on the edge of a 2p coin and align it with the zero mark on a ruler.
   b Roll the coin along the ruler to find the circumference of the coin.
   c Use the circumference to estimate the diameter of the coin.
   d Repeat parts **b** and **c**, but this time roll the coin 4 times.
   Discussion Which method should give you a more accurate answer for the diameter of the coin?
Explain your answer.
   e Measure the diameter of the coin.
     Which method was the most accurate?

5 Real / Modelling A penny-farthing bicycle has a large front wheel and a small back wheel. The radius of the front wheel is 74 cm.

a   i How far does the wheel travel in one revolution?
        Give your answer in metres to 1 decimal place.

   ii How many revolutions will it go through
        when travelling 100 m?

Over the same distance, the back
wheel rotates 108 times.

b   i What is the circumference
        of the back wheel?
        Round your answer to
        1 decimal place.

   ii What is the radius of the
        back wheel?
        Round your answer to 1 decimal place.

6 The diagram shows a square-based pyramid.

a Write the length of the distance x.
b Use Pythagoras' theorem to calculate l,
   the slant height of the pyramid.
c Calculate the area of one triangular face of
   the pyramid.
d Calculate the area of the base of the
   pyramid.
e Calculate the surface area of the pyramid.
f Calculate the volume of the pyramid.

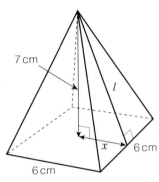

7 cm
l
x 6 cm
6 cm

> **Key point**
>
> Volume of a pyramid
> $= \frac{1}{3} \times$ area of base $\times$ height

7 Modelling The diagram shows a car wheel.

a Work out the circumference of the
   wheel to the nearest centimetre.

On a journey to work and back, the
wheel rotates 50 000 times.

b What is the total length of the journey?
   Give your answer in kilometres to
   1 decimal place.

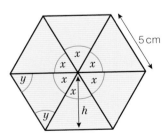

47.5 cm

> **Q7b hint**
>
> 1 m = 100 cm
> 1 km = 1000 m

8 The diagram shows a regular hexagon.

a Copy and complete
   $6x = \square$, so $x = \square$
b Copy and complete
   $x + 2y = \square$, so $y = \square$
c What type of triangle are each of the six triangles?
d Use Pythagoras' theorem to calculate h, the perpendicular height
   of one triangle.
e Calculate the area of one triangle.
f Calculate the area of the hexagon.

5 cm
x
x x
y x x
x
y h

9 Here is the outline of a circle and a sector with central angle 130°.

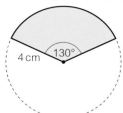

Work out
a the length of the arc
b the area of the sector.

Q9a hint

What fraction of the whole circle is the sector?

10 For each shape, work out
    i the arc length
    ii the sector area.

a

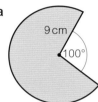

b

11 For each triangular prism, work out
  a **i** the surface area
    ii the volume.

Q11a hint

First use Pythagoras' theorem to calculate the length labelled x.

a

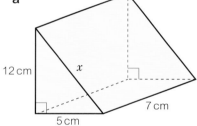

b

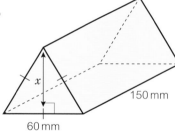

b Which prism has the larger surface area and volume?

12 Problem-solving

Q12 hint

Use Pythagoras' theorem to calculate the length of each line.

a Calculate the length of the lines
    i AB   **ii** BC   **iii** AC
b What type of triangle is ABC?

13 Real / Problem-solving The capacity of this cylindrical glass is 320 cm³.

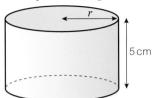

5 cm

a Work out the internal radius of the glass.
Four of these glasses fit exactly in this box.

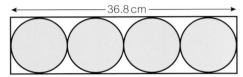

← 36.8 cm →

b How thick is the glass?
Round your answer to 2 decimal places.

Investigation   **Problem-solving**

A cake recipe asks for a 15 cm by 15 cm by 10 cm cuboid-shaped cake tin. You only have a circular tin with diameter 16 cm and height 10 cm. Will this tin be suitable? Show your working to explain.

a Investigate the diameter and height of other cylindrical cake tins that could hold all the cake mixture.
b Investigate other shapes and sizes of cake tins that would be suitable for making a novelty cake with this amount of mixture.

---

14 Each cylinder has a volume of 2000 cm³.
Work out the missing length for each one.
Round your answers to 2 decimal places.

a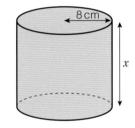
8 cm
x

b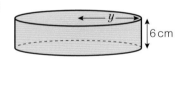
y
6 cm

---

15 Reflect The Ancient Greeks had a famous problem: How to draw a square whose perimeter was equal to the circumference of a circle.
They called the problem 'Squaring the circle'.
Explain why squaring the circle exactly is impossible.

2 Unit test

1 For each circle, work out
　　i the circumference
　　ii the area.
Round your answers to 2 decimal places.

a

2 cm

b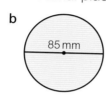

85 mm

2 For this semicircle, work out
　a the area
　b the perimeter.
Give your answers in terms of π.

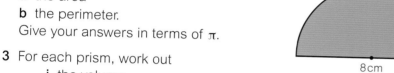

8 cm

3 For each prism, work out
　　i the volume
　　ii the surface area.

a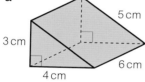

5 cm
3 cm
4 cm
6 cm

b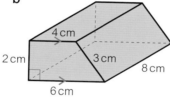

4 cm
2 cm
3 cm
8 cm
6 cm

4 Work out the missing length in each triangle. Give your answers correct to 3 significant figures.

a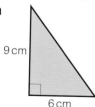

9 cm
6 cm

b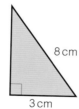

8 cm
3 cm

5 Work out the area of this triangle. Give your answer correct to 1 decimal place.

8 cm　8 cm
6 cm

6 Work out the length of the line AB in the diagram.
Give your answer correct to 3 significant figures.

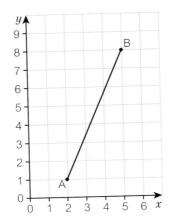

7 The volume of this pentagonal
prism is 135 cm³.
Work out the area of
the pentagon.

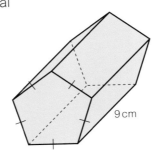

9 cm

8 For this cylinder, work out

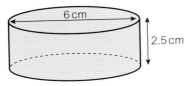

6 cm

2.5 cm

   a the volume
   b the surface area.
Round your answers to 2 decimal places.

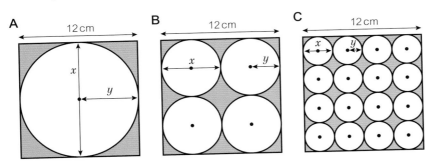

A 12 cm

x

y

B 12 cm

x

y

C 12 cm

x

y

9 a For each diagram A to C work out
    i the length of the line labelled *x*
    ii the length of the line labelled *y*
    iii the area of one circle
    iv the total area of the circles.
  b What can you say about the shaded area in each diagram?

10 Reflect This unit is about circles, prisms and Pythagoras' theorem.
Which of these topics did you like best? Why?
Which of these topics did you like least? Why?

3.1 Arithmetic and quadratic sequences

You will learn to:
- Use the nth term to generate a linear and quadratic sequence.
- Find the nth term of an arithmetic sequence.

Why learn this?
Sequences and patterns occur in nature and scientific experiments. They can be used to make predictions.

Fluency
What is the result of
- multiplying 1 by 3 and adding 7
- multiplying 2 by 3 and adding 7
- multiplying 3 by 3 and adding 7?

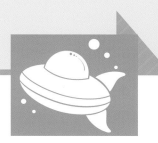

Explore
There are 100 rabbits on an island. How many will there be in 6 months' time?

Exercise 3.1

1 Work out the first four terms and the 10th term of the sequence with nth term
 a $6n$
 b $n - 7$
 c $3n + 2$
 d $2n - 3$

2 Work out the nth term of each sequence.
 a 5, 10, 15, 20, …
 b 5, 6, 7, 8, …
 c 2, 5, 8, 11, …
 d −3, 1, 5, 9, …

3 Decide whether each sequence is **arithmetic**.
 a 5, 9, 13, 17, …
 b 1, 4, 9, 16, …
 c −3, −1, 1, 3, …
 d 32, 28, 24, 20, …
 e 2, 8, 18, 32, …

4 Work out the first four terms and the 10th term of the **quadratic** sequence with
 a $T(n) = n^2$
 b $T(n) = 3n^2$
 c $T(n) = -2n^2$
 d $T(n) = 5n^2$

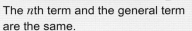

Literacy hint

The nth term and the general term are the same.

Key point

An nth term that includes n^2 (and no higher power of n) generates a **quadratic sequence**.

Q3 Literacy hint

An **arithmetic** sequence increases or decreases in equal steps.

Key point

$T(n)$ is another way of writing the nth term.

Q4a hint

$T(1) = 1^2 = \square$
$T(2) = 2^2 = \square$

Warm up

5 Work out the first four terms and the 10th term of the quadratic sequence with

   a $T(n) = 2n^2 + 4$

   b $T(n) = 3n^2 - 3$

   c $T(n) = -3n^2 + 7$

   d $T(n) = 4n^2 - 5$

6 For each nth term

   i work out the first four terms and the 10th term of the sequence

   ii state whether the sequence is arithmetic or quadratic.

   a $T(n) = 5n + 6$

   b $T(n) = 2n^2 - 6$

   c $T(n) = 2n - 6$

   d $T(n) = 100 - 2n^2$

7 **Reasoning** Find the 5th and 10th terms of the sequence with $T(n) = 2n^2 + 5$.

Explain why the 10th term is not double the 5th term.

8 The first two terms of an arithmetic sequence are 4, 6, …

   a Write down the next three terms.

   b Find the common difference.

   c Write down the nth term of the arithmetic sequence.

   d **Discussion** What is the relationship between the common difference and the nth term of an arithmetic sequence?

9 **Real / Problem-solving** A scientist thinks that the number of rabbits in a field will increase in the same way as an arithmetic sequence.

In year 1 he counts 12 rabbits.

In year 2 he counts 18 rabbits.

How many rabbits does he expect to see in

   a year 3   **b** year 5   **c** year 'n'?

Q8 hint

The sequence is arithmetic so it increases or decreases in equal steps.

Q8 hint

The common difference is the difference between consecutive terms in an arithmetic sequence.

For example, in the sequence 1, 6, 11, 16, … the common difference is 5.

Problem-solving

Investigation

1 The nth term of a sequence is $2n + a$, where a is an integer.

One of its terms is 20.

   a Choose a value for a.

   b What position is the term 20 with your choice of a?

   c How can you make the term 20 appear earlier in the sequence?

2 The nth term of a sequence is $an + 4$, where a is an integer.

One of its terms is 20.

   a Choose a value for a.

   b What position is the term 20 with your choice of a?

   c How can you make the term 20 appear earlier in the sequence?

10 **Explore** There are 100 rabbits on an island.

How many will there be in 6 months' time?

Is it easier to explore this question now that you have completed the lesson?

What further information do you need to be able to answer this?

11 **Reflect** Deepak says, 'A lot of maths is about looking for hidden patterns.'

Which questions in this lesson do you think Deepak was thinking of when he said this?

Active Learn   Homework, Year 9, Unit 3

3.2 Geometric sequences

You will learn to:
- Recognise and continue geometric sequences.
- Solve problems involving geometric sequences.

Why learn this?
Population growth could be modelled using a geometric sequence to work out how many schools and hospitals a town will need.

Fluency
Which of these sequences are arithmetic?
2, 4, 6, 8, …
2, 4, 8, 16, 32, …
8, 6, 4, 2, …
2, 4, 2, 4, 2, …

Explore
If you doubled the amount of money you earned every year, how much would you earn in the year in which you are 50? Do you think this is likely to happen?

Exercise 3.2

1 Work out

  a $\frac{1}{2} \times \frac{1}{2}$

  b $\frac{1}{4} \times \frac{1}{2}$

  c $\frac{1}{4} \times \frac{1}{4}$

  d $\frac{1}{2} \times \frac{3}{4}$

2 Work out

  a 3×0.1

  b 0.1×0.3

  c 0.3×0.3

  d 0.03×0.1

> **Key point**
>
> In a **geometric sequence** you find each term by multiplying the previous term in the sequence by a constant value. This value is called the common ratio.

Worked example

A geometric sequence starts 2, 6, …
What are the 3rd, 4th and 5th terms in the sequence?

$6 \div 2 = 3$
3rd term = $6 \times 3 = 18$
4th term = $18 \times 3 = 54$
5th term = $54 \times 3 = 162$

To find the common ratio divide the 2nd term by the 1st term.

3 Find the next three terms of the geometric sequences that start:

  a 1, 10, …

  b 1, 3, …

  c 100, 10, …

  d 400, 200, …

  e **Discussion** If the sequence is descending, what can you say about the common ratio?

> **Q3c hint**
>
> Sometimes the common ratio is a fraction or decimal,
> e.g. $10 \div 100 = 0.1$

4 Problem-solving The first term of a geometric sequence is 2.
The common ratio is 5.
How many terms in the sequence are smaller than 100?

5 Reasoning Decide whether these sequences are arithmetic,
quadratic geometric or neither.
   a 12, 15, 18, 21, ...
   b 12, 24, 48, 96, ...
   c 4, 7, 12, 19, ...
   d 12, 24, 36, 48, ...
   e 12, 0, 12, 0, ...
   f 1, 7, 17, 31, ...
   g 12, 8, 4, 0, ...

6 Look at this pattern.

How many drops will be in the 10th term?

7 Reasoning Look at the sequence: 3^0, 3, 3^2, 3^3
   a Discussion Explain why this is a geometric sequence.
   b Write down the 20th term in the sequence.

8 Write down the first five terms of the geometric sequence with

   a first term = –4   common ratio = –1

   b first term = 0.5   common ratio = 0.1

   c first term = $\frac{1}{2}$ common ratio = $\frac{1}{2}$

   d first term = $\frac{1}{4}$ common ratio = $\frac{3}{4}$

9 Explore If you doubled the amount of money you earned every
year, how much would you earn in the year in which you are 50? Do
you think this is likely to happen?
Is it easier to explore this question now that you have completed the
lesson? What further information do you need to be able to answer
this?

10 Reflect Write down definitions for an arithmetic sequence and a
geometric sequence. Write down one thing that is different about the
two sequences and one thing that is the same.

3.3 Expanding

You will learn to:
- Multiply pairs of brackets.
- Square a linear expression.
- Use quadratic identities.

Fluency
- What is $7(3 + 7)$?
- Expand $5(x - 6)$.
- Factorise $8x + 4$.

Explore
What is the area of a rectangle that is $(x + 2)$ by $(x - 2)$?

Why learn this?
Expanding brackets can help promoters work out what price to sell match tickets at for the greatest profit.

Exercise 3.3

Warm up

1 Expand and simplify
  a $5(x + 2) + 2x$
  b $6(a - 5) + 6$
  c $2(z + 3) + 3(z - 5)$
  d $5(3 - t) - 2(t + 4)$

2 Expand and simplify
  a $2x(x^2 + 2) + 3x$
  b $3y(4 - y) + y^2$
  c $2b + b^2(b + 3) + 3$
  d $w^3(3w - 2) - 2w(w + 3)$

Key point

When you **expand** double brackets, you multiply each term in one set of brackets by each term in the other set of brackets.
$$(a + b)(c + d) = ac + ad + bc + bd$$

Worked example

Expand and simplify $(x + 2)(x + 4)$.

$(x + 2)(x + 4) = x^2 + 4x + 2x + 8$
               $= x^2 + 6x + 8$

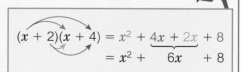

$(x + 2)(x + 4) = x^2 + \underline{4x + 2x} + 8$
              $= x^2 + \quad 6x \quad + 8$

3 Expand the double brackets and simplify.
  a $(x + 3)(x + 2)$
  b $(y + 2)(y + 3)$
  c $(d + 5)(d + 2)$
  d $(m + 3)(m + 4)$
  e $(v + 6)(v + 3)$
  f $(h + 6)(h + 7)$
  Discussion What do you notice about your answers to parts **a** and **b**?

4 Expand the double brackets and simplify.
  a $(p + 3)(p - 2)$
  b $(w - 3)(w + 2)$
  c $(x + 4)(x - 2)$
  d $(e - 3)(e + 6)$
  e $(s - 8)(s - 2)$
  f $(j - 5)(j - 4)$

Q4 hint

Be careful with negative numbers.
$-8 \times -2 = +16$

5 **Problem-solving / Reasoning** Adam and Kari both expand and simplify the quadratic expression $(x - 3)(-5 + x)$.
Adam says the answer is $x^2 + 2x - 15$.
Kari says the answer is $x^2 - 8x + 15$.
Only one of them is correct. Who is it? What mistakes were made?

6 Expand and simplify

  a $(x + 5)^2$

  b $(x + 6)^2$

  c $(x + 7)^2$

  d $(x - 1)^2$

  e $(x - 4)^2$

  f $(x - 7)^2$

Q6a hint

$(x + 5)^2 = (x + 5)(x + 5)$

7 Expand and simplify

  a $(x + 8)(x - 2) + x(4x - 2)$

  b $(n - 2)(n - 6) - 10(n + 4)$

Q7a hint

Expand $(x + 8)(x - 2)$.
Expand $x(4x - 2)$.
Add them together.

8 Problem-solving / Reasoning Show that
$$n(n + 8) - 2(n + 5) = (n + 4)(n - 2) + 2(2n - 1)$$

Problem-solving / Reasoning

Investigation

1 Expand and simplify

  a $(x + 1)(x - 1)$

  b $(x + 3)(x - 3)$

  c $(x + 4)(x - 4)$

  d $(x + 5)(x - 5)$

  e $(x + 6)(x - 6)$

  f $(x + 7)(x - 7)$

  g $(x + 8)(x - 8)$

2 What do you notice about your answers?

3 Why do you think expressions of the form $(x + n)(x - n)$ are called the **difference of two squares**?

9 Problem-solving / Modelling A farmer has a square-shaped field of length a metres.

  a Write an expression for the area of his field.

  b He changes the shape of the field by adding b metres to one pair of opposite sides, and subtracting b metres from the other pair of opposite sides. Write an expression for the area of this field.

  c What effect has changing the shape of the field had on the area?

10 Expand and simplify

  a $(2x + 7)(x - 5)$

  b $(2x - 4)(x - 3)$

  c $(x + 7)(2x - 2)$

  d $(3x + 6)(2x - 4)$

  e $(2x - 3)(4x + 5)$

  f $(3x - 7)(3x - 8)$

Q10 hint

Follow the same rules as you did in Q3–6.

11 Expand and simplify

  a $(3x + 7)^2$

  b $(2x - 4)^2$

  c $(5x + 6)^2$

  d $(4x + 9)^2$

  e $(7x - 3)^2$

  f $(8x - 9)^2$

12 Expand and simplify

  a $(2x + 1)(2x - 1)$

  b $(3x + 4)(3x - 4)$

  c $(2x - 5)(2x + 5)$

  d $(c + d)(c - d)$

13 Explore What is the area of a rectangle that is $(x + 2)$ by $(x - 2)$? Is it easier to explore this question now that you have completed the lesson? What further information do you need to be able to answer this?

14 Reflect Q9 is a pictorial example of the difference of two squares. Can you think of other examples where a picture helps to explain abstract ideas?

Reflect | **Explore**

Active Learn   Homework, Year 9, Unit 3

3.4 Factorising

You will learn to:

- Factorise quadratic expressions into two brackets.

Why learn this?
The path of a cricket ball can be described using a quadratic expression. It is useful to be able to factorise such expressions in order to find out more about the motion of the ball, such as the maximum height it reaches.

Fluency
Which pair of numbers
- add up to 7 and multiply to make 10
- add up to 13 and multiply to make 30
- add up to 5 and multiply to make −24?

Explore
Does $x^2 + a^2$ factorise?

Exercise 3.4

1 Expand and simplify
  a $(x + 4)^2$ **b** $(x - 3)^2$
  c $(x + y)^2$ **d** $(2x + 4)^2$
  e $(3x - 4)^2$ **f** $(2x + y)^2$

2 Expand and simplify
  a $(x + 5)(x - 5)$ **b** $(a + 7)(a - 7)$
  c $(y + 2)(y - 2)$ **d** $(x + y)(x - y)$

3 Factorise
  a $4x^2 + 12x$ **b** $25x^3 - 15x$
  c $y^2 - 9y^3$ **d** $3x^4 + 15x^2$

Worked example

Factorise $x^2 + 7x + 10$.

$2 + 5 \qquad 2 \times 5$

$x^2 + 7x + 10 = (x + 5)(x + 2)$

$x^2 + 7x + 10 = (x + 5)(x + 2)$

Check: $(x + 2)(x + 5) = x^2 + 5x + 2x + 5 \times 2$
$\qquad\qquad\qquad\quad = x^2 + 7x + 10$

The **factor pairs** of 10 are
1×10 and 2×5.
Only the 2 and 5 add together to make 7 so these are the numbers that go in the brackets.

Check your answer by expanding.

4 Factorise each quadratic expression. Check your answers.
  a $x^2 + 7x + 12$ **b** $x^2 + 9x + 18$
  c $x^2 + 9x + 14$ **d** $x^2 + 12x + 27$
  e $x^2 - 3x + 2$ **f** $x^2 - 7x + 12$

Q4f hint
Remember that $-3 \times -4 = 12$ as well as $3 \times 4 = 12$.

Warm up

5 Factorise each quadratic expression. Check your answers.
  a $x^2 + 3x - 18$
  b $x^2 + 4x - 12$
  c $x^2 + 8x - 33$
  d $x^2 - 7x - 44$
  e $x^2 - 9x - 36$
  f $x^2 - 12x - 28$

6 Match the equivalent expressions.

A $x^2 + 8x + 12$	i $(x - 7)(x - 4)$
B $x^2 + 9x + 20$	ii $(x + 9)(x - 4)$
C $x^2 - 11x + 28$	iii $(x + 2)(x - 5)$
D $x^2 - 7x + 10$	iv $(x + 4)(x + 5)$
E $x^2 + 5x - 36$	v $(x - 4)(x + 3)$
F $x^2 + 4x - 21$	vi $(x + 6)(x + 2)$
G $x^2 - x - 12$	vii $(x + 7)(x - 3)$
H $x^2 - 3x - 10$	viii $(x - 5)(x - 2)$

Key point

A **perfect square** is of the form
$(x + a)^2 = (x + a)(x + a) = x^2 + 2ax + a^2$

7 Write these as **perfect squares**.
  a $x^2 + 6x + 9$
  b $x^2 + 14x + 49$
  c $x^2 - 8x + 16$
  d $x^2 - 12x + 36$

Q7a hint

Find the value of a in this equation and then substitute it in.
$x^2 + 2ax + a^2 = x^2 + 6x + 9$

8 Factorise each quadratic expression. Check your answers.
  a $x^2 - 25$
  b $x^2 - 64$
  c $x^2 - 81$
  d $x^2 - 121$
  e $p^2 - q^2$

Q8 hint

The middle term has cancelled out when collecting terms.

9 **Problem-solving** The area of a rectangle is $x^2 + 11x + 24$.
  What could the side lengths of the rectangle be?

10 **Problem-solving** Ibrahim adjusts the sides of a quadrilateral so that
  its perimeter remains the same and its new area is $x^2 - 49$.
  a How did he change the two sides?
  b Describe the original shape.

11 **Explore** Does $x^2 + a^2$ factorise?
  Is it easier to explore this question now that you have completed the
  lesson? What further information do you need to be able to
  answer this?

12 **Reflect** Factorising quadratic expressions often involves 'trial and
  error'. Is trial and error simply guesswork, or can you devise a
  system to make it more efficient?

*Active*Learn   Homework, Year 9, Unit 3

3.5 Solving quadratic equations

You will learn to:
- Solve quadratic equations by factorising.

Why learn this?
The police solve quadratic equations to work out how fast cars were travelling before a collision.

Fluency
Work out x when
- $x - 8 = 14$
- $7x = 56$
- $3x + 4 = 19$

Work out
- 2×0
- $8 \times 0 \times 6$
- $15 \times -3 \times 0$
- 5×0

Explore
How far will a car travel once the brakes are applied?

Exercise 3.5

1 Write down the positive and negative square roots of 36.

2 Factorise each expression.
   a $x^2 - 3x + 2$ **b** $x^2 - 81$ **c** $x^2 - 2x - 35$ **d** $x^2 + 10x + 25$

3 Solve these equations. Give the positive *and* negative solutions.
   a $x^2 + 5 = 21$ **b** $x^2 + 9 = 58$ **c** $x^2 - 5 = 95$
   d $\dfrac{x^2}{2} = 32$ **e** $x^2 = 3^2 + 4^2$ **f** $x^2 - 5^2 = 12^2$

> **Key point**
> You can solve some quadratic equations by setting them equal to 0 and factorising.

> **Worked example**
> Solve the equation $x^2 + 9 = 90$, giving the positive and negative solutions.
> $$x^2 + 9 = 90$$
> $-9 \quad\quad -9$
> $$x^2 = 81$$
> $$x = \pm\sqrt{81} \quad \text{— Square root.}$$
> $$x = +9 \text{ or } x = -9$$

4 Solve each quadratic equation by factorising. Check your answers.
   a $x^2 + x = 2$ **b** $x^2 + 15x = -54$ **c** $x^2 + x = 20$
   d $x^2 + 4x = 21$ **e** $x^2 - 9x = 22$ **f** $x^2 - 14x = 51$

> **Q4 hint**
> Rearrange the equations so that they equal 0.

> **Worked example**
> Solve $x^2 + 6x = 27$.
> $$x^2 + 6x = 27$$
> $$x^2 + 6x - 27 = 0 \quad \text{— Rearrange the equation so it equals 0.}$$
> $$(x + 9)(x - 3) = 0 \quad \text{— Factorise the quadratic expression.}$$
> $$x + 9 = 0 \quad\quad x = -9$$
> $$x - 3 = 0 \quad\quad x = 3$$
> 0 multiplied by any number is 0.
> So either $x + 9 = 0$ or $x - 3 = 0$.
> $$x = -9 \text{ or } x = 3$$
> Check by substitution:
> $$x = -9: (-9)^2 + (6 \times -9) = 27 \quad\quad 81 - 54 = 27 \checkmark$$
> $$x = 3: 3^2 + (6 \times 3) = 27 \quad\quad 9 + 18 = 27 \checkmark$$

Warm up

5 Solve each quadratic equation by factorising. Check your answers.

   a $x^2 + 4x = -4$ **b** $x^2 + 14x = -49$

   c $x^2 - 6x = -9$ **d** $x^2 - 10x = -25$

6 **Problem-solving** The length of a rectangle is 4 m more than its width. The area is 96 m². What is the

   a length

   b width of the rectangle?

   Discussion How did you decide which solution to use?

7 **Problem-solving** Bonita is 2 years older than Kalila. The product of their ages is 399. How old are they both?

8 **Problem-solving** Bahir is 4 years younger than Jamal. The product of their ages is 437. How old are they both?

9 **Problem-solving** The square of a number is equal to 10 times the number subtract 24.
   Find two possible values for the number.

10 Solve these equations to work out x.

   a $x^2 + 11 = 47$ **b** $x^2 - 6 = 19$ **c** $x^2 - 24 = 25$

11 **Problem-solving** Shah thinks of a number, squares it and adds 9 to get an answer of 25.

   a Write an equation to show this.

   b Solve the equation.

   c Why can't you be sure about which number Shah thought of?

Investigation   Reasoning / Problem-solving

1 Without expanding and rearranging, solve $(x + 5)^2 = 16$.
2 Explain why the solutions are the same as $x^2 + 10x + 9 = 0$.
3 Write $x^2 + 4x + 4$ as a perfect square.
4 Use your answer to part **3** to solve $x^2 + 4x + 10$ in two different ways.

---

12 **Explore** How far will a car travel once the brakes are applied? Is it easier to explore this question now that you have completed the lesson? What further information do you need to be able to answer this?

13 **Reflect** This lesson has several problem-solving questions. How did your methods for solving them change as you progressed through the lesson? Did finding the solutions get easier by the time you reached the last question?

3 Check up

Arithmetic, quadratic and geometric sequences

1 Are these sequences arithmetic, geometric, quadratic or neither?

   a 1, 2, 4, 8, 16, …

   b 1, 2, 3, 4, 5, …

   c 1, 2, 1, 2, 1, 2, …

   d $1, \frac{1}{2}, \frac{1}{4}, \frac{1}{8}, …$

2 Write the next three terms in each sequence.
   a 0, 3, 8, 15, …
   b −1, 2, 7, 14, …
   c 3, 5, 9, 15, …
   d 3, 6, 12, 24, …
   e 81, 27, 9, 3, …

3 Work out the first four terms and the 10th term of the quadratic sequence with
   a $T(n) = 4n^2$
   b $T(n) = -7n^2$

4 Work out the first four terms and the 10th term of the quadratic sequence with
   a $T(n) = 4n^2 - 2$
   b $T(n) = -2n^2 + 4$
   c $T(n) = -3n^2 - 5$
   d $T(n) = -n^2 + 2n - 3$

5 The first term of a geometric sequence is 4.
   The common ratio is 3.
   How many terms in the sequence are less than 100?

6 Write down the first five terms of the geometric sequence with
   a first term = −3   common ratio = −1
   b first term = 6   common ratio = 0.2

Expanding

7 Expand and simplify
   a $(x + 2)(x + 7)$
   b $(x + 8)(x - 5)$
   c $(x - 4)(x + 6)$
   d $(x - 7)(x - 9)$

8 Molly has squared the expression $(x - 6)$ and written the answer $x^2 + 36$.
   Is Molly correct? Explain how you know.

9 Expand and simplify
   a $(x - 2)(x + 2)$
   b $(x + 7)(x - 7)$
   c $(x + 5)^2$

10 Expand and simplify

    a $(2x + 3)(x - 6)$

    b $(3x + 8)(2x - 5)$

    c $(4x - 3)(3x - 8)$

    d $(2x - 7)(2x + 7)$

11 A rectangle has a length of $2x + 1$ and a width of $3x - 2$.
Write an expression for the area of the rectangle.

Factorising

12 Factorise each quadratic expression.

    a $x^2 + 5x + 6$

    b $x^2 + 7x - 18$

    c $x^2 - 5x + 4$

    d $x^2 - 4x - 45$

13 Factorise each quadratic expression.

    a $x^2 + 6x + 9$

    b $x^2 - 10x + 25$

    c $x^2 - 49$

14 The area of a rectangle is $x^2 - 4x - 21$.
Write down an expression for the width and the length of
the rectangle.

Solving quadratic equations

15 Solve each equation.

    a $x^2 + 8x = -15$

    b $x^2 + 11x = -24$

    c $x^2 - x = 30$

    d $x^2 + 6x = 7$

16 Milo is 5 years older than Vlad.
The product of their ages is 414.
How old are they both?

17 **How sure are you of your answers? Were you mostly**
  😦 **Just guessing**   😐 **Feeling doubtful**   😊 **Confident**
**What next? Use your results to decide whether to strengthen or
extend your learning.**

Challenge

18 a Factorise each of the expressions in the grid.

$x^2 + 8x + 12$	$x^2 + 7x + 10$	$x^2 - 2x + 1$
$x^2 - 4x + 3$	$x^2 - 9$	$x^2 + 9x + 18$
$x^2 + 5x - 6$	$x^2 + 4x - 5$	$x^2 - x - 6$

    b Make a list of all the factors used.

    c Using only these factors, make as many new expressions as you
can.

3 Strengthen

You will:
* Strengthen your understanding with practice.

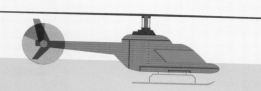

Arithmetic, quadratic and geometric sequences

1 Which of these are arithmetic sequences?

a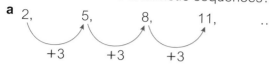
2,   5,   8,   11,   …
+3   +3   +3

Q1a hint

In an arithmetic sequence the difference between each consecutive term is constant.

b 5, 11, 17, 23, …
c 1, 2, 4, 7, …
d $\frac{1}{2}$, 1, 2, 4, …
e 10, 8, 6, 4, …
f 10, 7, 3, −2, …

2 Write the next three terms in these arithmetic sequences.
a 12, 15, 18, 21, …
b 112, 114, 116, 118, …
c 200, 190, 180, 170, …
d 9, 4, −1, −6, …

Q2a hint

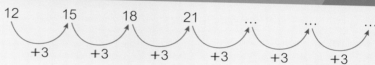
12   15   18   21   …   …   …
+3   +3   +3   +3   +3   +3

3 Which of these are geometric sequences?
a 10, 20, 40, 80, …
b 100, 10, 1, 0.1, …
c 20, 25, 30, 35, 40, …
d 19, 14, 9, 4, −1, …
e 3, 0.3, 0.03, 0.003, …

Q3a hint

In a geometric sequence the ratio between consecutive terms is constant.
$20 ÷ 10 = 2$
$40 ÷ 20 = 2$
$80 ÷ 40 = ….$

4 Write the next two terms in these geometric sequences.
a 1, 5, 25, …
b 2000, 200, 20, …
c 128, 64, 32, …
d 900, 90, 9, …

Q4a hint

$5 ÷ 1 = 5$; so the common ratio = 5.
$25 × 5 = 125$
$125 × 5 = ….$

5 A quadratic sequence has a general term $T(n) = n^2$.
a Work out the first four terms.
b Work out the 10th term.

Q5a hint

1st   term: $T(1) = 1^2$
2nd   term: $T(2) = 2^2$

6 Work out the first four terms and the 10th term of the quadratic sequence with
a $T(n) = n^2 + 4$
b $T(n) = n^2 − 3$
c $T(n) = 4n^2$
d $T(n) = 3n^2 + 7$
e $T(n) = −2n^2 + 5$

Q6 hint

Follow the same method as in Q5.

Expanding

1 Expand and simplify
  a $(a + 5)(a + 4)$
  b $(n + 3)(n + 2)$
  c $(x + 7)(x + 4)$
  d $(p + 3)(p + 2)$
  e $(y + 7)(y + 1)$

2 Expand and simplify
  a $(b - 6)(b + 3)$
  b $(y + 4)(y - 3)$
  c $(x - 8)(x + 2)$
  d $(a + 3)(a - 4)$
  e $(b - 6)(b - 5)$
  f $(x - 3)(x - 5)$
  g $(g - 3)(g - 7)$
  h $(n - 9)(n - 3)$

3 Expand and simplify
  a $(c + 7)^2$
  b $(y - 5)^2$
  c $(n + 8)^2$
  d $(n - 1)^2$
  e $(p - 6)^2$

4 Expand and simplify
  a $(x - 3)(x + 3)$
  b $(x + 2)(x - 2)$
  c $(x - 9)(x + 9)$
  d $(x + y)(x - y)$

5 Expand and simplify
  a $(2x + 4)(x - 3)$
  b $(2x - 5)(x - 2)$
  c $(x + 4)(2x - 3)$
  d $(2x + 7)(2x - 4)$
  e $(x + 2)(3x - 5)$
  f $(2x + 9)(3x - 2)$

Factorising

1 a Which two numbers
    i add together to make 8 and multiply together to make 15
    ii add together to make 11 and multiply together to make 28?
  b Factorise each quadratic expression.
    Check your answers by expanding the brackets.
    i $x^2 + 5x + 6 = (x + \square)(x + \square)$
    ii $x^2 + 12x + 35 = (x + \square)(x + \square)$
    iii $x^2 + 9x + 8 = (x + \square)(x + \square)$
    iv $x^2 + 10x + 24$
    v $x^2 + 11x + 24$
    vi $x^2 + 11x + 18$

Q1a hint

To expand $(a + 5)(a + 4)$, use a grid method like this:

×	a	+5
a	$+a^2$	$+5a$
+4	$+4a$	$+20$

Answer: $a^2 + 5a + 4a + 20$
Simplify: $\square + \square + \square$

Q2a hint

To expand $(b - 6)(b + 3)$, use a grid method like this:

×	b	−6
b	b^2	$-6b$
+3	$+3b$	-18

Q3a hint

$(c + 7)^2 = (c + 7)(c + 7)$

Q4 hint

Look at what happens to the middle two terms.

Q5 hint

$2x \times x = 2x^2$
$2x \times 2x = 2 \times x \times 2 \times x$
$\qquad\quad = 4 \times x^2$
$\qquad\quad = 4x^2$

Q1b i hint

Which two numbers add together to make 5 and multiply together to make 6?

2 a Which two numbers
    i add to make –5 and multiply to make 6
    ii add to make –10 and multiply to make 21?

b Factorise each quadratic expression.
    i $x^2 - 7x + 12 = (x - \square)(x - \square)$
    ii $x^2 - 6x + 8 = (x - \square)(x - \square)$
    iii $x^2 - 9x + 20 = (x - \square)(x - \square)$
    iv $x^2 - 8x + 7$
    v $x^2 - 15x + 44$
    vi $x^2 - 13x + 42$

Q2b hint

negative × negative = **positive**
negative + negative = **negative**

3 Factorise
a $x^2 - 2x - 8 = (x + \square)(x - \square)$
b $x^2 - 3x - 10 = (x + \square)(x - \square)$
c $x^2 - 3x - 18 = (x + \square)(x - \square)$
d $x^2 - 8x - 48$
e $x^2 - 6x - 27$
f $x^2 - x - 12$

Q3 hint

negative × positive = **negative**
negative + positive = **positive** or **negative**

4 Factorise
a $x^2 + 7x - 18 = (x - \square)(x + \square)$
b $x^2 + 2x - 24 = (x - \square)(x + \square)$
c $x^2 + x - 56 = (x - \square)(x + \square)$
d $x^2 + 3x - 54$
e $x^2 + 4x - 21$
f $x^2 + 5x - 24$

5 Factorise
a $x^2 + 4x + 4$
b $x^2 - 6x + 9$
c $x^2 + 12x + 36$
d $x^2 - 4x + 4$

Q6 hint

Any expression of the form $x^2 - y^2$
can be factorised as $(x + y)(x - y)$
and is known as the 'difference of
two squares'.
For example $x^2 - 9$ factorises as
$(x + 3)(x - 3)$.

6 Factorise
a $x^2 - 4$
b $x^2 - 16$
c $x^2 - 144$

Solving quadratic equations

1 Solve each quadratic equation by factorising.
a $x^2 + 6x = 0$
b $x^2 - 4x = 0$
c $x^2 - 8x = 0$
d $x^2 - 7x = 0$
e $x^2 + 5x = 0$

Q1 Strategy hint

Remember that anything multiplied
by zero is zero.
In the equation $x(x - 2) = 0$,
x is either 2 (because $2 - 2 = 0$)
or 0 (because 0 × the bracket is 0).

2 Solve each quadratic equation by factorising.

  a $x^2 + 3x = -2$
  b $x^2 + 5x = -4$
  c $x^2 + 3x = 10$
  d $x^2 - x = 12$
  e $x^2 + 9x = -20$
  f $x^2 - 7x = 18$
  g $x^2 + 12x = -36$
  h $x^2 - 6x = 16$

Q2a hint

Rearrange the equation so that it equals zero.

$x^2 + 3x = -2$ Add 2 to both sides of the equation.

$x^2 + 3x + 2 = 0$ Factorise the left-hand side.

$(x + 2)(x + 1) = 0$

The solutions are the values that make each bracket zero.

3 Problem-solving The length of a rectangle is 3 m more than its width. The area is 130 m².
Find the length and the width of the rectangle.

4 Problem-solving Hamid is 5 years older than his sister Shanaz. Their ages multiplied together come to 176.

  a How old is Hamid?
  b How old is Shanaz?

Q4 hint

Let Shanaz's age be x.
Create an expression for Hamid's age in terms of x.
Form an equation for their combined ages.
Factorise and solve.

Enrichment

1 Choose pairs of these linear expressions to expand. You can square expressions too.

  a How many different quadratic expressions can you make?
  b What are the similarities and differences between them?

  $x + 3$ $x - 2$ $x - 3$ $x + 2$

2 Reflect How would you explain the difference between linear and quadratic sequences to a friend who has missed out on this unit?

Reflect

3 Extend

You will:
• Extend your understanding with problem-solving.

---

1 Find the next three terms of each sequence.
a 7, 14, 23, 34, …
b 0, 9, 22, 39, …
c −6, 6, 30, 66, …
d 3, −7, −25, −51, …

2 Work out the first four terms, the 20th term and the 100th term of each sequence.
a $T(n) = n^2 + 6n − 2$
b $T(n) = 2n^2 + 3n − 1$
c $T(n) = 4n^2 − 2n + 5$
d $T(n) = −2n^2 − 2n + 4$
e $T(n) = −4n^2 + 2n − 3$
f $T(n) = 8n^2 + 2n − 16$

> **Q2 hint**
> Substitute the term number into each expression.

3 **Problem-solving / Reasoning** The first two terms of a sequence are 1, 2 …
What is the 5th term, if the sequence is
a arithmetic
b geometric?

4 **Problem-solving / Reasoning** The 5th and 6th terms of an arithmetic sequence are 20 and 17.
What is
a the 1st term?
b the nth term?
c the 10th term?

5 **Problem-solving / Reasoning / Modelling** A new website is launched. It has 240 hits on the first day.
On the second day it has 310 hits.
Assuming that the sequence continues arithmetically, how many hits will it have on day 10?

> **Q5 hint**
> 'Arithmetically' means that the sequence behaves like an arithmetic sequence.
> Work out the nth term of the sequence.

Investigation

Problem-solving

An ancient story tells of a ruler who liked to play chess. One day he challenged a wise man to a game and said that if the wise man won, he would pay him whatever he asked for. The wise man asked only for grains of rice, 1 in the first square on the chess board, 2 in the second square, 4 in the third square and so on.
Investigate how many grains of rice the ruler would have to give the wise man if he won the game.

> **Hint**
> There are 64 squares on a chess board.

6 The first four triangular numbers are shown below.

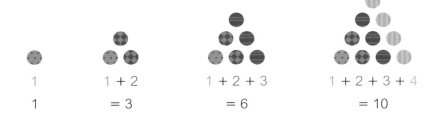

1   1 + 2   1 + 2 + 3   1 + 2 + 3 + 4

1   = 3   = 6   = 10

     a Find the next three triangular numbers.
     b Is the sequence of triangular numbers arithmetic, geometric or neither?

7 You can expand and simplify two sets of double brackets like this:
$$(x + 7)(x + 2) - (x + 3)(x + 8) = [x^2 + 2x + 7x + 14] - [x^2 + 8x + 3x + 24]$$
$$= [x^2 + 9x + 14] - [x^2 + 11x + 24]$$
$$= x^2 + 9x + 14 - x^2 - 11x - 24$$
$$= -2x - 10$$
$$= -2(x + 5)$$

Expand and simplify
     a $(x + 13)(x + 3) - (x + 10)(x + 4)$
     b $(x - 4)(x + 7) - (x + 5)(x - 3)$

8 You can expand three sets of brackets, $(x + 4)(x + 1)(x + 5)$, like this:
First expand and simplify the first two sets of brackets.
$(x + 4)(x + 1) = x^2 + x + 4x + 4 = x^2 + 5x + 4$
Then multiply the expression you get by the third set of brackets.

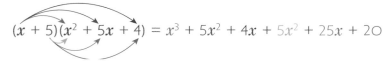

$$(x + 5)(x^2 + 5x + 4) = x^3 + 5x^2 + 4x + 5x^2 + 25x + 20$$

Expand and simplify
     a $(x + 2)(x + 3)(x + 4)$
     b $(x + 5)(x + 10)(x - 2)$
     c $(x - 6)(x + 2)(x - 9)$

9 Expand and simplify
     a $(2x + 4)(-3x - 6)$
     b $(3x + 4)(-6x - 5)$
     c $(-5x - 4)(3x + 7)$
     d $(-3x + 6)(-3x - 9)$
     e $(-2x - 4)(-4x - 2)$
     f $(-4x - 4)(-3x - 6)$

Q9 hint

Take care when squaring or multiplying negative numbers.

10 Expand and simplify
   a $(2x + 4)^2$
   b $(3x - 2)^2$
   c $(-4x - 3)^2$
   d $(-5x + 6)^2$
   e $(4x + 1)(4x - 1)$
   f $(-2x + 3)(-2x - 3)$
   g $(-4x - 7)(-4x + 7)$
   h $(ax + b)(ax - b)$

11 **Problem-solving** A square is changed into a rectangle by doubling two of the parallel sides and adding 2cm, and trebling the other parallel sides and subtracting 3cm.
   a Write an expression for the area of the rectangle.
   b The original side was 12cm. What is the difference between the area of the rectangle and the area of the original square?

> **Q11 hint**
> Form an expression for each side in terms of x.

12 **Problem-solving** A photograph with dimensions x cm by y cm is enlarged so that both sides are 4 times longer but with 1cm removed from each side to form a border.
   a Write an expression for the area of the new photograph.
   b What is the scale factor of the enlargement?

> **Q12 hint**
> The scale factor is the number that multiplies the original dimension to make the new one.

Investigation

Reasoning

1 a Expand $(x + 8)^2$.
  b Now expand $(x + 7)(x + 9)$.
  c What do you notice?
2 a Now expand $(x + 6)^2$ and $(x + 5)(x + 7)$.
  b What do you notice?
3 Try with other examples.
4 Write down a **generalisation**.
Check that your rule works for negative values.

> **Literacy hint**
> A **generalisation** usually uses only letters, for example, $(x + n)^2$.

13 Factorise each quadratic expression.
   a $2x^2 - 7x - 4 = (2x - \square)(x - \square)$
   b $3x^2 - 4x - 4 = (3x - \square)(x - \square)$
   c $5x^2 - 3x - 36$
   d $-5x^2 - 14x - 8$
   e $-3x^2 - 18x + 48$
   f $2x^2 - 11x + 12$

14 Factorise each quadratic expression.
   a $4x^2 + 4x - 3$
   b $6x^2 - 8x - 8$
   c $4x^2 - 1$
   d $12x^2 - 9x - 3$
   e $12x^2 - x - 6$
   f $9x^2 + 26x - 3$

> **Q14 hint**
> The factor pairs of $4x^2$ are x and $4x$, $2x$ and $2x$, $-x$ and $-4x$, and $-2x$ and $-2x$.

15 Problem-solving The area of a rectangular field is $6x^2 + x - 15$.
Write down an expression for the length and width of the field.

16 Problem-solving The area of a triangle is $2x^2 + 9x + 7$.
Write an expression for the base and the height of the triangle.

Q16 hint

Remember: the area of a triangle is
$\frac{1}{2}$ × base × height.

17 Solve each equation by factorising.
 a $x^2 + 10x = -16$
 b $x^2 + 20x = -36$
 c $x^2 + 6x + 5 = 0$
 d $x^2 + 16x = -28$
 e $x^2 + 14x = -40$

18 Problem-solving Abdullah thinks of a number. He squares it, then subtracts 15. His answer is twice his original number. What is his number?

Q18 hint

Start by forming an equation for the number.

19 Problem-solving There is a 5-year age difference between two brothers.
The product of their ages is 546 years.
How old are they both?

20 Two **consecutive** integers multiplied together make 306.
What are the integers?

Q20 Literacy hint

Consecutive means one after the other.

21 STEM The formula
$$s(t) = -\frac{1}{2} gt^2 + vt + h$$
is used in the study of moving objects.
$s(t)$ is an object's height after t seconds, v is the velocity in m/s, h is the initial height in metres and g is the acceleration due to gravity (9.8 m/s²).
An object is launched with a velocity of 29.4 m/s from a height of 78.4 m.
Use the formula to work out how long it will be (in seconds) before it hits the ground.

Q21 hint

Substitute the values you have into the equation.
The ground is at zero height.
Look for a common factor in each term. It could be a decimal.

22 STEM An object is launched from the ground at 41.65 m/s.
Use the formula in Q21 to work out how long it will be, in seconds, before the object returns to the ground.

23 Solve each equation by factorising.
 a $6x^2 + 13x = -6$
 b $9x^2 - 3x = 2$
 c $8x^2 + 14x = 15$
 d $-5x^2 - 57x = 22$
 e $9x^2 = 64$
 f $16x^2 + 22x = 20$

24 Reflect Jilsa says, 'You always need to sense check your answers when finding unknowns in real-life questions.' What do you think Jilsa means by 'sense check'? Can you think of any questions where you needed to do this?

Reflect

3 Unit test

1 Write the next three terms in each sequence.
 a 7, 12, 17, 22 …
 b 80, 40, 20, 10, …
 c −1, −3, −9, −27, …

2 Expand and simplify
 a $(x + 5)(x - 5)$
 b $(x + 10)(x - 10)$
 c $(a + b)(a - b)$

3 Expand and simplify
 a $(x + 3)(x + 1)$
 b $(x + 7)(x + 11)$
 c $(x + 13)(x + 3)$
 d $(x + a)(x + b)$

4 Expand and simplify
 a $(x + 8)(x - 2)$
 b $(x - 6)(x - 10)$
 c $(x - 9)(x + 3)$
 d $(x + a)(x - b)$

5 Expand and simplify
 a $(x + 5)^2$
 b $(x - 4)^2$
 c $(x + a)^2$
 d $(x - a)^2$

6 A geometric sequence starts 0.5, 1, …
 What are the next two terms in the sequence?

7 Work out the first term and the 10th term of the quadratic sequence
 with
 a $T(n) = -3n^2$
 b $T(n) = 2n^2 - 3$

8 Expand and simplify
 a $(2x + 7)(x - 2)$
 b $(4x - 5)(x - 3)$
 c $(2x - 5)(2x + 3)$
 d $(3x + 4)(2x - 3)$

9 A rectangle has side lengths $2x + 7$ and $4x - 1$.
 Write an expression, without brackets, for the area of the rectangle.

10 The diagram shows the start of a pattern.

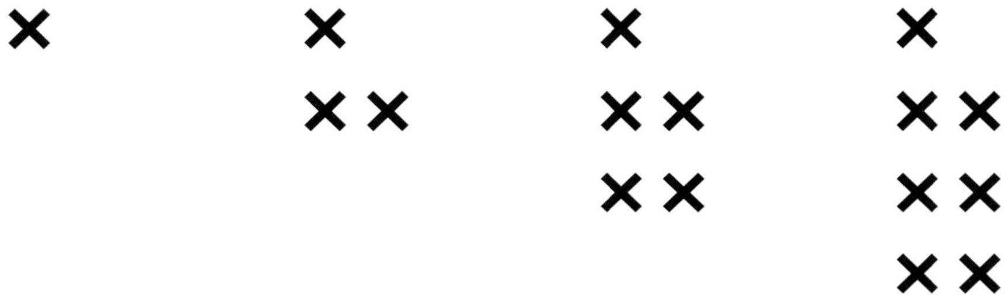

   a How many crosses will there be in the 10th term?
   b Write an expression for the number of crosses in the nth term.

11 Factorise
   a $x^2 + 6x$
   b $x^2 + 12x + 27$
   c $x^2 + 9x + 20$

12 Factorise
   a $x^2 + x - 30$
   b $x^2 - x - 12$
   c $x^2 - 11x + 24$
   d $x^2 + 3x - 54$

13 Factorise
   a $x^2 - 144$
   b $p^2 - q^2$
   c $4x^2 - 36$
   d $x^2 + 8x + 16$

14 Solve
   a $x^2 + x = 12$
   b $x^2 - 7x = -10$
   c $x^2 + 4x = 5$

15 Is 360 a term in the sequence with $T(n) = 2n^2 + 4$? Explain.

Challenge

16 Copy and complete the multiplication square below.

×		$(x - 3)$
	$x^2 + 10x + 21$	$x^2 - 9$
		$x^2 - 7x + 12$

17 Reflect Make a list of any topics in this unit that
   • you need more help with or
   • you could help another student to understand.

Reflect

Constructions

4.1 Constructing shapes

You will learn to:
* Draw accurate nets of 3D solids.
* Construct triangles using a ruler and compasses.
* Construct nets of 3D solids using a ruler and compasses.

Why learn this?
Packaging designers need to construct accurate nets for boxes.

Fluency
How many faces does each 3D solid have?
* cuboid
* triangular prism
* square-based pyramid

Explore
What area of cardboard is needed to make a box for a rolled-up poster?

Exercise 4.1

1 Here are the nets of some 3D solids.
Name the 3D solid made by each net.

a

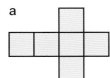

b

c

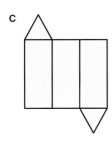

d

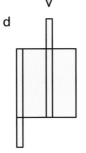

2 Use a ruler and protractor to accurately draw a net of each triangular prism.

a

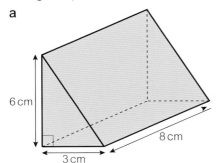

b

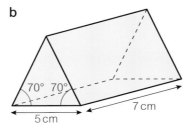

Q2 Strategy hint

Sketch the net first. Write all the lengths you know on your sketch. Mark the right angles.

Warm up

Worked example

Construct a triangle with sides 10 cm, 11 cm and 7 cm.

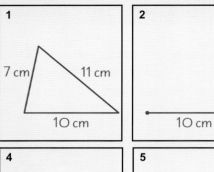

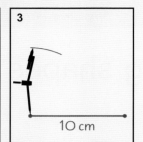

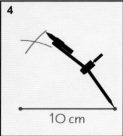

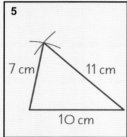

1 Sketch the triangle first.
2 Draw a 10 cm line.
3 Open your compasses to 7 cm.
  Place the point at one end of the 10 cm line.
  Draw an arc.
4 Open your compasses to 11 cm.
  Draw an arc from the other end of the 10 cm line.
  Make sure your arcs are long enough to intersect.
5 Join the intersection of the arcs to each end of the 10 cm line.
  Don't rub out your construction marks.

3 Construct each triangle ABC.
  a AB = 9 cm, BC = 6 cm and CA = 6 cm
  b AB = 7 cm, BC = 3 cm and CA = 8.5 cm
  c AB = 12.8 cm, BC = 11.9 cm and CA = 3.2 cm

4 Draw an equilateral triangle with sides 7.5 cm.
  Check the angles using a protractor. What should they measure?
  Discussion How could you construct an angle of 60° without using a protractor?

Topic links: Parts of a circle

5 **Real** The diagram shows a 700 cm ladder leaning against a wall.
The foot of the ladder is 270 cm from the wall.
The ladder reaches a height of 640 cm up the wall.

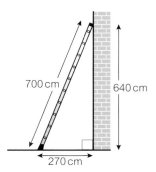

700 cm   640 cm   270 cm

    a Use a ruler and compasses to make an accurate scale drawing.
    Use a scale of 1 cm to 100 cm.
    b Safety guidelines say that a ladder should make a maximum angle
    of 75° to the ground.
    Use your protractor to check if this ladder is safe.

6 Each face of a four-sided dice is an
equilateral triangle.
Use a ruler and compasses to construct
a net of the dice.

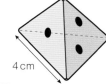

4 cm

7 The Great Pyramid of Khafre has a square
base of side 220 m and a sloping edge of length 210 m.

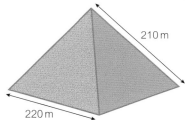

210 m

220 m

Construct a net of the pyramid on squared paper.
Use a scale of 1 cm to 50 m.

Q7 hint

Start by drawing two sides of the
square base.
Then draw two arcs to find the other
corner of the square.

8 **Explore** What area of cardboard is needed to make a box for a
rolled-up poster?
Look back at the maths you have learned in this lesson.
How can you use it to answer this question?

9 **Reflect** In this lesson you drew constructions and accurate diagrams.
What were you good at?
What were you not so good at?
Write yourself a hint to help you with the constructions or diagrams
you are not so good at.

4.2 Constructions 1

You will learn to:
- Bisect a line using a ruler and compasses.
- Construct perpendicular lines using a ruler and compasses.

Confidence

Why learn this?
Constructions reduce measurement error.

Fluency
What do these words mean?
- perpendicular
- intersect
- arc

Explore
What is the shortest distance from a point in a field to the edge?

Exercise 4.2

Warm up

1 Use a ruler and compasses to construct this triangle.

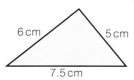

6 cm   5 cm
7.5 cm

2 a What is the name of this quadrilateral?
  b How many lines of symmetry does it have?
  c Sketch the quadrilateral and draw the diagonals.
  d Write on the diagram any information you know about its angles, lengths, parallel sides and right angles.

3 a Draw two intersecting circles with radius 5 cm.

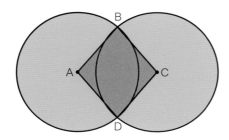

  b Join the centres to the points of intersection, B and D.
  c What is the name of the quadrilateral ABCD?
    Explain your answer.
  d Join the centres A and C using a straight line.
    Join the points of intersection B and D using a straight line.
  e What can you say about the point of intersection of AC and BD?

Q3e hint

Measure the lines and angles.

Worked example

Draw a line 7 cm long.
Construct its **perpendicular bisector**.

  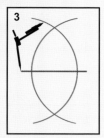 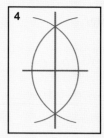

1. Use a ruler to draw the line.
2. Open your compasses to more than half the length of the line.
   Place the point on one end of the line and draw an arc above and below.
3. Keeping the compasses open to the same distance, move the point to the other end of the line and draw a similar arc.
4. Join the points where the arcs intersect.
   Don't rub out your construction marks.
   This vertical line is the perpendicular bisector.

Key point

A **perpendicular bisector** cuts a line in half at right angles.

Literacy hint

To **bisect** means to cut in half.

4. a Draw a straight line AB 8 cm long.
     Construct its perpendicular bisector.
   b Use a ruler and protractor to check that it bisects your line at a right angle.
   c Mark any point P on your perpendicular bisector.
     Measure its distance from A and from B.
   Discussion What do you notice about point P?

5. In triangle ABC, AB = 5 cm, AC = 7 cm and BC = 7 cm.
   a Use a ruler and compasses to construct the triangle.
   b What kind of triangle is ABC?
   c Construct the perpendicular bisector of AB.
   d Describe the shapes you have made.

Q5d hint

Use mathematical words.

6. a Draw a straight line AB 12 cm long.
     Mark the point P on AB 7 cm from A.
   b Follow these steps to construct a line through P that is perpendicular to AB.
     i Open your compasses to less than the distance PB.
     ii Put the point of the compasses at point P.
     iii Draw the two red arcs centred on P. Label them Q and R.
     iv Open your compasses a little more.
     v Construct the perpendicular bisector of QR.

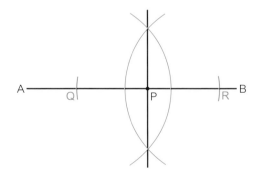

7. Use the method in Q6 to construct each pair of perpendicular lines.

a    b

Q7a hint

Label your diagram with letters as in Q6.

Q7b hint

Draw your starting line much longer than 10 cm, so that you can construct the arcs.

8 Use a ruler and compasses to construct
   a a rectangle with length 9 cm and width 6 cm
   b a right-angled triangle ABC where angle ABC = 90°,
     AB = 7.5 cm and BC = 4 cm
   c a square of side 6.2 cm.

Q8 hint

Sketch each shape first. Label
it with the information you know.
Think through the steps you need to
carry out.

9 **Reasoning** Danilo is drawing the
   perpendicular from point P to line AB.
   He has drawn an arc centred on P.
   a Draw the line AB and point P.
     Draw your own arc.
     Label the points Q and R.

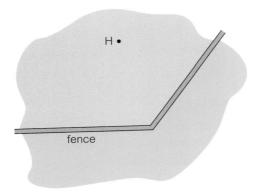

   b Construct the perpendicular bisector of QR.
     What do you notice?
   Discussion What is the shortest distance from P to the line AB?

Q9a hint

Choose a large arc to make Q and
R far apart. This makes it easier to
bisect QR.

10 The diagram shows the plan of part of a prison.
   The scale is 1 cm to 10 m.

   fence

   The prisoners want to dig two tunnels from their hut H to each
   section of fence.
   The tunnels must be as short as possible.
   a Trace the diagram.
   b Use a ruler and compasses to construct the route of each tunnel.
   c Work out the difference in the lengths of the tunnels.

Literacy hint

A hut is a small shelter.

Investigation   **Problem-solving**

How many different triangles ABC can you construct with   **Hint**
AB = 8 cm, BC = 4 cm and angle CAB = 30°?   There is more than one.
Use a ruler and compasses to construct your triangles.

11 **Explore** What is the shortest distance from a point in a field
   to the edge?
   Look back at the maths you have learned in this lesson.
   How can you use it to answer this question?

12 **Reflect** Look back at the investigation.
   What was the first step you took in solving the problem?
   Is it possible to write a similar problem where there are more
   possible triangles?
   Explain your answer.

Explore

Reflect

4.3 Constructions 2

You will learn to:
- Bisect angles using a ruler and compasses.
- Draw accurate diagrams to solve problems.

Why learn this?
A ruler and compasses can be used to draw angles and solve problems without using a protractor.

Fluency
Describe a trapezium.
How can you work out the area of a trapezium?

Explore
Which regular polygons can you draw using only a ruler and compasses?

Exercise 4.3

1 Construct a 60° angle.

2 Use only a ruler and compasses to construct each diagram.

a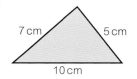
7 cm 5 cm
10 cm

b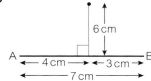
P
6 cm
A 4 cm 3 cm B
7 cm

Q2 hint
Remember to show all your construction marks.
Don't rub them out.

3 In a scale drawing 1 cm represents 4 m.
  a What does a 3 cm line on the scale drawing represent in real life?
  b How long is 10 m in real life on the scale drawing?

Worked example

Draw an angle of 70°.
Construct the **angle bisector**.

1	2	3	4	5
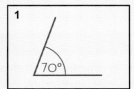		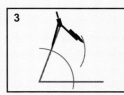		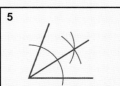

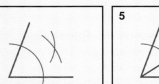

1 Draw the 70° angle using a protractor.
2 Open your compasses and place the point at the vertex of the angle. Draw an arc that cuts both arms of the angle.
3 Keep the compasses open to the same distance.
  Move them to one of the points where the arc crosses the arms.
  Make an arc in the middle of the angle.
4 Do the same from the point where the arc crosses the other arm.
5 Join the vertex of the angle to the point where the two small arcs intersect. Don't rub out your construction marks. This line is the angle bisector.

Key point

An **angle bisector** cuts an angle exactly in half.

Topic links: Area

4 For each angle
  i draw the angle using a protractor
  ii bisect the angle using a ruler and compasses
  iii check your two smaller angles using a protractor.

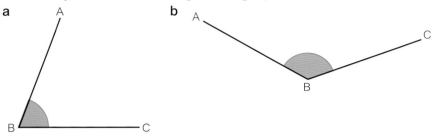

a

b

Q4 hint

Measure each angle first, using a protractor.

5 **Problem-solving** Use a ruler and compasses to construct each angle. Check your angles using a protractor.
  a 30°   **b** 45°
  Discussion What is the same about constructing a perpendicular to a line and bisecting a 180° angle?

Q5 Strategy hint

Start by constructing a larger angle, then bisect it.

6 **STEM / Problem-solving** The diagram shows a rectangular room with a burglar alarm sensor in one corner. Any movement activates the sensor.
  a Make a scale drawing of the rectangle on squared paper.
  b Use a ruler and compasses to construct the angle.
  c Calculate the shaded area.

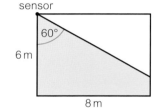

Q6 hint

Choose a suitable scale.

7 **Problem-solving** Two wires connect the mast AB to the deck of a yacht.
The wire CD bisects angle ACB.
  a Use a ruler and compasses to construct a scale drawing. Use a scale of 1 cm to 2 m.
  b Work out the length of the wire CD.

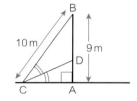

Q7 hint

Start by constructing the perpendicular AB.

8 **Problem-solving** Use a ruler and compasses to construct this kite.

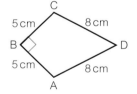

9 **Problem-solving / Reasoning** Sketch a quadrilateral for a classmate to construct. Make sure you can construct it yourself first.

Q9 hint

Think of the different quadrilaterals you've learned to construct, and the facts you know about them.

10 **Explore** Which regular polygons can you draw using only a ruler and compasses? Look back at the maths you have learned in this lesson. How can you use it to answer this question?

12 **Reflect** Look back at the constructions you did in this and the previous lesson.
Which do you find easier
  • using a straight edge and compasses to construct, or
  • using a ruler and protractor to measure lengths and angles accurately?
Explain your answer.

Explore

Reflect

4 Check up

Constructing shapes

1 Construct a net of this triangular prism on centimetre squared paper.

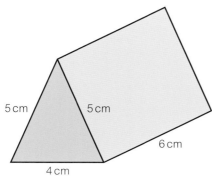

2 Use a ruler and compasses to construct this triangle.

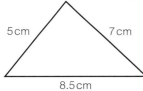

3 Construct an equilateral triangle with sides 6 cm using a ruler and compasses.

Constructions

4 a Draw an angle of 120° using a protractor.

  b Construct the angle bisector.

5 a Draw a line AB 10 cm long.
  b Construct the perpendicular bisector of AB.

6 a Construct this isosceles triangle using a ruler and compasses.

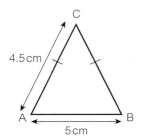

  b Construct the perpendicular bisector of the line AB.

7 Raafid has constructed an angle bisector of angle ABC.
Raafid knows that he has made a mistake.
Use the diagram to explain what he has done wrong.

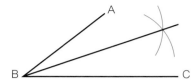

8 Copy this diagram. Use a ruler and compasses to construct a line
perpendicular to line XY that passes through the point P.

• P

X ——————————————————— Y

9 An adventure park has two zip wires attached to the same tower.
One is set at 12 m high the other at 7 m high. Both lines are
anchored to the same point. Using a scale of 1 cm to 2 m, construct
an accurate diagram and use it to calculate the real length of the
lower zip wire, AC.

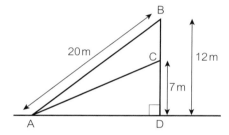

10 a Draw a line AB of length 8 cm.
b Draw a circle of radius 4 cm with centre A.
c Draw a circle of radius 6 cm with centre B.
d Join points A and B to the points where the two circles meet to
form a quadrilateral.
e What is the name for this quadrilateral?

11 How sure are you of your answers? Were you mostly
☹ **Just guessing**   😐 **Feeling doubtful**   🙂 **Confident**
What next? Use your results to decide whether to strengthen or
extend your learning.

Challenge

12 a Construct triangle ABC with sides of length 15 cm, 12 cm and 9 cm.
b Construct the perpendicular bisectors of sides AB, BC and AC.
c The perpendicular bisectors should meet at a point P.
d Draw a circle with centre P and with radius AP. What do you
notice?
e What is the radius of the circle?
f Measure and write down the size of angle ACB.

Reflect

4 Strengthen

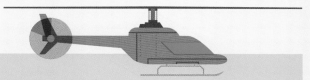

You will:
- Strengthen your understanding with practice.

Constructing shapes

1 Follow these instructions to accurately construct a triangle with sides 7 cm, 8 cm and 9 cm.

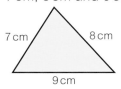

7 cm   8 cm

9 cm

a Use a ruler to draw the 9 cm side accurately.

b The 7 cm side starts at the left-hand end of this line. Open your compasses to exactly 7 cm and draw an arc from the left-hand end of the line.

c Open your compasses to exactly 8 cm and draw an arc from the other end.

d Use the point where the arcs cross to create the finished triangle.

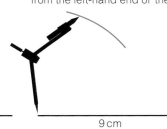

9 cm

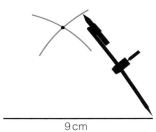

9 cm

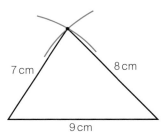

7 cm   8 cm

9 cm

2 Construct this triangle.

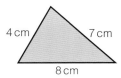

4 cm   7 cm

8 cm

3 Construct a scale diagram of this triangle. Use the scale 1 cm to 1 m.

8.2 m   8.2 m

6.8 m

4 Construct an accurate net of this triangular prism.

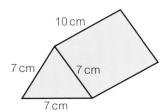

10 cm
7 cm, 7 cm
7 cm

Q4 Strategy hint

Sketch the net and write the measurements on it.
Make an accurate drawing of the rectangles using a ruler and protractor.
Construct the triangles using compasses.

5 Construct an accurate net for this square-based pyramid.

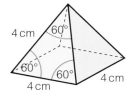

4 cm 60°
60° 60° 4 cm
4 cm

Constructions

1 Draw a line 14 cm long.
Follow these instructions to construct the perpendicular bisector of this line.

a Draw the line.
Open your compasses to more than half the length of the line.

b Draw the first arc.

c Draw the second arc.

d Draw the perpendicular bisector.

14 cm

Q1 Strategy hint

Remember this diagram.

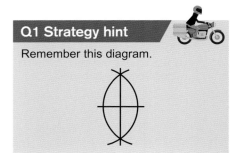

Q1 hint

Check by measuring that the angle is 90° and the line is cut in half.

2 Use a ruler to draw a line 11.5 cm long.
Construct the perpendicular bisector of this line.

3 Use a protractor to draw an angle of 60°.
Follow these instructions to construct the bisector of this angle.

Q3 Strategy hint

Remember this diagram.

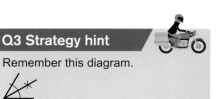

a Draw the angle.

b Draw an arc from the vertex of the angle.

c Draw another arc between the two sides of the angle.

60°

d Draw a second arc.　　**e** Draw the angle bisector.

　　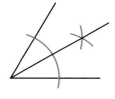

4 Use a protractor to draw an angle of 120°.
Construct the bisector of this angle.

5 Draw a line and point A above the line.
Follow these instructions to construct a perpendicular line from the point A to the line.

a Draw an arc from point A that intersects the line twice.

b Keep your compasses open the same distance. Draw an arc from each of the two points where the first arc crosses the line.

c Join the points where these two arcs intersect.

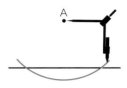
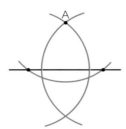
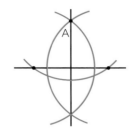

6 The diagram shows a sketch plan of a garden with a washing line pole. Construct an accurate plan showing the washing line meeting the house at right angles.

Q6 hint

Use the perpendicular construction you used in Q5. Start by drawing an arc from the pole.

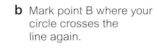

7 Point P is close to the end of a line.
Follow the instructions to construct a perpendicular to the line at point P.

a Mark point A to the right of point P. Point A should be near to, but not on the line. Put your compasses on point A and draw a circle through point P.

b Mark point B where your circle crosses the line again.

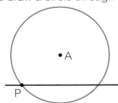
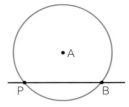

c Draw a line across the circle through point A and point B.

d Join point P to the circle.

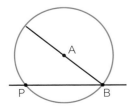
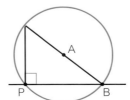

4 Extend

You will:
- Extend your understanding with problem-solving.

1 Reasoning

  a Construct triangle ABC where AB = 8 cm, BC = 6 cm and
  AC = 7.5 cm.

  b Construct the perpendicular bisectors of AB and BC.
  Mark the point P where they cross.

  c Construct the perpendicular bisector of AC.
  What do you notice?

  d Draw accurately a circle with centre P and radius PC.
  What do you notice?

  e Draw another triangle ABC, this time with an obtuse angle.
  Repeat the steps in parts **b** to **d**.

2 Problem-solving Use a ruler and compasses to construct
these angles.
Check your angles using a protractor.

  a 15°   **b** 105°

Q2 hint

How do these relate to angles you
know such as 60° and 90°?

3 a Use a ruler and compasses to construct triangle ABC.

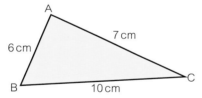

  b Construct the perpendicular from A to the base BC.

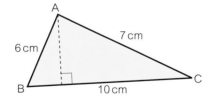

 c Work out the area of the triangle.

4 Problem-solving

  a Construct these two sides of triangle ABC.
  Join AC.

  b Use your triangle to construct the quadrilateral
  ABCD where CD = 4 cm and AD = 7 cm.

  c Construct another quadrilateral ABCD where AB = 7.7 cm,
  BC = 5.2 cm, CD = 6.4 cm, AD = 7.7 cm.

Q4b hint
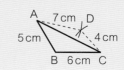

Topic links: Scale, Area, Circles, Pythagoras' theorem   **Subject links:** Sport (Q6)

5 a Sketch this kite ABCD.
  b Split it into two congruent
    triangles.
  c Construct the kite using
    the method in Q4.

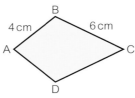

6 Problem-solving The diagram shows the penalty area of a
football pitch.

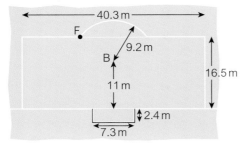

  a Make a scale drawing of the penalty area.
    Use a scale of 1 cm to 4 m.
  b A footballer at F runs straight to the ball B on the penalty spot
    and kicks it towards the goal at an angle of 120° to FB.
    Could she score a goal?

Q6b hint

Draw the line and angle on your
diagram.

7 Problem-solving
  a Draw the right-angled triangle ABC on squared paper where
    AB = 8 cm, BC = 6 cm and angle ABC = 90°.
  b Construct the perpendicular bisector of the hypotenuse AC.
    Mark the point P where the bisector intersects AC.
  c Draw the circle with centre at point P with radius PA.
    What do you notice?

8 Problem-solving
  a Draw accurately an isosceles triangle OAB with OA = OB = 8 cm
    and angle AOB = 50°.
  b Draw an arc of a circle with centre O and radius 8 cm that passes
    through the points A and B.
  c Write down the name of the shape formed by sides OA and OB
    and the arc of the circle.

9 The diagram shows three sides of a regular octagon.
  ABP is a straight line. The length of each side is 5 cm.

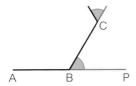

  a Work out the marked exterior angle.
  b Draw accurately the sides AB and BC.
  c Continue in the same way to complete the octagon.

10 Problem-solving The diagram shows a rolled-up poster inside a cardboard box. The box is a triangular prism.

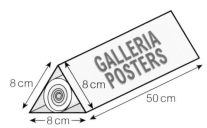

a Construct the triangular cross-section.
b Bisect two of its angles.
Mark the point P where the angle bisectors cross.
c Bisect the third angle of the triangle.
What do you notice?
d Construct a perpendicular from P onto one of the sides.
Mark the point Q where it meets the side.
e Draw a circle with centre P and radius PQ.
f Another poster is rolled up with a diameter of 8 cm.
Construct the triangular cross-section of a box for it.

11 Problem-solving / Reasoning The diagram shows a hexagonal-based pyramid. The base is a regular hexagon.

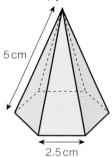

Q11 hint

Hexagonal base:

Sketch one face. What type of triangles are the faces?

Construct the net of a hexagonal-based pyramid using a ruler and compasses.

12 a Construct this triangle.
b Measure the hypotenuse.
c Use Pythagoras' theorem to check your answer.

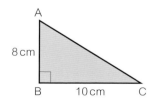

13 Reflect Look back at the questions in these Extend lessons.
a Write down the question that was the easiest to answer. What made it easy?
b Write down the question that was the most difficult to answer. What made it difficult?
c Look again at the question that you wrote down for part **b**. What could you do to make this type of question easier to answer?

Q13 hint

Ask your classmates how they answered this question. Do they have some hints for you?

4 Unit test

1 Use a ruler and compasses to construct these triangles.

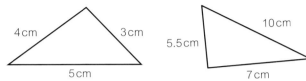

2 **a** A shape is made using an equilateral triangle and an isosceles triangle.
   Use a ruler and compasses to construct the shape.

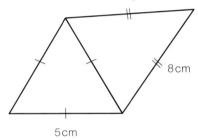

   b What is the name of this shape?

3 **a** Draw this angle accurately using a protractor.
   b Construct the angle bisector.

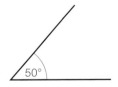

4 **a** Construct this parallelogram.

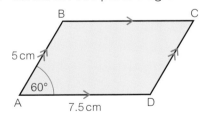

   b Construct the perpendicular from B to AD.

5 Draw a line 9.5 cm long and construct the perpendicular bisector.

6 Use a ruler and compasses to construct an angle of 30°.

7 The line AB is of length 10 cm.
   a Construct the perpendicular bisector of AB.
   b Draw accurately the circle that passes through A and B.

8 Real Karl builds a semi-circular pond against a wall in his back garden.
The garden is rectangular.
The radius of the pond is 1.5 m.
Construct a scale diagram of the garden and the pond using a ruler and compasses.
Use a scale of 1 cm to 0.5 m.

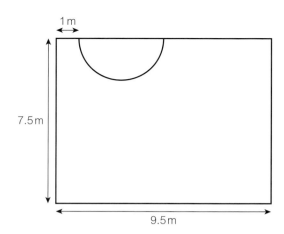

9 Construct an accurate net of this triangular prism on squared paper.

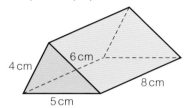

Challenge

10

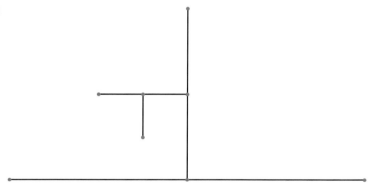

  a Draw a straight line which is 16 cm long.
  b Draw a perpendicular bisector half the length of the first line and above it.
  c Draw a perpendicular bisector half the length of the second line and to its left.
  d Keep repeating this process as far as you can, halving the line length each time, and mark the end point of each line segment in red.
  e What shape do the red points make?
  f What shape do other starting lengths make?
  g What shape would be formed if the process was continued and all the red points were joined together?

11 Reflect For this unit, copy and complete these sentences.
  I showed I am good at ....
  I found .... hard.
  I got better at .... by ....
  I was surprised by ....
  I was pleased that ....
  I still need help with ....

Master | Check P108 | Strengthen P110 | Extend P115 | Test P119

5.1 Substitution

You will learn to:
- Substitute values into expressions and formulae involving powers, roots and brackets.
- Write expressions and formulae involving more than one variable.
- Solve problems involving formulae and expressions.

Why learn this?
Formulae can help describe situations that work in the same way for different numbers. The cost of hiring a vehicle depends on its type, how long you have it and how far you travel.

Fluency
What is x^2 when x is
- 3
- 2.4
- −3
- 5
- −10.5?

Explore
How long does it take to walk up a mountain?

Exercise 5.1

1 Match each statement to the correct expression.

A 2 more than x	**1** $\dfrac{x}{2}$
B twice x	**2** $2x + 2$
C 2 less than x	**3** $2 - x$
D half x	**4** $x + 2$
E x less than 2	**5** $2x$
F 2 more than double x	**6** $x - 2$

2 Modelling A plumber charges a call-out fee of $72, plus $40 per hour.
 a How much does he charge for a 2-hour job?
 b Write a formula to work out the total charge, C, when the plumber is called out for h hours.

3 Modelling A horse-riding stables charges $65 for an adult and $50 for a child to go riding.
 a How much does it cost a family of 2 adults and 2 children to go riding?
 b Write a formula for the total cost, T, for A adults and C children to go riding.

Warm up

Worked example

You can work out a waiter's daily pay using the number of hours worked, h, the hourly rate of pay, r, the total amount of tips, t, and the number of staff who share the tips, s.

a Write an expression for the daily pay in terms of h, r, t and s.

$$hr + \frac{t}{s}$$

> hourly rate × number of hours worked
> $+$ $\dfrac{\text{total amount of tips}}{\text{number of staff who share the tip}}$

b Write a formula for the daily pay, P, in terms of h, r, t and s.

$$P = hr + \frac{t}{s}$$

> The formula has '$P =$' in front of the expression.

4 Modelling A worker's daily pay depends on the number of hours worked, h, the hourly rate of pay, r, and a travel allowance, t. The travel allowance is the same however many hours worked.

  a Work out how much a worker is paid for a 7-hour day at an hourly rate of $22.50 and a travel allowance of $18.

  b Write an expression for his daily pay in terms of h, r and t.

  c Write a formula for his daily pay, P, in terms of h, r and t.

  d Use your formula to work out P when $h = 6.5$, $r = 19$ and $t = 14$.

5 Real / Modelling Wooden flooring costs $65 per square metre. The floor is then edged with a narrow wooden strip which costs $8 per metre.

  a How much does it cost for a 6 m by 4 m room, including the edging?

  b Write a formula for the cost, C, of a wooden floor in a rectangular room of width w metres and length l metres (remember to include the edging).

  c Use your formula to work out C when $w = 3.5$ and $l = 5$.

  Discussion What assumptions did you make when writing this formula?

Worked example

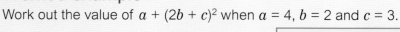

Work out the value of $a + (2b + c)^2$ when $a = 4$, $b = 2$ and $c = 3$.

$$a + (2b + c)^2 = 4 + (2 \times 2 + 3)^2$$
$$= 4 + (4 + 3)^2$$
$$= 4 + 7^2$$
$$= 4 + 49$$
$$= 53$$

> Substitute the values of a, b and c.
> Work out the brackets.
> Work out the index (power).
> Add to get the final value.

6 Work out the value of these expressions when $c = 3$ and $d = 2$.

  a $4d + c^2$ **b** $4c^2$ **c** $3d^3$

  d $5c^3 + 2d^3$ **e** $10d^3 - 6c$ **f** $2c^3 - 9$

  g $-5c + 2d^2$ **h** $(5d)^2$ **i** $(2c + d)^2$

  j $(5d - c)^2 + 1$ **k** $cd + (2c - d)^3$ **l** $(4d - 2c)^2 - cd$

  Discussion Is $(5d)^2 = 25d^2$ always, sometimes or never true?

Investigation

Problem-solving

1 Use the formula cards to work out the value of each letter.

$I = 12$ $K + I = G$ $4H = I$ $G + 4 = 2I$

$N = H^3 - I$ $A = (W - H)^2$ $K + I = 4W$

2 Write the letters in order of value from the smallest to the biggest.
What famous scientist's surname do they spell?

7 Work out the value of these expressions.
  a $3a^2b$ when $a = 3$ and $b = 4$
  b $35 - (b^3 - a)$ when $a = 2$ and $b = 3$
  c $(a + b)^2 - c$ when $a = 5$, $b = 2$ and $c = 1$
  d $\frac{ab + cd}{b + c}$ when $a = 6$, $b = 3$, $c = 1$ and $d = 4$

Q7d hint

$\frac{ab + cd}{b + c}$ is the same as
$(ab + cd) \div (b + c)$.

8 **STEM / Modelling** You can use this formula to work out the height of a ball when it is thrown upwards:
$s = ut + \frac{1}{2}at^2$
where
s = height (m)
u = starting speed (m/s)
a = acceleration (m/s²)
t = time (s).
Work out the value of s when
  a $u = 30$, $t = 6$ and $a = -10$
  b $u = 40$, $t = 8$ and $a = -9.8$

9 **STEM** Use the formula $v = u + at$ to work out the value of
  a u when $v = 34$, $a = 5$ and $t = 3$
  b t when $v = 50$, $u = 20$ and $a = 5$
  c a when $v = 22$, $u = 8$ and $t = 7$

Q9a hint

Substitute the values into the formula and then solve the equation to find u.

10 Use the formula $y = mx + c$ to work out the value of
  a m when $y = 31$, $x = 7$ and $c = -4$
  b c when $y = 0.02$, $x = 3.4$ and $m = -1.2$

11 Find the value of each expression when $x = 4$, $y = 2$ and $z = -5$.
  a $3(x^3 + y)$
  b $3x(x + z)$
  c $y^2(z + x^3)$
  d $4x(3 - z) + y$
  e $5(x^2 + y) + x(3x + 2)$
  f $5y(x + y^3 + z) + 3y^2(x + 3z)$
  g $y\sqrt{x}$
  h $\sqrt[3]{xy} + z^2$
  i $\sqrt{xyz + 76}$

12 **Explore** How long does it take to walk up a mountain? Is it easier to explore this question now that you have completed the lesson? What further information do you need to be able to answer this?

13 **Reflect** What is different and what is the same about formulae and equations?

Reflect Explore

5.2 Inequalities

You will learn to:
- Solve linear inequalities and represent the solution on a number line.
- Multiply both sides of an inequality by a negative number.

Confidence

Why learn this?
Businesses use inequalities to work out maximum and minimum profits based on different sales.

Fluency
Write < or > between each pair of numbers.
- 5 ☐ 1
- 4 ☐ 2
- −3 ☐ −5
- −10 ☐ −20
- 3 ☐ −9

Explore
How are inequalities used in optimisation problems?

Warm up

Exercise 5.2

1 Work out
  a −4 + 9
  b 10 − 17
  c −8 − −3
  d 5 × −2
  e $-\dfrac{6}{3}$
  f −4 × −8

2 Solve each of these equations.
  a $x + 12 = 19$
  b $5x = 45$
  c $2x - 5 = 9$
  d $\dfrac{x}{3} + 7 = 16$

Key point

You can show **inequalities** on a number line.
An empty circle ○ shows that the value is not included.
A filled circle ● shows that the value is included.
An arrow ○—→ shows that the solution continues to plus or minus infinity.

Worked example

Use a number line to show the values that satisfy these **inequalities**.
  a $x < 4$
  b $5 > y \geqslant -2$

a $x < 4$

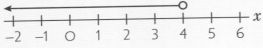

> This includes all the numbers less than 4 (*excluding* 4).

b $5 > y \geqslant -2$

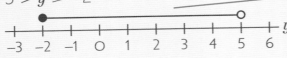

> This includes all the numbers less than 5 (*excluding* 5) and greater than or equal to −2 (*including* −2).

3 Show each of these inequalities on a number line.
  a $x > 5$
  b $x \leqslant 2$
  c $-3 \leqslant y < 3$
  d $7 > y \geqslant 1$
  e $-4 \leqslant z \leqslant -1$
  f $6 \geqslant z \geqslant -2$

4 Write inequalities for each of these and show them on a number line.
  a a number less than or equal to 5
  b a number greater than −4
  c a number less than 6 and greater than or equal to −2
  d a number greater than or equal to −8 and less than or equal to −1

Q4 hint

Choose a letter to represent the number.

5 Write the inequalities shown by each of these number lines.

  a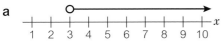

  b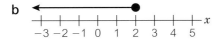

  c

6 Solve these inequalities. Show each solution on a number line. The first one has been started for you.

  a $x + 12 \geqslant 15$

$$x \geqslant 15 - 12$$

$$x \geqslant \square$$

Key point

You can solve inequalities in a similar way to solving equations.

  b $x + 9 < 11$ c $y - 4 \geqslant -9$
  d $2y \leqslant 14$ e $3z > -15$
  f $\dfrac{x}{5} \geqslant -1$ g $\dfrac{x}{2} < 3$

7 **STEM** In a science experiment, Gohar mixes vinegar and calcium carbonate to make a 'volcano'.
  He uses 150 ml of vinegar. In order to get the volcano to erupt Gohar must use x grams of calcium carbonate, where $3x \leqslant 150$.
  a Solve the inequality.
  b Gohar has 35 g of calcium carbonate. Does this satisfy the inequality?

8 Solve these inequalities. Show each solution on a number line.
  a $-2 < x + 4 < 5$ b $0 \leqslant y - 5 \leqslant 3$

  c $8 \geqslant 2y > 2$ d $2 > \dfrac{x}{4} \geqslant -1$

  Discussion Is $3 \geqslant z > -1$ the same as $-1 < z \leqslant 3$?

Q8 hint

Do the same operation to all three parts of the inequality so that the variable is on its own in the middle.

9 **Problem-solving** Kiann says, 'I think of an integer and double it. The answer is greater than 2 but smaller than 14'.
  a Write an inequality to represent this information.
  b Solve the inequality and show the solution on a number line.
  c Write down all the numbers that Kiann could have chosen.

Q9 hint

$\square < 2x < \square$

10 Solve these inequalities. Show each solution on a number line.
  a $2n + 1 \leqslant 5$ b $3n - 8 > 1$

  c $\dfrac{x}{2} + 7 < 11$ d $\dfrac{x}{3} - 2 \geqslant -4$

11 Solve these inequalities. Show each solution on a number line.
The first one has been started for you.

a $-1 \leqslant 2y + 3 < 9$

$$-1 - 3 \leqslant 2y < 9 - 3$$
$$-4 \leqslant 2y < 6$$
$$-\frac{4}{2} \leqslant y < \frac{6}{2}$$
$$\square \leqslant y < \square$$

b $1 \leqslant 3x - 2 < 10$

c $19 > 5n - 1 > 4$

d $29 \geqslant 4p + 1 \geqslant -7$

12 Problem-solving Ling says, 'I think of an integer, multiply it by 3 and then subtract 5. The answer is greater than 7 but smaller than 12'.

a Write an inequality to represent this information.

b Solve the inequality and show the solution on a number line.

c Write down all of the numbers Ling could have chosen.

Investigation   Reasoning

On a number line you can see that $-6 < -4$.

1 Multiply both sides of the inequality $-6 < -4$ by -1.
Is the statement you wrote as your answer to part **1** still true?

2 Divide both sides of the inequality $-6 < -4$ by -1.
Is the statement you wrote as your answer to part **1** still true?

3 a For what values of x is $x < 5$?
   b For what values of x is $-x < -5$?

4 a For what values of x is $2x < 10$?
   b For what values of x is $-2x < -10$?

Discussion What happens to the inequality sign when you multiply or divide both sides by a negative number?

---

13 Solve these inequalities.

a $-x < 8$

b $-3x > 15$

c $-2x \leqslant -18$

d $8 - x < 3$

e $3 < -x < 5$

f $-12 \leqslant -4x \leqslant 20$

> **Q13a hint**
>
> $-x$ is less than 8, so x is greater than $\square$.

14 Explore How are inequalities used in optimisation problems?
Is it easier to explore this question now that you have completed the lesson?
What further information do you need to be able to answer this?

15 Reflect In what ways are inequalities similar to equations?
In what ways are they different?

5.3 Using index laws

You will learn to:
* Use index laws with zero and negative powers.

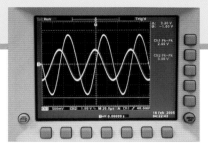

Fluency

Work out
* 4^2
* 4^{-2}
* 4^0

Explore
What expressions will simplify
to x^{-4}

Why learn this?
Negative indices are used in lots of mathematical functions and terms.

Exercise 5.3

1 Work out the value of these expressions when $x = 1$.

  a $12x - 15$ **b** $11 - 8x$ **c** $\dfrac{15x + 21}{9x}$

2 Write each fraction in its simplest form.

  a $\dfrac{3}{24}$ **b** $\dfrac{18}{22}$ **c** $\dfrac{14}{6}$

3 Write each of these as a single power.

  a $5^2 \times 5^4$ **b** $3^3 \times 3^4$ **c** $4^9 \div 4^3$

  d $7^{11} \div 7^2$ **e** $10^4 \times 10^{-2}$ **f** $10^2 \div 10^{-3}$

4 **Reasoning** Write down the value of

  a 1^0 **b** 2^0 **c** 3^0 **d** 4^0 **e** a^0 **f** x^0 **g** $2p^0$ **h** $5t^0$

> **Key point**
>
> Any number to the power of zero is 1.

5 Write true (T) or false (F) for each of these statements.

  a $5^0 = 5$ **b** $2 \times 3^0 = 2$ **c** $3.1 \times 10^0 = 3.1$ **d** $a^0 = 1$

  e $5c^0 = 1$ **f** $(z^0)^5 = 1$ **g** $(2f^0)^2 = 4$ **h** $(3y^3)^0 = 27$

6 Work out the value of each of these expressions.

  a $7x^0 - 4y^0$

  b $4m^0 \times 8n^0$

  c $\dfrac{45}{5y^0}$

  d $\dfrac{36 - 4a^0}{8b^0}$

  e $18c^0 - \dfrac{10^2}{5d^0}$

  f $8z^0 \left(12^0 - \dfrac{12y^0}{2^2} \right)$

> **Q6 hint**
>
> $x^0 = 1$ and $y^0 = 1$

1 Copy and complete.

a $\dfrac{7^3}{7^6} = 7^{3-6} = 7^\square$

$\dfrac{7^3}{7^6} = \dfrac{7 \times 7 \times 7}{7 \times 7 \times 7 \times 7 \times 7 \times 7} = \dfrac{1}{7^\square}$

b $\dfrac{x^2}{x^3} = x^{2-3} = x^\square$

$\dfrac{x^2}{x^3} = \dfrac{x \times x}{x \times x \times x} = \dfrac{1}{x^\square}$

c $\dfrac{y^6}{y^{10}} = y^{6-10} = y^\square$

$\dfrac{y^6}{y^{10}} = \dfrac{1}{y^\square}$

2 Write down what it means when a number has a negative power.

Discussion For what values of x is $x^{-1} < 1$?

7 Simplify these expressions. Write each one as a negative power and as a fraction. The first one has been started for you.

a $\dfrac{x^4}{x^7} = x^{4-7} = x^\square = \dfrac{1}{x^\square}$

b $\dfrac{y^2}{y^8}$ **c** $\dfrac{p^4}{p^5}$ **d** $\dfrac{z}{z^9}$

> **Q7 hint**
>
> $z = z^1$

Worked example

Simplify $\dfrac{20x^5}{4x^8}$. Write your answer as a negative power and as a fraction.

$\dfrac{20x^5}{4x^8} = \dfrac{20}{4} \times \dfrac{x^5}{x^8}$ ⟶ Write the fraction as the product of two simpler fractions.

$\dfrac{20}{4} \times \dfrac{x^5}{x^8} = 5 \times x^{-3} = 5x^{-3}$ ⟶ Simplify the two fractions.
$20 \div 4 = 5$
$\dfrac{x^5}{x^8} = x^{5-8} = x^{-3}$

$5x^{-3} = 5 \times \dfrac{1}{x^3} = \dfrac{5}{x^3}$ ⟶ A negative power as a fraction is 1 over the positive power. $x^{-3} = \dfrac{1}{x^3}$.

---

8 Simplify these expressions. Write each one as
   i a negative power   **ii** a fraction.

a $\dfrac{6x^7}{2x^9}$ **b** $\dfrac{24y^3}{4y^7}$ **c** $\dfrac{56y}{7y^8}$ **d** $\dfrac{7p^8}{21p^{12}}$ **e** $\dfrac{8r^3}{72r^{10}}$ **f** $\dfrac{9q}{45q^{11}}$

> **Q8a hint**
>
> $\dfrac{6x^7}{2x^9} = \dfrac{\square}{x^\square}$

9 Simplify these expressions. The first one is started for you

a $\dfrac{9x^3}{3x^3} = 3x^\square =$ **b** $\dfrac{25x^2}{5x^2}$ **c** $\dfrac{12x^3}{3x^3}$ **d** $\dfrac{5x^7}{15x^7}$

10 **Explore** What expressions will simplify to x^{-4}?
   Is it easier to explore this question now that you have completed the lesson?
   What further information do you need to be able to answer this?

11 **Reflect** What was familiar to you in this lesson and what surprised you?

5.4 Expressions, equations, identities and formulae

You will learn to:
- Distinguish between expressions, identities, equations and formulae.
- Expand and factorise expressions involving powers.

Why learn this?
Scientists factorise expressions to solve equations. For example, they work out how long an object stays above a certain height when it is kicked.

Fluency
Write down the highest common factor of
a 12 and 8
b x and x^2
c y and y^2
d $12xy^3$ and $8x^2y^2$

Explore
In how many different ways can you write $12xy + 8x^2y^3$ using brackets?

Exercise 5.4

1 Simplify
a $3x \times 2y$
b $4x^2 \times x$
c $5x^2y \times 2y$
d $3x^3y \times 5xy^2$

2 Expand and simplify
a $3(x + 5) + 4(x - 1)$
b $8(p - 7) - 3(p + 2)$
c $5m^2 + m(7m - 2)$
d $2y(y + 4) + 6(5 - 3y)$

3 Write down whether each of these is an expression or a formula.
a $3x + 4y$
b $P = 4t + 5$
c $s = 5d - 2x$
d $v + 10t$
e $8x^2 - 7x + 24$
f $t = 4m^2 - 3n + mn$

4 **Reasoning** The = and ≡ signs are not printed with these statements. Decide whether each one is an **equation** or an **identity**.
a $3m + 6 \square 21$
b $x + x + x + x \square 4x$
c $5 \times r \times r \square 5r^2$
d $6n^2 \square 13n + 5$
e $9y + 9 \square 2y + 7y + 4 + 5$
f $5 \times p \times p + 3 \times p - 2 \square 5p^2 + 5p + 2$

5 Decide whether each of these is an equation, an identity or a formula.
a $2x + 3 \square 11$
b $A = \dfrac{(a + b)h}{2}$
c $3x + 2x \square 5x$
d $F = ma$
e $3x + 5 \square 32$
f $2x(x + 1) \square 2x^2 + 2x$

6 Expand these brackets.
a $y(y^2 + 5y)$
b $x(x^3 + 3x + 7)$
c $a(a^2 - 8a + 1)$
d $b(b^3 + 5b^2 - 6)$
e $2p(4 + 5p + p^2)$
f $3y(8y - 2y^3)$
g $6z(z^3 - 4z^2 + 9)$
h $a^2(2a^2 + 3a - 4)$
i $3k(k^3 - 6k - 7)$

Warm up

Q2 hint

An **expression** doesn't have an equals sign. A **formula** is a rule showing a relationship between two or more variables.

Key point

An **equation** has an equals (=) sign. It is true for particular values.
For example $2x + 5 = 11$ is only true for $x = 3$.
The **identity** symbol (≡) shows that two expressions are always equivalent.
For example $x + x + 5 \equiv 2x + 5$.

Q5e hint

$2p \times 4 + 2p \times 5p + 2p \times p^2$

7 Expand and simplify
   a $x(x^2 + 3x) + 2x(x^2 + 4x)$
   b $4b(b^2 + 7b) - b(b^2 + 9b)$
   c $5d(d^3 - 3) - d(2d^3 - 9)$
   d $y(y^2 + 4y + 5) + y(2y^2 - 7)$
   e $z(z^3 + 8z^2 - 3) + 4z(z^3 - 3z^2 - 1)$
   f $4p(p^2 + 5p + 12) - p(3p^2 + 17p - 2)$
   g $7q(8 + 4q - 3q^2) - 2q(5 - 3q + 12q^2)$
   h $6a(2a + 3a^2 - 1) + 4(a^2 - 3a^3 + a)$

Q7 hint

Expand both sets of brackets separately, then simplify by collecting like terms.

Q7 Strategy hint

Expand and simplify each side of the equation to show that both expressions are the same.

8 **Problem-solving / Reasoning**
   Show that $3x^3 + x(4x^2 + 9x) \equiv 7x^2(x + 3) - 12x^2$.

9 **Reasoning**
   a Show that $2^2 + 2^2 \equiv 2^3$.
   b Is $x^2 + x^2 \equiv x^3$ true for all values of x?
     Explain your answer.

Q9 hint

Work out the value of both sides.

10 **Reasoning / Modelling** The diagram shows a cuboid.

   Show that an expression for the volume of the cuboid is $x^3 + 7x^2$.

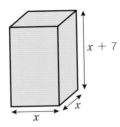

Q10 Literacy hint

'Show that' means 'Show your working'.

Key point

To **factorise** an expression completely, take out the **highest common factor** (HCF) of its terms.

11 Factorise each expression completely. Check your answers by expanding.
   a $4x + 8$ b $4x^2 + 8x$ c $4x^3 + 8x^2$ d $6x - 2x^3$
   e $y^2 + 5y^3$ f $9y^5 - 3y^3$ g $10y^4 - 5y^2$ h $12y^7 + 9y^5$

12 Factorise each expression completely. Check your answers.
   a $3x + 6y + 9z = 3(x + \Box y + \Box z)$ b $xy + 5y + yz$
   c $x^2 + 6xy + 9xz$ d $5x^2 + 10xy + 15xz$
   e $x^3 + 2x^2y + 5x^2z$ f $12xy - 4x^2y^2 + 8yz$

Q12b hint

What is the HCF of xy, $5y$ and yz?

13 **Problem-solving / Reasoning**
   a Work out the missing terms from this factorised expression.
     $\Box x^2y + \Box y^2 + 9\Box = 3x\Box(\Box + 4y + \Box)$
   b Is there only one answer to this problem? Explain your answer.

14 **Explore** In how many different ways can you write $12xy + 8x^2y^3$ using brackets?
   Is it easier to explore this question now that you have completed the lesson?
   What further information do you need to be able to answer this?

15 **Reflect** Look back at Q11.
   Rakesh says, 'I worked from left to right. I thought about what could go in the box before x^2y first.'
   Rekha says, 'I began with the $3x\Box$ outside the bracket and the $4y$ inside the bracket. This meant I was only working with one box.'
   What did you do first?
   Which is the best first step, Rakesh's, Rekha's or yours? Why?

Explore

Reflect

5.5 Solving equations

You will learn to:

- Construct and solve complex equations.

Why learn this?
Engineers designing roller coaster rides have to solve equations to make sure the ride is safe.

Fluency
Work out the value of these expressions when $x = 4$.
- $5x - 3$
- $7(2x + 1)$
- $\dfrac{x + 5}{3}$
- $\dfrac{5x - 2}{7}$

Explore
Do all equations have a solution?

Exercise 5.5

1 Solve these equations.

  a $3(y + 5) = 9$

  b $7(p - 3) = 2(2p + 6)$

  c $\dfrac{y + 9}{4} = 5$

2 Solve these equations.

  a $3x - 11 = \dfrac{4x + 2}{3}$

  b $2x + 5 = \dfrac{5x + 1}{2}$

  c $\dfrac{11x + 6}{5} = 3x - 2$

  d $\dfrac{8x - 2}{6} = 2x - 5$

3 Problem-solving Ahlam and Fiona are thinking of the same number.
Ahlam multiplies it by 3, then adds 5.
Fiona multiplies it by 12, subtracts 3, then divides the result by 3.
They both get the same answer.
What number did they start with?

4 Problem-solving The diagram shows an equilateral triangle.

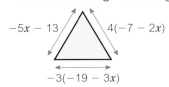

Work out the perimeter of the triangle.
Discussion Does it matter which two sides of the triangle you used?
How can you check that your answer is correct?

Warm up

Q2a hint

Start by multiplying both sides by 3.
$3(3x - 11) = 4x + 2$

Q3 Strategy hint

Use a letter to represent the number.
Write expressions for Ahlam's and Fiona's calculations.

Worked example

Solve the equation $\dfrac{3x + 6}{2} = \dfrac{x - 4}{2}$.

$$\frac{6(3x + 6)}{3} = \frac{6(x - 4)}{2}$$

> To remove the fractions, multiply both sides of the equation by the LCM of 2 and 3, which is 6.

$$\frac{^{2}\cancel{6}(3x + 6)}{\cancel{3}} = \frac{^{3}\cancel{6}(x - 4)}{\cancel{2}}$$

> Cancel the denominators: $6 \div 3 = 2$ and $6 \div 2 = 3$.

$$2(3x + 6) = 3(x - 4)$$
$$6x + 12 = 3x - 12$$

> Expand the brackets.

$$6x - 3x = -12 - 12$$

> Collect like terms.

$$3x = -24$$
$$x = -8$$

> $-24 \div 3 = -8$

Check:

LHS: $\dfrac{3x + 6}{3} = \dfrac{3 \times (-8) + 6}{3} = \dfrac{-18}{3} = -6$

RHS: $\dfrac{x - 4}{2} = \dfrac{-8 - 4}{2} = \dfrac{-18}{2} = -6$

> Check that the solution is correct by substituting $x = -8$ into both sides of the equation.

5 Solve

a $\dfrac{x - 2}{3} = \dfrac{x + 3}{6}$

b $\dfrac{11x + 6}{3} = \dfrac{3x + 8}{2}$

c $\dfrac{4x - 9}{3} = \dfrac{3x + 2}{3}$

d $\dfrac{4x + 23}{3} = \dfrac{2x + 4}{6}$

Q5 Strategy hint

Check your solutions are correct by substituting.

6 The diagram shows an isosceles triangle ABC.

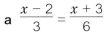

In triangle ABC, $\angle ABC = \dfrac{11x - 10}{10}$ and $\angle ACB = \dfrac{7x + 46}{8}$.

a Write an equation using the fact that $\angle ABC = \angle ACB$.

b Solve your equation to find the value of x.

c Work out the sizes of $\angle ABC$ and $\angle ACB$.

d Work out the size of $\angle BAC$.

7 **Problem-solving** The diagram shows a square.

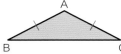

Work out the perimeter of the square.

Q7 Strategy hint

Write an equation using the fact that the sides of a square are the same length. Solve it to find the value of x. Then work out the side length of the square.

8 Problem-solving / Reasoning The diagram shows a square, a rectangle and two triangles.

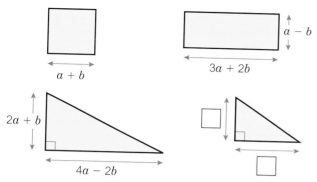

$a - b$

$3a + 2b$

$a + b$

$2a + b$

$4a - 2b$

The total area of the square and the rectangle is the same as the total area of the two triangles.

a Write an expression for the length and the height of the small triangle in terms of a and b.

b Is your answer to part **a** the only answer? Explain why.

9 Explore Do all equations have a solution?
Is it easier to explore this question now that you have completed the lesson?
What further information do you need to be able to answer this?

10 Reflect Q8 is tagged as a Problem-solving and Reasoning question.
What is the difference between Problem-solving and Reasoning?
Which part of the question is which, or do both parts need both skills?

Explore

Reflect

5.6 Changing the subject

You will learn to:
• Change the subject of a formula.

Why learn this?
If you know the formula for convert °C to °F, you can also converting °F to °C by changing the subject.

Fluency
Match each blue expression with its equivalent red expression.

$6x + 3$ $x(x + 2)$
$4y - 6$ $3(2x + 1)$
$x^2 + 2x$ $2y(4x - 5)$
$8xy - 10y$ $2(2y - 3)$

Explore
How can you work out the radius of a sphere from the volume?

Exercise 5.6

1 Solve these equations.

a $5x = 20$

b $\dfrac{x}{3} = 8$

c $2x + 1 = 9$

d $5x - 6 = 4$

2 Factorise these expressions.

a $7x + 14$

b $9y - 6$

c $4ab + 8ac$

d $3x^2 - 9xy$

3 Make x the **subject** of each formula.

a $y = x + 5$

b $z = x - 12$

c $h = 5x$

d $k = \dfrac{x}{4}$

4 **STEM** The formula to work out the force (F) acting on an object is $F = ma$, where m is the mass and a is the acceleration of the object.

a **i** Make a the subject of the formula.
  ii Work out the value of a when $F = 24$ and $m = 3$.

b **i** Make m the subject of the formula.
  ii Work out the value of m when $F = 35$ and $a = 10$.

5 Make x the subject of each formula.

a $y = 2x + 3$

b $t = 5x - 9$

c $v = 3x + 8m$

Key point

The **subject** of a formula is the variable on its own on one side of the equals sign.
A is the subject of $A = l \times b$.

Q3a hint

Rearrange the formula so it starts '$x =$'.

Q4a i hint

$F = m \times a$
$m \times a = F$

$a = \dfrac{\square}{\square}$

Q5a hint

$y - 3 = 2x$

$x = \dfrac{y - 3}{\square}$

6 The equation of a straight line can be written in the form $y = mx + c$.
Make y the subject of each of these by writing them in the form $y = mx + c$.
  a $y - 5x = 12$ **b** $y + 4x - 11 = 0$ **c** $2y - 6x = 18$
  Discussion In what order did you rearrange the terms in part **c**?

7 Make r the subject of each formula.
  a $C = 2\pi r$
  b $A = \pi r^2$
  c $A = 4\pi r^2$
  d $V = \pi r^2 h$
  Discussion What are each of these formulae for?

Q7b hint

$r^2 = \dfrac{A}{\pi}$

$r = \square$

8 **Problem-solving** The diagram shows a trapezium with area $72\,\text{cm}^2$.

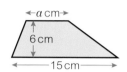

  a Write down the formula for the area of a trapezium.
  b Rearrange the formula to make a the subject.
  c Work out the value of a.

9 **Problem-solving** A company wants to make a cylindrical tin with radius $8\,\text{cm}$ and capacity 1 litre.
  Work out the smallest integer height of the tin.

Q9 hint

1 litre = $1000\,\text{cm}^3$

10 **Reasoning** Jacinda rearranges the formula for the surface area of a cylinder to make h the subject.
  This is what she writes.

$$A = 2\pi r^2 + 2\pi rh$$

$$h = \frac{A - \cancel{2\pi r^2}}{2\pi r}$$

$$h = A - r$$

  a Explain the mistake that Jacinda has made.
  b Work out the value of h when $A = 205\,\text{cm}^2$ and $r = 3.4\,\text{cm}$.
    Give your answer correct to 3 significant figures.

Worked example

Make x the subject of this formula.

$$ax + 7 = bx + c$$

$ax + 7 = bx + c$	
$ax - bx = c - 7$	Get all the terms in x onto one side.
$x(a - b) = c - 7$	x is a common factor of both terms, so factorise.
$x = \dfrac{c - 7}{a - b}$	Divide both sides by $(a - b)$ to make x the subject.

Key point

The subject of a formula should only appear once in the formula.

---

11 Make x the subject of each formula.

  a $5x = kx + p$

  b $mx + t = x + 10$

  c $xy - 5 = 12 + 4x$

  d $r^2x = m^2x + mr$

12 **STEM** In an experiment, Ghasan works out the speed of two balls after they collide.

This is one of the formulae that he writes.

$$6eu - ev = 2v + u$$

  a Make u the subject of this formula.

  b Work out the value of u when $v = 4$ and $e = 0.5$.

13 Make y the subject in each of these formulae.

  a $a = 2b + \sqrt{y}$

  b $T = 2x + \sqrt{y}$

  c $L = 2x + \dfrac{\sqrt{5y}}{k}$

Q13 Strategy hint

Rearrange each formula to make $\sqrt{y}$ or $\sqrt{5y}$ the subject first. Then square both sides of the equation.

14 **STEM** Two formulae used in physics are

$$w = \sqrt{\dfrac{k}{m}} \text{ and } b = a\sqrt{1 - e^2}$$

  a Make k the subject of the first formula.

  b Make e the subject of the second formula.

Q14a hint

Square both sides of the equation first.

15 This formula is used to work out the distance, d, travelled by an object that starts from rest.

$$d = \dfrac{at^2}{2}$$

where a is the acceleration and t is the time taken.

  a Rearrange the formula to make a the subject.

  b Work out the acceleration when $d = 100$ and $t = 8$.

  c Work out the time taken when $a = 25$ and $d = 50$.

16 **Explore** How can you work out the radius of a sphere from the volume?

Is it easier to explore this question now that you have completed the lesson?

What further information do you need to be able to answer this?

17 **Reflect** Choose one of the formulae in Q13 to write out as a Worked Example for another student.

Do you think this is a useful way to strengthen your learning?

Explore

Reflect

5 Check up

Substitution and formulae

1 Find the value of each expression when $x = 2$, $y = -3$ and $z = 4$.

  a $5(x^2 + y)$ **b** $y^2(4 + 2x^3)$

  c $5z(6 - x) - y$ **d** $y(x + \sqrt{z})$

2 A car hire company charges $\$x$ per day to hire a car for d days.
They also charge a one-off fuel cost of $\$f$.

  a Work out the total cost of hiring a car for 7 days if it costs $15 per day with a one-off fuel cost of $55.

  b Write an expression for the total amount a customer pays in terms of x, d and f.

  c Write a formula for the total amount a customer pays, T, in terms of x, d and f.

  d Use your formula to work out T when $x = 18$, $d = 10$ and $f = 65$.

3 Use the formula $L = \dfrac{5x^2}{v}$ to work out the value of L when $x = 4$ and $v = 10$.

4 Use the formula $P = mv + t$ to work out the value of

  a t when $P = 50$, $m = 6$ and $v = 5$

  b v when $P = 28$, $m = 10$ and $t = 12$

5 Make x the subject of each formula.

  a $u = x + v$ **b** $y = 4x - 9$ **c** $A = 7x^2$

6 Make x the subject of each formula.

  a $xy - a = x + b$ **b** $p^2x = q^2x + pq$ **c** $T = \sqrt{\dfrac{x}{2}}$

Inequalities

7 Write the inequalities shown by each of these number lines.

  a 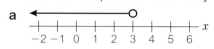   **b**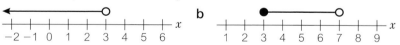

8 Represent each of these inequalities on a number line.

  a $x > 4$ **b** $-4 < y < 2$

9 Solve these inequalities.

  a $x + 2 < 5$ **b** $2y < -6$

  c $-5 < y - 3 < 1$ **d** $2 > \dfrac{x}{3} > -1$

10 Solve these inequalities.

  a $4n + 1 < 9$ **b** $\dfrac{x}{2} - 3 > -1$

  c $2 < 3y + 5 < 17$ **d** $6 > 2n - 2 > -6$

11 Solve these inequalities.

a $-x > 2$

b $-5x < -30$

c $5 > -x > 8$

d $-4 < -x < 7$

Expanding, factorising and indices

12 Work out the value of $4y^0$.

13 Write $\dfrac{x^2}{x^4}$ as a single power of x.

14 Expand

a $y(y^3 + 7y)$

b $x^2(2x^2 + 5x - 7)$

15 Expand and simplify $x(x^2 + 5x) + 3x(x^2 + 9x)$.

16 Factorise each expression completely. Check your answers.

a $9x - 3x^3$

b $20y^6 + 15y^4$

c $9x + 12y + 18z$

d $x^2 + 8xy + 2xz$

17 This is how Alisha factorises the expression $8x^2y^2 - 4xy^2z$ completely.

$8x^2y^2 - 4xy^2z = 2xy(4xy - 2yz)$

a Explain the mistake that she has made.

b Factorise the expression correctly and completely.

Equations and identities

18 Solve these equations.

a $3x + 7 = \dfrac{9x - 1}{2}$

b $\dfrac{15x + 1}{4} = 2x - 5$

19 The diagram shows an isosceles triangle.

$4(7 - 2x)$ $-3(5x - 14)$

a Work out the value of x.

b What is the length of the equal sides in this isosceles triangle?

20 Solve $\dfrac{x - 4}{3} = \dfrac{x + 2}{4}$.

21 The $=$ and $\equiv$ signs are not printed in these statements.
Decide whether each one is an equation or an identity.

a $y + y + 3y \ \square \ 5y$

b $m + 7 \ \square \ 3m - 7$

Challenge

22 Here are two inequalities.

A $\square < 5x - 7 \leqslant \square$ B $\square < \dfrac{x}{3} + 5 \leqslant \square$

The solution to both of the inequalities is $-3 < x < 6$.
What are the missing numbers in each of the inequalities?

23 How sure are you of your answers? Were you mostly
😟 Just guessing   😐 Feeling doubtful   🙂 Confident
What next? Use your results to decide whether to strengthen or extend your learning.

5 Strengthen

You will:
- Strengthen your understanding with practice.

Substitution and formulae

1 Work out the value of these expressions when $x = 3$ and $y = 4$.

  a $2x + y^2 = 2 \times \square + \square^2 =$

  b $5x^2 = 5 \times \square^2 =$

  c $6x^3 - 12 = 6 \times \square^3 - 12 =$

  d $2y^3 - 15x = 2 \times \square^3 - 15 \times \square$

  e $3xy - y^2$ **f** $2(x + y)$ **g** $3(4x - y)$ **h** $4(y^2 - x^2)$

> **Q1a hint**
>
> $2 \times \square + \square^2 = \ldots$

2 This is how Carrie and Dai substitute $a = -2$ and $b = -3$ into the expression $6a^2 - 4b$:

Carrie
$$6a^2 - 4b = 6 \times (-2)^2 - 4 \times -3$$
$$= 6 \times 4 + 12$$

Dai
$$6a^2 - 4b = 6 \times (-2)^2 - 4 \times -3$$
$$= 6 \times -4 - 12$$

  a Who is correct so far?

  b Explain the mistakes that the other one has made.

  c Work out the correct final answer.

3 **STEM / Modelling** The formula to change a temperature in degrees Celsius to degrees Fahrenheit is

    $F = 1.8C + 32$

where C in the temperature in degrees Celsius and F is the temperature in degrees Fahrenheit.

Work out the value of F when

  a $C = 10°C$ **b** $C = 28°C$ **c** $C = -5°C$ **d** $C = -20°C$

> **Q3a hint**
>
> $F = 1.8 \times 10 + 32 = \square + \square = \square$

4 Find the value of each expression when $x = 5$, $y = 4$ and $z = -3$.

  a $xy + 2z$ **b** $z^2 + 3xy$ **c** $5y^2 - xz$

  d $6(4x - 9z)$ **e** $3(y^3 + 4xz)$ **f** $\dfrac{x - z}{2y}$

> **Q4a hint**
>
> $5 \times 4 + 2 \times -3 = 20 + -6 = 20 - 6 = \square$

> **Q4b hint**
>
> $z^2 = (-3)^2 = -3 \times -3 = \square$

> **Q4d hint**
>
> Work out the brackets first, then multiply the answer by 6.

5 **Modelling** A bicycle hire company charge an amount per day to hire a bicycle. The amount depends on the size and quality of the bicycle.

  a Work out the total cost to hire a bicycle for

    i 3 days at $18 per day

    ii 5 days at $24 per day.

  b Write an expression for the total cost of hiring a bicycle for d days at c per day.

  c Write a formula for the total cost, T, in terms of d and c.

  d Use your formula to work out T when $d = 10$ and $c = \$9.50$.

> **Q5b hint**
>
>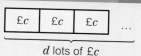
>
> | £c | £c | £c | ... |
>
> d lots of £c

> **Q5c hint**
>
> Write '$T =$' in front of the expression you wrote in part **b**, to make it a formula.

6 STEM / Modelling You can use this formula to calculate the energy stored in a stretched string.

$$E = \frac{kx^2}{2l}$$

Work out the value of E when

a $k = 30$, $x = 2$ and $l = 12$ b $k = 60$, $x = 3$ and $l = 18$

7 Use the formula $R = mu + p$ to work out the value of

a p when $R = 20$, $m = 4$ and $u = 2$
b p when $R = 25$, $m = 2$ and $u = 7$
c m when $R = 23$, $u = 3$ and $p = 14$
d m when $R = 40$, $u = 5$ and $p = 20$
e u when $R = 28$, $m = 6$ and $p = 16$
f u when $R = 79$, $m = 8$ and $p = 7$

8 Make x the subject of these formulae. $b = x + m$ $x \rightarrow \boxed{+m} \rightarrow b$
The first one has been done for you. $x = b - m$ $x \leftarrow \boxed{-m} \leftarrow b$

a $b = x + m$
b $y = 3x$
c $y = mx + c$
d $h = gx - 2$
e $T = 2x^2$
f $h = px^2$

9 Make x the subject of these formulae.
Some of them have been started for you.

a $5x = bx + c$ b $xp + m = x + n$
   $5x - bx = c$
   $x(5 - b) = c$
   $x = \dfrac{c}{\square + \square}$

c $7x + 12 = 20 - xy$ d $a^2x = b^2x + cd$

e $R = \sqrt{\dfrac{x}{4}}$ f $M = \dfrac{\sqrt{2x}}{3}$
   $R^2 = \dfrac{x}{4}$
   $x = \square R^2$

Inequalities

1 Match each of these inequalities with the correct number line diagram.

a $x < 2$ b $x \geqslant 2$
c $-2 < x \leqslant 2$ d $2 > x \geqslant -2$

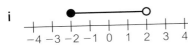 

 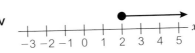

Q6a hint

$$E = \frac{30 \times 2^2}{2 \times 12} = \frac{30 \times \square}{\square} = \frac{\square}{\square} = \square$$

Q7a hint

Substitute the values into the formula, then use a function machine to solve $20 = 4 \times 2 + p$

Q7c hint

Use a function machine to solve $23 = 3m + 14$

Q8e hint

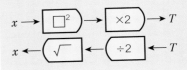

Q9b hint

Rearrange to get only the terms in x on the left-hand side of the equation.

Q1 hint

○ shows that the value is not included.
● shows that the value is included.

Q1d hint

$2 > x \geqslant -2$ is the same as $-2 \leqslant x < 2$

2 Write whether A, B or C is the correct inequality shown by each of these number lines.

a

$A\ x \leqslant 1$ $B\ 1 < x$ $C\ x < 1$

b [number line from 4 to 12, filled circle at 6, open circle at 10]

$A\ 6 \leqslant x \leqslant 10$ $B\ 6 \leqslant x < 10$ $C\ 6 < x < 10$

Q2a hint

Choose any number that fits your inequality. Add 7. Is it less than 12?

3 Write inequalities for each of these sentences and show them on a number line.
Some of them have been started for you.

a A number is less than or equal to -1.

[number line from -4 to 4, filled circle at -1 with arrow to left] $x\ \square\ -1$

b A number is greater than or equal to 3.

c A number is less than 4 and greater than or equal to -3.

[number line from -3 to 5, filled circle at -3, open circle at 4] $-3\ \square\ x\ \square\ 4$

Q3c hint

Rewrite as $-1 < \frac{x}{3} < 3$.

d A number is greater than or equal to -7 and less than or equal to 0.

4 Solve these inequalities.
Represent each solution on a number line.

a $x + 7 < 12$
$x < 12 - 7$
$x < \square$

b $n - 4 > 9$

c $3y \leqslant 15$

d $\frac{z}{5} \geqslant -1$

e $8n + 3 < 19$

f $2z - 8 > 4$

Q4a hint

Add x to both sides so it is no longer negative.

5 Mia uses this method to solve a double inequality.

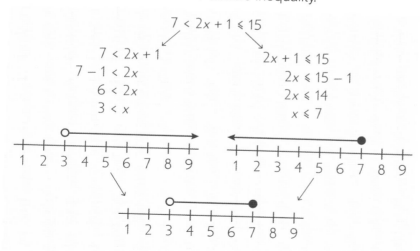

$$7 < 2x + 1 \leqslant 15$$

$7 < 2x + 1$
$7 - 1 < 2x$
$6 < 2x$
$3 < x$

$2x + 1 \leqslant 15$
$2x \leqslant 15 - 1$
$2x \leqslant 14$
$x \leqslant 7$

Solve these double inequalities. Represent each solution on a number line.

a $-1 \leqslant y + 2 \leqslant 8$

b $4 < 2x < 16$

c $3 \geqslant \frac{x}{5} > -1$

d $-7 \leqslant 2y + 3 < 15$

e $14 > 3n - 1 > 5$

6 Solve these inequalities.

a $8 - x < 3$

b $12 - y > 18$

c $-7x \geqslant -21$

d $-3y \leqslant 24$

e $2 < -x < 9$

f $-18 \leqslant -6x \leqslant 30$

Expanding, factorising and indices

1 You can use a grid method to expand brackets like this:

$a(a^3 - 4a + 3)$

×	a^3	$-4a$	$+3$
a	a^4	$-4a^2$	$+3a$

Answer: $a^4 - 4a^2 + 3a$

Expand

a $d(d^2 + 8d + 6)$ **b** $a(a^3 + 9a^2 - 2a)$

c $2b(3b^2 + 4b + 8)$ **d** $c^2(3c^2 - 2c - 1)$

2 Expand and simplify

  a $a(a^2 + 4a) + 2a(a^2 + 6a)$

  b $y(y^2 + 2y + 8) + y(y^2 + 3y + 5)$

  c $a(3a^2 + 6a - 8) + a(2a^2 - a - 4)$

  d $5b(b^2 + 3b + 5) - b(3b^2 + b - 2)$

3 Simplify

  a $(5a)^3$

  b $(3b)^2$

  c $(2x)^4$

  d $\left(\dfrac{x}{7}\right)^2$

  e $\left(\dfrac{y}{9}\right)^2$

  f $\left(\dfrac{b}{2}\right)^3$

4 Copy and complete

  a $2^{-2} = \dfrac{1}{2^\square}$ **b** $2^{-3} = \dfrac{1}{2^\square}$ **c** $x^{-2} = \dfrac{1}{x^\square}$ **d** $y^{-3} = \dfrac{1}{y^\square}$

5 Simplify these expressions.

  a $\dfrac{x^2}{x^3}$

  b $\dfrac{y^4}{y^6}$

  c $\dfrac{z^3}{z^8}$

  d $\dfrac{w}{w^7}$

6 What is the highest common factor of

  a $3x$ and 6

  b $4x^2$ and $12x$

  c $10x^2$ and $15x^3$?

7 Factorise each expression completely.
Take out the highest common factor and put it in front
of the brackets.
Check your answers by expanding the brackets.

  a $10x + 5 = 5(\square + \square)$ **b** $12x - 9x^2 = 3x(\square - \square)$

  c $25y^5 + 10y^2 = 5y^2(\square + \square)$ **d** $14a^3 - 10a = \square(\square - \square)$

  e $b^2 + 3b^4 = \square(\square + \square)$ **f** $12c^2 + 18c^3 = \square(\square + \square)$

Q1a hint

×	d^2	$+8d$	$+6$
d			

Q1d hint

×	$3c^2$	$-2c$	-1
c^2			

Q2a hint

×	a^2	$+4a$
a		

$+$

×	a^2	$+6a$
$2a$		

$\square + \square + \square + \square = \square + \square$

Q2d hint

Watch out for the '$-b$'.

Q3a hint

$(5a)^3 = 5a \times 5a \times 5a$

$= 5 \times a \times 5 \times a \times 5 \times a$

$= 5 \times 5 \times 5 \times a \times a \times a$

$= \square a^3$

Q3d hint

$\left(\dfrac{x}{7}\right)^2 = \dfrac{x}{7} \times \dfrac{x}{7} = \dfrac{x \times x}{7 \times 7} = \dfrac{x^2}{\square}$

Q4 hint

$2^{-4} = \dfrac{1}{2^4}$

Q5a hint

$\dfrac{x^2}{x^3} = x^{2-3} = x^\square = \dfrac{1}{x^\square}$

Q5d hint

$\dfrac{w}{w^7} = w^{1-7} = w^\square = \dfrac{1}{\square}$

Q6b hint

The HCF of 4 and 12 is 4.
x is also a common factor.
So $4\square$ is the HCF of $4x^2$ and $12x$.

Q7d hint

The HCF of 14 and 10 is 2.
a is also a common factor of $14a^3$
and $10a$.
So $2\square$ is the HCF of $14a^3$ and $10a$.

8 Factorise each expression completely.
Check your answers by expanding the brackets.
a $4x + 14y + 8z = 2(\square + \square + \square)$
b $x^2 + 3xy + 5xz = x(\square + \square + \square)$
c $3a^2 + 9ab - 6ac = 3a(\square + \square - \square)$
d $5mn + 15m^2 + 10m^3 = \square(\square + \square + \square)$
e $8wx^2 + 4w^2x + 12wx = \square(\square + \square + \square)$
f $6b + 24ab^3 - 12bc = \square(\square + \square + \square)$

Q7d hint

The HCF of 5, 15 and 10 is 5.
m is also a common factor of $5mn$, $15m^2$ and $10m^3$.
So $5\square$ is the HCF of these terms.

Equations

1 Solve these equations.
a $5x + 3 = \dfrac{11x + 2}{2}$ b $\dfrac{10x + 9}{3} = 6x - 5$

Q1a hint

First multiply both sides by 2.
$2(5x + 3) = \dfrac{2(11x + 2)}{2}$

2 The diagram shows a square.

$-3x + 2$

$4(-8 - 5x)$

a Write an equation involving x.
b Solve your equation to work out the value of x.
c Work out the side length of the square.

Q2c hint

Substitute your value for x into one of the expressions.

3 Follow these steps to solve $\dfrac{2x + 3}{3} = \dfrac{5x + 2}{6}$
a What is the lowest common multiple (LCM) of 3 and 6?
b Multiply $\dfrac{2x + 3}{3}$ by the LCM of 3 and 6.
c Multiply $\dfrac{5x + 2}{6}$ by the LCM of 3 and 6.
d Solve $\dfrac{2x + 3}{3} = \dfrac{5x + 2}{6}$

4 Solve these equations. Check that your solutions are correct by substituting.
a $\dfrac{x + 3}{3} = \dfrac{3x + 7}{5}$ b $\dfrac{5x - 1}{8} = \dfrac{2x + 1}{4}$ c $\dfrac{3x - 2}{6} = \dfrac{4x - 1}{9}$

Enrichment

1 Here are two inequalities involving x.
$2x + 1 < 7$ $4x - 9 > -5$
x is a whole number. What is the value of x?

Q1 Strategy hint

Solve each inequality and represent both solutions on the same number line.

2 Becky says, 'I think of a number, add 2 then divide the result by 5. This gives me the same answer as when I start with the same number, subtract 4 and divide the result by 3'.
a Write an equation using x to represent the number Becky thinks of.
b Solve the equation to work out the value of x.

3 **Reflect** How would you explain index notation to someone who has never used it?

5 Extend

You will:
• Extend your understanding with problem-solving.

1 Problem-solving

a Match each lettered expression with the correct numbered answer. Use the value of the letters given in the table.

a	b	c	d	e	f	g	h	i
3	−2	−5	16	25	−27	−4	4	12

A $4a^2 - \sqrt{e}$

B $b(\sqrt{d} + \sqrt{ai})$

C $\sqrt[3]{f} - 8c$

D $\dfrac{hi}{3} + 3b^2c$

E $\dfrac{b^2 + g^2}{h}$

F $\sqrt[3]{dh} - 2c^2$

1 −44

2 −20

3 37

4 −46

5 31

6 5

7 12

b One answer card has not been used. Write an expression for this answer card. Use at least three of the letters from the table, and include a power or a root in your expression.

2 Problem-solving The area of the grey rectangle is twice the area of the yellow rectangle.

a Work out the value of x.

b Work out the areas of the two rectangles.

4 cm

$(3x - 7)$ cm

Area = $(36 - 4x)$ cm²

3 Simplify

a $\dfrac{18x^7}{4x^{10}}$

b $\dfrac{22x^4}{6x^7}$

c $\dfrac{12m}{14m^5}$

d $\dfrac{y^2 \times y^2}{y^9}$

e $\dfrac{x^5}{x^3 \times x^6}$

f $\dfrac{8p^3}{6p \times p^4}$

> **Q3e hint**
>
> Simplify the denominator first.

4 Solve these inequalities. Write each answer as a mixed number. Represent each solution on a number line.

a $x + 1\frac{1}{3} \geqslant 5\frac{2}{3}$

b $x - 3\frac{3}{4} < 2\frac{1}{8}$

c $3x > 13$

d $\dfrac{x}{2} \leqslant 1\frac{2}{5}$

> **Q4a hint**
>
> $x \geqslant 5\frac{2}{3} - 1\frac{1}{3}$

5 Real Arjay makes a fertiliser from nettle juice. He mixes $\frac{1}{4}$ litre of nettle plant juice with some water.
So that the fertiliser is not too strong, he must mix the nettle juice with w litres of water, where $4w \geqslant 10$.
  a Solve the inequality.
  b i What is the smallest whole number of litres of water that he can use?
   ii How much fertiliser will this make?
  c i What is the smallest whole number of litres of fertiliser that he can make?
   ii How much water will he use for this amount of fertiliser?

6 Solve these inequalities. Write your answers as decimals. Represent each solution on a number line.
  a $2 \leqslant 10x < 8$ **b** $-6 < 4x \leqslant 10$

7 Problem-solving Ella solves the inequality $\square < 8x \leqslant \square$. The number line shows her solution.

What is the inequality that Ella solved?

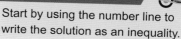

Q7 Strategy hint

Start by using the number line to write the solution as an inequality.

8 Solve these inequalities. Write your answers as mixed numbers or decimals. Represent each solution on a number line.

  a $4n + 3 \leqslant 16$

  b $\dfrac{x}{3} - \dfrac{1}{2} < \dfrac{1}{8}$

  c $2 \leqslant 3x - 5 < 6$

  d $9 > 5n + 3 > -1$

9 STEM / Modelling You can use this formula to calculate the energy, E joules, in a moving object:
  $E = \frac{1}{2}mv^2$
  where m is the mass of object (kg) and v is the speed (metres per second, m/s).
  Work out the speed, v, of the object when
  a $E = 96$ and $m = 12$
  b $E = 625$ and $m = 8$
  c $E = 1470$ and $m = 15$

Q9a hint

When you know v^2, take the square root to find v.

10 Reasoning Carlos is substituting values into the expression $3x^2y + z^3$.
The values he uses for x, y and z are always negative.
Carlos says, 'The value of my expression will never be a positive number.' Is he correct? Explain your answer.

Q10 Strategy hint

Substitute different negative number values for x, y and z into the expression.

11 Substitute $a = -2$ and $b = -4$ into each expression and simplify the answer.

  a $a^4 - b^3$ **b** $\sqrt{a^6}$ **c** $\sqrt[3]{b^6 - 2a^2}$ **d** $ab^2 - a^2b - (ab)^2$

  e $\left(\dfrac{5}{2}b\right)^2$ **f** $\left(\dfrac{a}{b}\right)^3$ **g** $\dfrac{a^2b^2}{a^2 + b^2}$ **h** $\dfrac{\sqrt[3]{ab} + ab}{a^2 - b^2}$

12 **STEM / Problem-solving** You can use this formula to calculate the elastic potential energy, E joules, stored in a stretched string:

$$E = \frac{kx^2}{2l}$$

where k is the stretch factor, x is the distance stretched (m) and l is the normal length (m).

a Work out the value of E when

   i $k = 40$, $x = 3$ and $l = 15$

   ii $k = 32$, $x = 5$ and $l = 20$

You can use this formula to calculate the tension, T newtons, in a stretched string

$$T = \frac{kx}{l}$$

where k is the stretch factor, x is the distance stretched (m) and l is the normal length (m).

b Work out the value of k when

   i $T = 6$, $x = 2$ and $l = 5$

   ii $T = 15$, $x = 2.5$ and $l = 8$

c Use both of these formulae to work out the value of E when $T = 12$, $x = 1.5$ and $l = 4$.

13 Make m the subject of each formula.

  a $x = 2hm$ **b** $P = mgh$ **c** $r = \dfrac{m}{2l}$

  d $y = \dfrac{3m}{4x}$ **e** $y = m^2$ **f** $x = m^2 + 2n$

14 Make x the subject of these formulae.
Some of them have been started for you.

  a $\dfrac{1}{x} = y - 8$ **b** $\dfrac{1}{x} = \dfrac{1}{y} + \dfrac{1}{z}$ **c** $\dfrac{1}{x} - \dfrac{2}{p} = \dfrac{3}{q}$ **d** $\dfrac{5}{x} + \dfrac{3}{m} = \dfrac{1}{k}$

    $1 = x(y - 8)$ $\dfrac{1}{x} = \dfrac{\square + \square}{yz}$

    $x = \dfrac{1}{\square - \square}$ $yz = x(\square + \square)$

                          $x = \square$

15 **STEM** You can use this formula to calculate the distance, s, travelled by a body that starts from rest:

$$s = \frac{at^2}{2}$$

where a is the acceleration (m/s²) and t is the time (s).

a **i** Make a the subject of the formula.

    ii Make t the subject of the formula.

b Work out the value of s when $a = 10$ and $t = 3$.

c Use your answer to part **b** and the values given for a and t to check that your rearranged formulae in part **a** are correct.

16 The diagram shows a regular pentagon and a regular octagon.
The perimeter of the pentagon is given by $3x - 4$
and the perimeter of the octagon $4x + 8$.

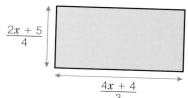 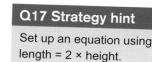

  a Write an expression for the side length of the
    i pentagon
    ii octagon.
  b The side length of the pentagon is the same as the side length of
    the octagon. Write an equation to show this.
  c Solve your equation to find the value of x.
  d Work out
    i the side length of each shape
    ii the perimeter of each shape.

17 Problem-solving This rectangle is
made of two squares joined together.
Work out the value of x. Write your
answer as a mixed number in its
simplest form.

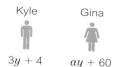

Q17 Strategy hint

Set up an equation using
length = 2 × height.

18 Problem-solving The diagram shows a
semicircle.
  a Write a formula for the perimeter (P) of the semicircle.
  b Work out the radius of the semicircle when $P = 33$ cm.
    Give your answer correct to 1 decimal place.

19 Problem-solving / Reasoning The diagram shows
the ages of two people in terms of x and y.
Gina is three times the age of Kyle.

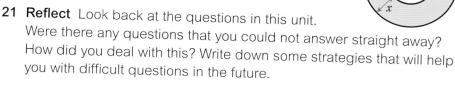

  a Write an equation using the information given
    and make y the subject of the formula.
  b When $a = 1$, work out the value of y and the ages of Kyle and
    Gina.
  c When $a = 2$, work out the value of y and the ages of Kyle and
    Gina.
  d Explain why a cannot be equal to 6.

Q19a Strategy hint

Start by writing an equation which
includes brackets.

20 Problem-solving / Reasoning The diagram shows a
small circle cut out from a larger circle.
Show that the formula for the shaded area (A) can
be written as $A = \pi x(2R - x)$.

Q20 hint

Shaded area = area of large circle
           – area of small circle
Radius of small circle = □ – □

21 Reflect Look back at the questions in this unit.
Were there any questions that you could not answer straight away?
How did you deal with this? Write down some strategies that will help
you with difficult questions in the future.

Reflect

5 Unit test

1 Work out the value of each of these expressions.

  a $2a + b^2$ when $a = 5$ and $b = 2$

  b $40 - (a + b^3)$ when $a = 8$ and $b = 3$

  c $(a + b)^2 - 4c$ when $a = 3$, $b = 5$ and $c = 5$

  d $\dfrac{2a^2}{bc}$ when $a = 6$, $b = 4$ and $c = 3$

2 A wedding venue company charges an amount per person for food plus an amount per hour for the room hire.
  a Work out the total cost of food for 80 people at $30 per person plus room hire at $50 per hour for 6 hours.
  b Write an expression for the cost of food for p people at $x per person plus room hire for h hours at $y per hour.
  c Write a formula for the total cost, T, in terms of x, p, y and h.
  d Use your formula to work out T when $x = 35$, $p = 100$, $h = 8$ and $y = 30$.

3 Solve the equation
  $2x + 1 = \dfrac{7x - 19}{2}$

4 A cube has a mass of $3(-5x - 7)$ kg.
  A cuboid has a mass of $-2(7x + 9)$ kg.
  The mass of the cube is the same as the mass of the cuboid.
  a Work out the value of x.
  b What is the mass of the cube and the cuboid?

5 Represent each of these inequalities on a number line.
  a $x \leqslant -2$
  b $-1 < y < 5$

6 Write the inequality that each number line represents.

  a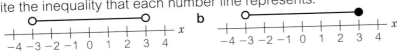
  b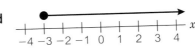

  c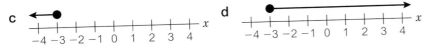
  d

7 Work out the value of $7x^0 \times 5y^0$.

8 Write $\dfrac{q^8}{q^{15}}$ as a single power of q.

9 Write down true (T) or false (F) for each of these statements
  a $3e^0 = 3$
  b $0a^0 = 1$
  c $(h^4)^0 = h^4$
  d $(3c^2)^0 = 1$

10 Find the value of each expression when $x = 4$, $y = -2$ and $z = 3$.

    a $x^2(3 - y) - 4z$

    b $z(8x - z^3) + 2(3x + 2y)$

11 Factorise each expression completely. Check your answers.

    a $24x + 8$

    b $12x^3 - 9x^5$

    c $y^2 + 15xy + 10yz$

    d $4x^2 - 14xy - 2xyz$

12 Use the formula $R = mg - T$ to work out the value of m when $R = 40$, $g = 12$ and $T = 8$.

13 Solve these inequalities.

    a $x + 3 < 7$ **b** $3y \leqslant -3$

    c $5 > \dfrac{x}{2} > 3$ **d** $-5 \leqslant 2x + 3 < 7$

    e $-x > -6$ **f** $2 - x < -3$

14 Solve the equation

$$\frac{7x + 1}{6} = \frac{9x + 3}{8}$$

15 Make x the subject of each formula.

    a $m = x + t$ **b** $F = ax$

    c $g = 3x - 5$ **d** $T = rx^2$

16 Make t the subject of the formula $w = r + 2t^2$.

17 Make x the subject of each formula.

    a $12x = xy + p$ **b** $mx - 4 = nx + 9$

    c $a^2x = bx + 5d$ **d** $P = \dfrac{\sqrt[3]{3x}}{r}$

Challenge

18 The diagram shows a rectangle and a triangle.

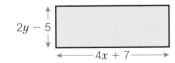 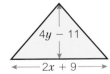

Carrie makes this pattern using the triangle and the rectangle.

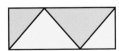

    a Write two equations using the information given and solve them to work out the values of x and y.

    b Work out the area of the rectangle and the triangle.

    c What can you say about the areas of the rectangle and the triangle?

19 **Reflect** This unit covered equations, formulae, inequalities and indices. Which topics did you like most and which did you like least? Can you explain why?

6.1 STEM: Planning a survey

You will learn to:
* Identify sources of primary and secondary data.
* Choose a suitable sample size.
* Understand how to reduce bias in sampling and questionnaires.
* Identify a random sample.

Confidence

Why learn this?
Governments carry out surveys called censuses to find out information about the population of the country.

Fluency
Round 5.56 cm to the nearest
* mm
* cm
* m

Work out 10% of
* 50
* 400
* 2000

Explore
When the government carries out a census, what sample of the population does it ask? What proportion respond?

Exercise 6.1

Warm up

1 What unit would you use to measure
  a the distance between two cities
  b the length of a caterpillar
  c the width of a garden?

2 Michelle wants to test whether this spinner is **biased**. Should she spin it 5, 30 or 100 times?

Literacy hint
Biased means it is more likely to land on one colour than another.

3 **Real / STEM** Choose the most appropriate measurement from the cloud for these investigations.
  a How deep in the ocean can fish survive?
  b Do genetically engineered fish grow longer than wild fish?
  c How far can a remote-controlled helicopter fly?

mm   km   metres   cm

4 **Real / STEM** Select an appropriate level of accuracy for these investigations.
  a The times taken to run 800 m at your school sports day to the nearest
    A millisecond   **B** second   **C** minute.
  b The masses of frogs to the nearest
    A gram   **B** 0.1 kg   **C** kg.
  c The speeds of vehicles on the motorway to the nearest
    A 0.1 mph   **B** 1 mph   **C** 10 mph.

Subject links: Science (Q3–5, Q7), Geography (Q7)

5 **Real / STEM** Decide on an appropriate level of accuracy for these investigations.

   a The times taken to run 800 m at an Olympic Games.

   b The capacity of petrol tanks.

   c The masses of sunflower seeds.

6 For the following data:

   i decide whether it is **primary** or **secondary data**

   ii if it is primary data, give a suitable method for collecting it.

   a The total time spent in the Emergency Department in every hospital in Australia from April 2018 to June 2019.

   b Numbers given by people who were asked to choose their favourite number.

   c Percentage of the Indian population that used the internet in 2019.

   d IGCSE results of all pupils in New Zealand in 2019.

   e The percentage of people who write with their right hand.

   f The number of people in cars on a main road.

Key point

Primary data is data I collect myself.
Secondary data is collected by someone else.
Different ways of collecting primary data include questionnaires, surveys and data logging.

Key point

The total number of items your survey relates to is called the **population**.
The group of items you test is called a **sample**.
Sampling can be time consuming and expensive but the bigger the sample, the more reliable it can be.
For a sample to be reliable and unbiased, it should
* be at least 10% of the population
* represent the population.

7 **STEM / Reasoning** Select the most appropriate **sample size** for each survey. Explain your choice.

   a There are 50 000 trees in a forest. Researchers want to find out what proportion of trees are taller than 20 m.

     i 5000   **ii** 1000

     iii 500   **iv** 10

   b The **population** of a country is approximately 64 000 000. An organisation wants to find out how many people have had a flu vaccination.

     i 100   **ii** 10 000

     iii 1 000 000   **iv** 20 000 000

   c The population of a city is 510 000. The council wants to find out how many people visit the doctor at least once a year.

     i 100 000   **ii** 6000

     iii 100   **iv** 5

8 **Real** A hospital wants to know the ages of people in the local area. They put questionnaires in the local pet shop. Why will this give a biased sample?

9 **Real** A town council wants to know how much the public library is being used. They give questionnaires to everyone in the library every Thursday afternoon for a month. Why is this sample biased?

10 A school wants to investigate the type of food students eat at lunchtime.

There are 1500 students at the school.

a Suggest a sensible number of students to be sampled.

b Which of these surveying methods will give a biased result? Explain your answers.

   i Sending a questionnaire to all Year 10 email accounts.

   ii Sending a questionnaire to all students.

   iii Asking students in the lunch queue at the beginning of lunchtime.

   iv Asking students with a packed lunch.

c Will the data be primary or secondary?

11 Explain why each of these **leading questions** is unsuitable to use in a survey.

For each question write a more suitable question to replace it.

a What methods of travel have you used in the last 12 months?

   car   bus   train   taxi   none

   ☐   ☐   ☐   ☐   ☐

b Petrol prices keep rising, so do you intend to use your car less during the next year?

c What do you do at weekends?

d Should the inadequate bus service in our town be improved?

e The main cause of bad behaviour in lessons is because the

   lesson is boring   teacher is not strict enough   lesson is too long

   ☐   ☐   ☐

f Because killing animals is cruel, should more people become vegetarians?

g What kind of food do you eat most of?

12 **Real / Reasoning** The table shows some survey questions and the sampling method used for each one. For each survey

a write down the population

b decide if the sample is **random**. Explain your answer.

	Survey	Sample
1	How long do patients spend in the Emergency Department at a hospital?	Every person leaving the Emergency Department on a Saturday night
2	What is the most common second language of people living in Denmark?	Students at a university in Denmark
3	What proportion of UK secondary school teachers are male?	Teachers at the local secondary school
4	What proportion of UK secondary school teachers are male?	Teachers in secondary schools in Leicester, Birmingham, Swansea and Aberdeen

13 **Explore** When the government carries out a census, what sample of the population does it ask? What proportion respond?

Is it easier to explore this question now that you have completed the lesson? What further information do you need?

14 **Reflect** Look back at the questions you have answered in this lesson. What mathematical skills do you need when planning a survey?

Literacy hint

A **leading question** encourages people to give a particular answer.

Key point

A question in a survey can be biased if it encourages people to give a particular answer.

A good survey question should not be

• unclear

• **leading**

• restrictive.

Key point

In a **random** sample, the whole population has an equal chance of being chosen, so it reduces the chances of bias.

Reflect Explore

6.2 Collecting data

You will learn to:
- Design a good questionnaire.
- Design and use data collection sheets and tables.

Why learn this?
Computers process large amounts of data by grouping the data in order to spot trends.

Fluency
$b = 5$
Which group should it be in?
$0 \leqslant b < 5$
$5 \leqslant b < 10$
$10 \leqslant b < 15$

Explore
What makes a good survey question?

Exercise 6.2

1 **Real** Here are the ages of 50 users of a leisure centre.
18, 23, 27, 36, 45, 42, 20, 8, 1, 17, 23, 45, 27, 29, 45, 60, 62, 35, 33,
41, 26, 25, 26, 68, 10, 19, 15, 23, 28, 30, 33, 36, 19, 18, 24, 26, 30,
41, 59, 65, 18, 34, 37, 36, 44, 45, 44, 37, 40, 44

 a Copy and compete the tally chart for the data.

Age (years)	Tally	Frequency
0–10		
11–20		
21–30		
31–40		
40+		

 b What percentage of customers are over 40?

Key point
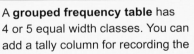
A **grouped frequency table** has 4 or 5 equal width classes. You can add a tally column for recording the data.

2 In which class does 0.5 cm go for each of these frequency tables?

 a
Length, l (cm)	Frequency
$0 \leqslant l < 0.5$	
$0.5 \leqslant l < 1$	
$1 \leqslant l < 1.5$	
$1.5 \leqslant l < 2$	

 b
Length, l (cm)	Frequency
$0 < l \leqslant 0.5$	
$0.5 < l \leqslant 1$	
$1 < l \leqslant 1.5$	
$1.5 < l \leqslant 2$	

Q2 Strategy hint

For values that are at the limits of a class, check the $\leqslant$ and $<$ symbols carefully.

3 The table shows the driving test results of 50 people.

	Men	Women
Pass	11	10
Fail	15	14

 a What percentage of the drivers passed their driving test?

 b What fraction of the men failed their driving test?

 c Work out the pass : fail ratio.

Key point

A **two-way table** shows data sorted in two ways, e.g. gender and age.

Warm up

4 Here are some records from a hospital database.

  a Design a grouped frequency table to record the masses.

  b **i** Copy and complete this two-way table to show the masses and ages of the patients.

		Age (years)		
		10–29	30–49	50+
Mass, *m* (kg)	$50 \leqslant m < 70$			
	$70 \leqslant m < 90$			
	90+			

    ii How many patients who are 50+ have a mass less than 70 kg?

    iii What proportion of the patients are aged between 10 and 29 years?

    iv What proportion of patients are in the middle mass group?

5 Year 8 and Year 9 students choose to learn French, Spanish or Mandarin. Design a two-way table to record each possible choice.

6 The numbers of people using a supermarket each day in one month were
123, 179, 235, 189, 207, 199, 145, 154, 198, 132,
201, 99, 134, 245, 207, 198, 164, 157, 149, 183,
172, 175, 188, 192, 184, 167, 203, 201, 188, 181

  a Is the data **discrete** or **continuous**?

  b Design a grouped frequency table to record this data.

  c Which group has the highest frequency?

7 A post office employee recorded the masses in kilograms of 15 parcels.
2.00, 4.54, 9.75, 8.21, 4.53,
3.45, 6.00, 1.24, 5.22, 3.30,
0.99, 6.12, 5.44, 6.23, 7.12

  a Design a grouped frequency table to record this data.

  b Which group has the highest frequency?

Name	Age	Mass, *m* (kg)
Hall	35	63
Field	25	56
Aintree	17	67
Kingley	34	80
Firbrand	56	77
Ruvierra	72	66
Huckelberry	61	70
Tudoristo	43	56
Franklin	45	73
Murphy	81	80
Orringe	34	88
Fruitry	47	93
Smith	65	67
Frankless	32	82
Harrison	45	91
Amberly	63	110
Kingston	45	84
Ocra	35	92
Savile	72	72
Dengel	56	88

Strategy hint

Think about the possible results.

Key point

Discrete data can only take particular values. For example, dress sizes are usually only even numbers. For discrete data you can use groups like 1–10, 11–20, …
Continuous data is measured and can take any value. Length, mass and capacity are continuous. For continuous data there are no gaps between the groups. You must use the $\leqslant$ and $<$ symbols.

Worked example

Here are three questions used in an online survey.
Explain what is wrong with each question and rewrite it.

a How old are you?
☐ 0–10   ☐ 10–20   ☐ 20–30   ☐ 30–50   ☐ 50+

The groups overlap. For example, if you are 20 years old, which box do you tick?
Change to: ☐ 0–10   ☐ 11–20   ☐ 21–30   ☐ 31–50   ☐ 51+

b Do you agree that exercise is enjoyable?   ☐ Yes   ☐ No
Saying, 'Do you agree?' encourages the answer 'Yes'.
Change to: Do you enjoy exercise?

Topic links: Upper and lower limits, Percentages

c Do you exercise enough?
'Enough' is not precise and means different things to different people.
Change to: How much do you exercise each day?
☐ Less than 1 hour   ☐ 1–2 hours   ☐ More than 2 hours

8 Anti animal-cruelty campaigners want to find out how people feel about killing animals for fur. They ask, 'It is cruel to kill animals for fur, isn't it?'

a What do you think most people will answer?

Discussion Why is this a leading question?

b Rewrite the question to find out what people really think about killing animals for fur.

9 a Explain what is wrong with each question and rewrite them.

   i How many portions of fruit or vegetables do you eat a day?
     ☐ 0–2　☐ 4–6　☐ 6–8

   ii Do you eat a healthy diet?
     ☐ Yes　☐ No

   iii Do you agree that fruit and vegetables are good for you?
     ☐ Yes　☐ No

b Imagine you are carrying out a survey using your new questions. Design a data collection sheet with tables to collect together all the answers.

10 Design your own questionnaire to test this hypothesis.
'Most people watch at least two hours of television a day.'

> **Key point**
>
> A **hypothesis** is a statement that you can test by collecting data.

Investigation
Problem-solving

Choose a topic that you are interested in. It could be sport, music, school activities – anything you like.

1 Write a hypothesis related to your topic.

2 Design a questionnaire to collect the information you need for testing your hypothesis.

3 Test your questionnaire on a friend.

4 Collect data from a suitable sample.

5 Record your findings in a two-way table or spreadsheet.

11 **Explore** What makes a good survey question?
Is it easier to explore this question now that you have completed the lesson? What further information do you need to be able to answer this?

12 **Reflect** You have learned lots of new terminology so far in this unit.
For example
• primary data and secondary data　• hypotheses　　• bias
• random samples　　　　　　　• discrete and continuous data
Work with a classmate. Discuss what you think 'primary data' and 'secondary data' are. Now write definitions for 'primary' and 'secondary data'. Try to be as accurate as possible.
Look at the key point for primary and secondary data in lesson 6.1 to see if you got them right. If not, rewrite the definitions to help you remember.
Do the same for the other words in the list.

> **Q12 Literacy hint**
>
> 'Terminology' is the special words or 'terms' used in a subject.

6.3 Calculating averages and range

You will learn to:
- Estimate the mean and range from a grouped frequency table.

Confidence

Why learn this?
Scientists use grouped data to analyse geographical features.

Fluency
What is the range of this set of data?
5 cm, 3 cm, 0 cm, 2 cm, 10 cm, 5 cm, 6 cm

Explore
Is it better to have a high average with a large range or a low average with a small range?

Exercise 6.3

Warm up

1 The frequency table shows how many siblings (brothers or sisters) each pupil in a class has.

Number of siblings	0	1	2	3	4
Frequency	5	13	7	4	1

a Work out the mean.   **b** How many pupils have 2 siblings?

> **Key point**
> When data has been grouped, you cannot work out the exact mean but you can work out an **estimate**.

Worked example

The table shows the results of a survey into the lengths of long rivers in the United Kingdom.
Work out an **estimate** for   **a** the mean   **b** the range.

a

Length of river, L (km)	Frequency	Midpoint of class (km)	Midpoint × frequency
$110 \leqslant L < 140$	17	125	2125
$140 \leqslant L < 170$	5	155	775
$170 \leqslant L < 200$	3	185	555
$200 \leqslant L < 230$	2	215	430
$230 \leqslant L < 260$	1	245	245
$260 \leqslant L < 290$	0	275	0
$290 \leqslant L < 320$	1	305	305
$320 \leqslant L < 350$	1	335	335
$250 \leqslant L < 380$	1	365	365
Total	**31**	**Total**	**5135**

> You don't know the exact value of each length, so estimate it as the midpoint of each class.
> Draw a column for the midpoints.
> Calculate an estimate of the total length for each class (midpoint × frequency).

> Calculate the total number of rivers and an estimate for the sum of their lengths.

Estimated mean = Estimated sum of lengths ÷ total number of rivers
= 5135 ÷ 31
= 165.65 km (to 2 d.p.)

> From the frequency table, the smallest possible value is 110 km and the largest possible value is 380 km.

b An estimate of the range is 380 − 110 = 270 km

Topic links: Imperial measures

Subject links: Geography (Q2, Q4)

2 The table shows the results of a survey into the lengths of river systems in Europe.
Work out an estimate for
 a the range
 b the mean.

Length of river, L (miles)	Frequency
$0 \leqslant L < 300$	5
$300 \leqslant L < 600$	13
$600 \leqslant L < 900$	8
$900 \leqslant L < 1200$	1
$1200 \leqslant L < 1500$	2
$1500 \leqslant L < 1800$	1
$1800 \leqslant L < 2100$	0
$2100 \leqslant L < 2400$	1

3 **Problem-solving** Class 9Y carried out a survey to find out how many miles people drive each year. The table shows their results.
Work out an estimate for
 a the range
 b the mean.

Distance driven each year, d (thousands of kilometres)	Frequency
$0 < d \leq 5$	9
$5 < d \leq 10$	26
$10 < d \leq 15$	35
$15 < d \leq 20$	20
$20 < d \leq 25$	9
$25 < d \leq 30$	1

4 The table shows the results of a survey into the lengths of rivers in North America.

Length of river, L (miles)	Frequency
$0 < L \leqslant 400$	21
$400 < L \leqslant 800$	18
$800 < L \leqslant 1200$	4
$1200 < L \leqslant 1600$	3
$1600 < L \leqslant 2000$	3
$2000 < L \leqslant 2400$	2
$2400 < L \leqslant 2800$	1
$2800 < L \leqslant 3200$	2

Key point

You can't work out the median from grouped data but you can find out which group the median value is in.

 a How many items are there in the sample?
 b Which number item is the median?
 c In which group will the median value be?
 d What is the modal class?
 e Work out an estimate for
  i the mean **ii** the range.

5 **Explore** Is it better to have a high average with a large range or a low average with a small range?
Look back at the maths you have learned in this lesson.
How can you use it to answer this question?

6 **Reflect** Edhita says, 'On average, a human has slightly less than two legs.' What point do you think Edhita is trying to make with this statement?

6.4 Displaying and analysing data

You will learn to:
- Construct and use a line of best fit to estimate missing values.
- Identify and explain outliers in data.
- Identify further lines of enquiry.
- Construct and use frequency polygons.

Why learn this?
A good scientist can spot any outliers in data and suggest what might have caused them.

Fluency
Find the midpoint of each group.
- $2 < e \leqslant 8$
- $0.5 < e \leqslant 1$
- $5 < e \leqslant 12$

Explore
What is a temperature anomaly map?

Exercise 6.4

1 **Real** The table shows the age and number of visits of patients at a doctor's surgery from April to September for 20 people.

Age (years)	25	67	35	92	35	48	72	18	25	63	28	19	26	50	38	78	93	38	1
Number of visits	2	7	4	12	3	6	8	0	2	7	3	1	4	8	5	13	12	4	8

a Draw a pair of axes with the horizontal axis from 0 to 100 labelled 'Age' and the vertical axis from 0 to 15 labelled 'Number of visits'. Plot a scatter graph showing this data.

b What type of correlation does the graph show?

c Draw a line of best fit.

2 a **Modelling** Use the line of best fit in Q1 to estimate the number of visits a 40-year-old would make between April and September.

b Use the line of best fit to estimate the age of a patient who visited the doctor 11 times between April and September.

c A doctor suggests this hypothesis.
'The older you are, the more times you visit the doctor per year.'
Does the data collected match the hypothesis?

d Explain what you would need to do to investigate this hypothesis further.

Discussion Did everyone in your class get the same answer to parts **a** and **b**?

3 Identify an outlier in Q1 and suggest what might have caused it.

Q2a hint

Find 40 on the correct axis. Draw a line up to the line of best fit and then across to the other axis.

Q2d Strategy hint

Is the sample size suitable?

Key point

An **outlier** is a value that doesn't follow the trend or pattern.

4 Real / Modelling The manager of a shop wants to work out when she needs the most staff in her shop.

She records the number of customers in a shop at half-hourly intervals one Monday.

She draws this graph.

a At which times is she most likely to need extra staff?

b Suggest a reason why these times might be the busiest.

c How could she investigate further?

Worked example

Draw a frequency polygon to represent this data.

Age, a	Frequency
$0 \leqslant a < 10$	12
$10 \leqslant a < 20$	15
$20 \leqslant a < 30$	2
$30 \leqslant a < 40$	11

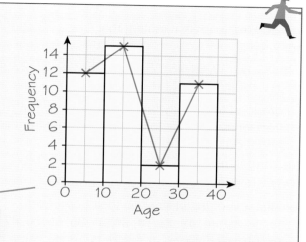

First draw a frequency diagram. Then join the midpoints of the tops of bars.

Key point

You can draw a **frequency polygon** by joining the midpoints of the tops of the bars in a frequency diagram.

5 Samarah constructs a frequency polygon for this data.

Earnings (per year), e	Number of employees
$0 < e \leqslant £10\,000$	3
$£10\,000 < e \leqslant £20\,000$	52
$£20\,000 < e \leqslant £30\,000$	29
$£30\,000 < e \leqslant £40\,000$	27
$£40\,000 < e \leqslant £50\,000$	5
$£50\,000 < e \leqslant £60\,000$	3

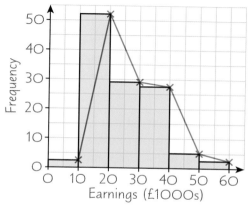

a Explain what she has done wrong.

b Construct an accurate frequency polygon for the data.

Discussion Can you see a shortcut for drawing a frequency polygon?

6 A leisure centre records the number of customers hourly through the day.

Leisure centre A

Time	9–10 am	10–11 am	11–12 pm	12–1 pm	1–2 pm	2–3 pm	3–4 pm	4–5 pm
Number of customers	35	79	182	23	31	245	90	118

a Draw a pair of axes with the horizontal axis showing time from 9 am to 5 pm and the vertical axis from 0 to 250 labelled 'Number of customers'. Construct a frequency polygon for the data.

Another leisure centre records this data.

Leisure centre B

Time	9–10 am	10–11 am	11–12 pm	12–1 pm	1–2 pm	2–3 pm	3–4 pm	4–5 pm
Number of customers	127	23	65	213	189	34	21	17

b Construct a frequency polygon for the second leisure centre on the same axes as part **a**.

c Compare the busiest times for the two leisure centres.

Q6b hint

Do you need to draw a frequency diagram first or can you simply construct a frequency polygon?

7 A teacher recorded the time (in minutes) that Class 2B spent on their maths homework.

34, 29, 3, 55, 16, 23, 30, 39, 59, 45, 35, 48, 33, 56, 29, 51, 23, 41, 31, 45

a Identify any outliers in the data.

b Construct a grouped frequency table, ignoring any outliers.

c Construct a frequency polygon to display the data from your frequency table.

d What is the modal class?

e Work out the range and mean from your frequency table.

Discussion How could the outliers have occurred?

Class 3C spent these lengths of time on their homework.
44, 51, 34, 62, 34, 56, 49, 44, 48, 23, 54, 34, 35, 36, 55, 56, 47, 44, 41, 20

f Construct a frequency polygon of this data on the same axes.

g What is the modal class for Class 3C?

h Work out the range and mean.
Are these accurate values or estimates?

i Compare the times spent on homework by the two classes.

Q7i hint

Use the averages and range, and look at the shape of the frequency polygons.

Investigation

Problem-solving

Construct a graph to present your findings from your investigation in lesson 6.2.

You may choose any graph you know how to draw: scatter graph, pie chart, frequency diagram, frequency polygon, bar chart.

Think about what you wish to display and how easy it will be to read the mean, mode, median and range from it.

8 Explore What is a temperature anomaly map?
Is it easier to explore this question now that you have completed the lesson?
What further information do you need to be able to answer this?

9 Reflect In this lesson you used a
- scatter diagram (for Q1, Q2 and Q3)
- line graph (for Q4)
- frequency polygon (for Q5, Q6 and Q7)

a Which type of diagram do you find easiest? Why?

b Which type of diagram do you find hardest? Why?

c What could you do to make it easier to work with the diagram you chose in part **b**?

Explore

Reflect

6 Check up

Planning a survey

1 A student wants to find out about the type of food students prefer. She collects two sets of data.

    A A survey of students about the food they like.

    B A record of food sold in the canteen.

  a Are A and B primary data or secondary data?

  b There are 1500 students at the school.
    What size sample should she use: 20, 200 or 1000?

Collecting data

2 A school has 1800 students. It wants to investigate how its students travel to school. Select the most appropriate sample size for the survey.

  A 1000   **B** 500   **C** 200   **D** 20

3 A library has 3860 members. How big should a sample of the library members be?

4 Fiona is researching the amount of time teenagers spend on the computer

  a Say whether each of these is primary or secondary data.

    A Sending a survey to the students of a local school.

    B Using information from the internet.

  She gives questionnaires to all the Year 10 students at her school.

  b Why will the sample be biased?

  c How could Fiona reduce bias in her sample?

5 Explain what is wrong with each question.

  a What is your shoe size?

    ☐ 1–3   ☐ 3–5   ☐ 5–7   ☐ 7+

  b Do you agree that it is harder to buy shoes for larger feet?

6 This question appears in a survey:
  'Do you watch too much TV'?
  Explain what is wrong with this question and rewrite it.

7 A farmer logs the mass (in grams) of 20 eggs laid by her chickens.
  70.5 61.2 75.3 77.7 79.7 80.0 84.3 69.9 70.5 91.3
  90.0 68.9 73.8 80.4 78.4 81.9 70.1 73.3 82.3 79.9

  a Design a frequency table to record the data.

  b Complete your frequency table.

Calculating averages and range

8 This table shows the weights of 50 children when they are two years old.

  a Estimate the mean weight.

  b Estimate the range.

Weight, w (kg)	Frequency
$10 < w \leqslant 11$	8
$11 < w \leqslant 12$	14
$12 < w \leqslant 13$	15
$13 < w \leqslant 14$	7
$14 < w \leqslant 15$	5
$15 < w \leqslant 16$	1

9 These frequency polygons show the heights of 50 boys and 50 girls on their second birthday.
Calculate the mean height for each frequency polygon.

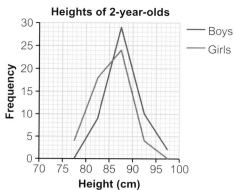

Displaying and analysing data

10 a Draw two frequency polygons on the same axes to show the lifespans of butterflies and moths.

Lifespan, l (days)	Butterflies	Moths
$0 < l \leqslant 5$	3	1
$5 < l \leqslant 10$	88	123
$10 < l \leqslant 15$	76	91
$15 < l \leqslant 20$	83	35

b Describe the main differences.

11 The scatter graph shows the number of driving lessons plotted against the number of driving tests taken before a successful pass.
  a Identify an outlier.
  b Suggest a reason for this outlier.
  c Adil has 36 lessons. Estimate how many tests he would take before passing.

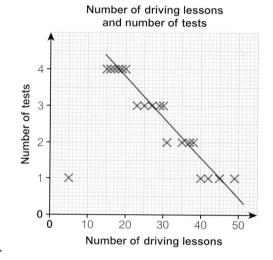

12 How sure are you of your answers? Were you mostly
  ☹ **Just guessing**   😐 **Feeling doubtful**   ☺ **Confident**
What next? Use your results to decide whether to strengthen or extend your learning.

Challenge

13 This table shows information about UK house prices.

Quarter-year	Average price (£)			
	Flat	Terraced house	Semi-detached house	Detached house
Jan–Mar 2012	96 769	98 754	124 269	173 607
April–June 2012	96 875	96 775	129 324	173 754
July–Sep 2012	100 154	99 286	129 143	176 108
Oct–Dec 2012	97 344	94 761	128 157	173 991
Jan–Mar 2013	91 942	96 964	123 998	176 580
April–June 2013	102 165	99 666	128 507	173 490

Source: Land Registry

  a Write two questions that the data could help you to answer.
  b What further data could you collect for your investigation?

Reflect

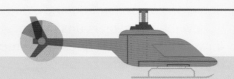

6 Strengthen

You will:
• Strengthen your understanding with practice.

Planning a survey

1 Rahni is doing a geography investigation on soil types in her area.
  a She tests 10 different samples of soil.
    Is this primary or secondary data?
  b She asks the Environment Agency for data on the soil.
    Is this primary or secondary data?

2 A large supermarket is planning a survey on the nation's favourite food.
  How many people should they interview: 10, 500 or 30 000?

3 The head teacher of a school wants to find out how long students spend on their homework. There are 1000 students in the school.
  a How many students should he ask: 1, 10 or 100?
  b What should he ask pupils to round their answers to?
    A the nearest hour
    B the nearest 10 minutes
    C the nearest minute
  c He decides to ask only students from Year 11. Is this a good idea? Explain your answer.

> **Q1 hint**
> **I** collect **pri**mary data for my investigation. **S**omeone else collects **s**econdary data.

> **Q2 hint**
> The results will be more reliable when more people are surveyed, but you need to think about whether it is practical or not.

> **Q3b hint**
> Think about how long you spend on your homework. What would you answer?

Collecting data

1 A light bulb manufacturer wants to check the quality of its products.
  It produces 5000 light bulbs a day.
  What is the most appropriate sample size?
  A 5
  B 50
  C 500
  D 5000

2 For each place, suggest a suitable sample size for surveying the number of people who use public transport.
  a Corby Glen   (population   1017)
  b Bangor   (population   17 988)
  c Luton   (population   211 228)
  d Birmingham   (population 1 085 810)

3 Would you use primary or secondary data to investigate
  a the number of birds of prey in the UK
  b how much money students at your school spend on lunch
  c how often people in your neighbourhood exercise?

> **Q1 hint**
> In general, 10% of the total population is a good sample size.

> **Q2a hint**
> Work out 10% of 1017.
> Round to the nearest 10.

> **Q3 hint**
> If you could obtain the data yourself, then it is primary data.

4 For each question
   i choose an option from the cloud to describe how the question is unsuitable
   ii write an unbiased question to replace it.

> not all options included
> leading question   too unclear
> too many possible answers

   a What is the best time of the year?
   b Do you disagree with the plans for a great big new motorway?
   c What sport do you do?
      football   cricket   tennis   none
   d Most students want to have less homework. Do you?
   e What is the best kind of holiday?

5 **Reasoning** A research organisation wants to find out how much fruit and vegetables people eat.
Explain how each sample is biased.
   a Only people leaving a health club.
   b Only people shopping in a health food shop.
   c Only people at an old people's home.

Q5a hint

People at a health club don't represent the whole population because …

6 A student wants to record the lengths of pebbles in a stream to the nearest centimetre. He suggests the following groups.
   0–10 cm   10–20 cm   20–30 cm
   a In which groups could he record a 10 cm long pebble?
   b What is the problem with his choice of groups?
      He redesigns his groups.
   c Copy and complete the new groups.
      0–9 cm   ☐–19 cm   ☐–29 cm

7 The times (in minutes) that 10 people spent in the gym are 65, 34, 49, 58, 23, 45, 40, 36, 55, 69
Copy and complete the frequency table.
All groups must be the same width.

Time, t (minutes)	Tally	Frequency
$20 < t \leq 30$		
$30 < t \leq \square$		
$\square < t \leq \square$		
$\square < t \leq \square$		
$60 < t \leq 70$		

8 Design a frequency table to record the times (in minutes) that people spend making mobile phone calls.

Q8 hint

Think about the answers you would expect to get to your question.

Calculating averages and range

1 **Real** The table shows the heights of major waterfalls around the world.
   a How high could the tallest waterfall be?
   b How high could the shortest waterfall be?
   c Use your answers to parts **a** and **b** to estimate the range.
   d How many waterfalls were surveyed?
   e The midpoint of $650 < H \leq 700$ is 675. Work out the midpoints for the other groups and write them in a new column in your table.
   f Work out midpoint × frequency for each row.
   g Use your table from parts **d** and **f** to estimate the mean.

Height, H (metres)	Frequency
$650 < H \leq 700$	7
$700 < H \leq 750$	11
$750 < H \leq 800$	6
$800 < H \leq 850$	4
$850 < H \leq 900$	4
$900 < H \leq 950$	3
$950 < H \leq 1000$	1

2 The table shows the times that members of a Year 9 class spent on maths homework.
Work out estimates for
   a the range
   b the mean.

Time, t (minutes)	Frequency
$0 < t \leq 10$	3
$10 < t \leq 20$	13
$20 < t \leq 30$	8
$30 < t \leq 40$	5
$40 < t \leq 50$	1

Displaying and analysing data

1 A nurse recorded the heights of 14 children in Year 3.

Height, h (cm)	Frequency
$130 < h \leqslant 135$	3
$135 < h \leqslant 140$	4
$140 < h \leqslant 145$	7

Polly is drawing a frequency polygon for this data.
She starts by drawing the bars.
What does Polly need to do next?

2 A vet recorded the masses of some kittens in a litter.

Mass, m (kg)	Midpoint	Frequency
$0.4 \leqslant m < 0.6$	0.5	1
$0.6 \leqslant m < 0.8$	☐	6
$0.8 \leqslant m < 1$	☐	2

a Copy the axes.
b Draw a frequency polygon for this data.

3 The scatter graph shows the times taken for 20 students to run 200 m plotted against their times taken to run 100 m.

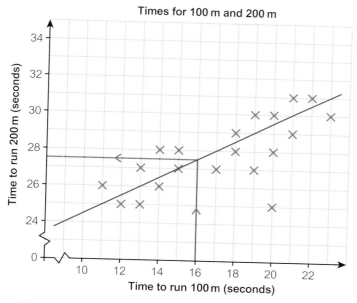

Times for 100 m and 200 m

a Describe the type of correlation.
b **Modelling** Use the line of best fit to predict the 200 m time for a student who ran the 100 m in
  i 16 seconds
  ii 19 seconds
  iii 17 seconds
c One point is an outlier. What were the times for 100 m and 200 m for this student?

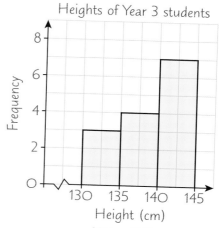

Heights of Year 3 students

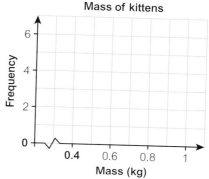

Mass of kittens

Q3a Literacy hint

Positive correlation means that as one value increases, so does the other.
Negative correlation means that as one value increases, the other decreases.

Q3b i hint

Find 100 m in 16 seconds on the correct axis.
Draw a line up to the line of best fit and then across to the other axis.
Read off the value.

Q3b Literacy hint

Outliers are points that don't follow the trend.

4 A school records the exam results of 9 pupils in Mandarin and maths.

Mandarin	75%	81%	45%	24%	57%	91%	89%	93%	63%
Maths	83%	92%	35%	30%	62%	25%	80%	84%	59%

a Draw a scatter graph for this data.

b Draw a line of best fit.

c Predict the maths score for a student whose Mandarin score was

    i 30%

    ii 50%

    iii 90%

d Predict the Mandarin score for a student whose maths score was

    i 60%

    ii 40%

    iii 70%

e Put a ring around the data point that is an outlier.

> **Q4a hint**
>
> Put Mandarin marks on the horizontal axis. What is the highest value you need to plot?

Enrichment

1 A supermarket only buys batches of trout from a supplier if the mean mass of the fish is at least 3.5 kg.
The tables show the same mass data grouped differently.

Table A

Mass, m (kg)	Freq.
$0 < m \leqslant 1$	4
$1 < m \leqslant 2$	14
$2 < m \leqslant 3$	22
$3 < m \leqslant 4$	91
$4 < m \leqslant 5$	49
$5 < m \leqslant 6$	6

Table B

Mass, m (kg)	Freq.
$0 < m \leqslant 1.5$	11
$1.5 < m \leqslant 3$	29
$3 < m \leqslant 4.5$	116
$4.5 < m \leqslant 6$	30

Table C

Mass, m (kg)	Freq.
$0 < m \leqslant 2$	18
$2 < m \leqslant 4$	113
$4 < m \leqslant 6$	55

a Which table should the supplier use to show that his fish meet the supermarket's requirements?

b Which table should the supermarket use to negotiate a lower price?

2 Reflect Gabby says, 'When I see a question with a table:
- I cover the question with my hand, so I can only see the table
- then I look for a title or a description of the table
- then I read any row or column headings
- finally, I randomly pick a number in the table and ask myself what this number tells me.

It only takes a minute, and stops me panicking about all the information I am being given.'

Look back at any Strengthen question that has a table in it. Use Gabby's method.

Now find an Extend question with a table. Use Gabby's method again.

Is Gabby's method helpful?

Reflect

6 Extend

You will:
- Extend your understanding with problem-solving.

1 A company is designing an online survey to find out whether their employees are happy in their work.
Which data should they collect about each employee? Explain why you did or didn't choose each one.
A name
B age
C level of satisfaction with the company
D number of years with the company
E how their working conditions should be improved

2 **Real / Reasoning** A yearly competition held in Bognor Regis for human-powered flying machines started in 1971.
Table A shows the distances travelled in 2004 and 2006.
Table B shows the time spent in the air.

Table A

Distance, D (metres)	Frequency	
	2004	**2006**
$0 \leqslant D < 2$	1	0
$2 \leqslant D < 4$	4	1
$4 \leqslant D < 6$	10	5
$6 \leqslant D < 8$	5	12
$8 \leqslant D < 10$	5	5
$10 \leqslant D < 12$	1	1

Table B

Airtime, T (seconds)	Frequency	
	2004	**2006**
$1 \leqslant T < 1.25$	2	4
$1.25 \leqslant T < 1.5$	15	7
$1.5 \leqslant T < 1.75$	6	9
$1.75 \leqslant T < 2$	0	2
$2 \leqslant T < 2.25$	1	2
$2.25 \leqslant T < 2.5$	2	0

Source: Birdman

a Using the same axes, draw frequency polygons for distance travelled in 2004 and in 2006.
b On a new set of axes, draw frequency polygons for airtime in 2004 and 2006.
c Compare the distances and the airtime for the 2 years.
d What can you say about distance and airtime?

Q2a hint

Use a different colour for each frequency polygon and give a colour key.

3 **Real** A council wants to find out what facilities the people living in the town would like to improve.
a Explain what is wrong with the following question.
'Do you agree this town needs more play parks for children?'
b Write some questions you might ask instead.

4 **Reasoning** Samir wrote a questionnaire about bullying.

	Questionnaire about bullying
Question A	How often have you been bullied?
Question B	What do you do when you see someone being bullied?
Question C	Do you agree that bullies should be sent to prison?

a Say why each of Samir's questions needs to be improved.

b Choose three questions from this list to replace questions A, B and C.

Question P	Why is bullying wrong?
Question Q	If you saw someone being bullied would you ☐ do nothing ☐ try to stop it ☐ tell someone in authority, such as a teacher?
Question R	When were you last bullied?
Question S	When do you think bullying usually happens? ☐ in lessons ☐ after school ☐ on the way home ☐ during lunch break ☐ on the school bus ☐ every day
Question T	Do you agree that bullies should be ignored?
Question U	Tick the option that best describes your experience. During the past year I have been bullied ☐ never ☐ once ☐ between 2 and 12 times ☐ at least once per month ☐ at least once a week ☐ daily
Question V	Do you defend people who are being bullied?
Question W	Tick the option that is closest to your view. School bullies should be ☐ sent to prison ☐ dealt with by a teacher who knows them well ☐ made to apologise to the person they bullied ☐ expelled from the school ☐ kept in after school for an hour for a whole term ☐ ignored ☐ banned from all sports

5 In a survey into eating habits, students recorded the number of portions of fruit and vegetables they ate for a week.
The results are shown in the table.

Number of portions per week	Frequency
0–9	6
10–19	17
20–29	15
30–39	48
40–49	21
50–59	3

a Work out an estimate for the mean number of portions eaten each week.

b Which class contains the median number of portions?

6 Real The tables show the populations (in millions) of Asia and Europe, by age and gender.

Asia

Age, a (years)	Male	Female
$0 \leqslant a < 20$	757	700
$20 \leqslant a < 40$	655	615
$40 \leqslant a < 60$	415	400
$60 \leqslant a < 80$	155	180
$80 \leqslant a < 100$	17	33

Europe

Age, a (years)	Male	Female
$0 \leqslant a < 20$	84	80
$20 \leqslant a < 40$	105	103
$40 \leqslant a < 60$	100	104
$60 \leqslant a < 80$	54	71
$80 \leqslant a < 100$	8	18

a Construct two pie charts to show the age distributions in Asia and in Europe.

b Find the modal age group for each continent.

c Calculate an estimate of the mean for each continent.

d Write three sentences comparing the populations of Asia and Europe.

7 Finance Two investment funds record the percentage increase in the value of their investments over the past 20 years.

Company A

Percentage increase in investment, I	Frequency
$0 \leqslant I < 2$	3
$2 \leqslant I < 4$	11
$4 \leqslant I < 6$	5
$6 \leqslant I < 8$	1

Company B

Percentage increase in investment, I	Frequency
$0 \leqslant I < 2$	0
$2 \leqslant I < 4$	15
$4 \leqslant I < 6$	5
$6 \leqslant I < 8$	0

a Can you use the tables to find out how many percentage increases were exactly 4%?

b Can you use the tables to find out the exact value of the biggest percentage increase?

c By plotting frequency polygons and calculating the estimated mean, explain which investment fund you would use and why.

> **Q7 hint**
>
> You might wish to think about where your money would be safest or where you could invest to make the most profit.

8 These frequency tables are for the same data grouped in two different ways.

Class	Frequency
$0 \leqslant b < 20$	7
$20 \leqslant b < 40$	25
$40 \leqslant b < 60$	15
$60 \leqslant b < 80$	3

Class	Frequency
$0 \leqslant b < 15$	3
$15 \leqslant b < 30$	11
$30 \leqslant b < 45$	21
$45 \leqslant b < 60$	12
$60 \leqslant b < 75$	3

For each set of data

a give the modal class

b estimate the range

c estimate the mean.

9 These graphs show facts about percentages of populations who turned out to vote in UK General Elections.

Graph A shows the percentage of the whole UK population that voted in elections between 1945 and 2010.

Graph B shows the percentages of the population for a random sample of UK **constituencies**.

Graph A

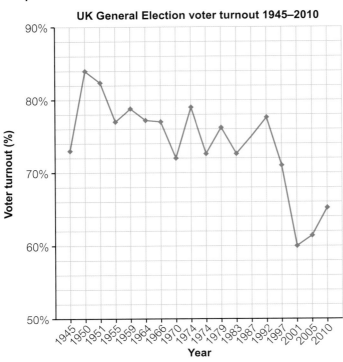

Graph B

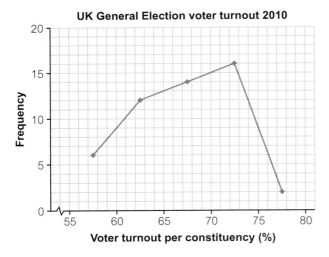

Source: House of Commons

Q9 Literacy hint

A **constituency** is an area that votes for a single Member of Parliament.

a Explain why graph A is not a frequency polygon.

b Work out an estimate of the mean percentage of eligible people in each constituency who voted in the 2010 General Election.

10 Reflect This extend section included a lot of questions using real data. Do you find it easier or harder to understand statistics when real data is used? Explain your answer.

6 Unit test

1 An insurance company suggests, 'Men are better drivers than women.'
It uses these questions in a survey.
   A How many accidents have you had in the last 10 years?
   ☐ 0–2   ☐ 2–4   ☐ 4–6   ☐ 6+
   B Would you agree that women have more accidents than men?
   a Explain what is wrong with the questions.
   b Rewrite the questions.

2 For a 'Stop Speeding' campaign, Brendan measures the speed that
cars travel along his road. The road has a 30 mph limit.
   a How accurately should he record the data to state his case to the
   council?
   A nearest 10 mph   **B** nearest 1 mph   **C** nearest 0.1 mph
   b Design a frequency table to record his data.

3 Students at a school can choose one sport from each group.
   Group A Tennis, Badminton, Squash
   Group B Swimming, Athletics, Gymnastics
   Design a two-way table to record the results.

4 The table shows the results of a survey into how old people were
when they first flew on a plane.
Construct a frequency polygon for this data.

Age, a (years)	Frequency
$0 < a \leqslant 10$	16
$10 < a \leqslant 20$	32
$20 < a \leqslant 30$	27
$30 < a \leqslant 40$	8
$40 < a \leqslant 50$	5
$50 < a \leqslant 60$	2

5 These frequency polygons show the number of people employed at
companies in two towns.

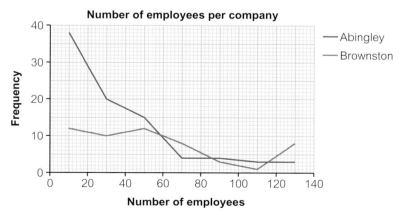

Number of employees per company

— Abingley
— Brownston

   a Calculate the mean number of employees per company for
   each town.
   b Write a sentence to compare the size of the companies in the
   two towns.

6 The table shows the diameters of some asteroids.
Estimate
  a the range   **b** the mean.

Diameter, D (metres)	Frequency
$0 < D \leqslant 30$	1600
$30 < D \leqslant 100$	2700
$100 < D \leqslant 300$	2800
$300 < D \leqslant 1000$	3150
$1000 < D \leqslant 2000$	880

7 The scatter graphs show the relationship between the maximum daily temperature and the number of ice creams sold in a shop. They show the same data but have different lines of best fit.

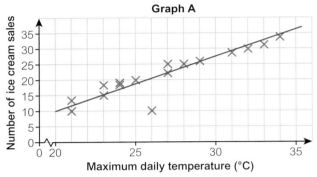

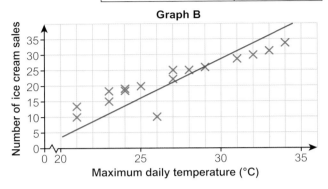

  a What type of correlation do the graphs show?
  b What is the temperature for the outlier in Graph A?
  c Which graph has the most accurate line of best fit?
  d Use this line of best fit to estimate
    i the maximum daily temperature when the shop sells 20 ice creams
    ii the number of ice creams the shop will sell when the temperature is 30 °C.

8 Two airline companies record the number of people travelling on their Airbus 320s for 200 flights.

Airline A

Number of passengers, p	Frequency
$0 \leqslant p < 40$	20
$40 \leqslant p < 80$	43
$80 \leqslant p < 120$	112
$120 \leqslant p < 160$	25

Airline B

Number of passengers, p	Frequency
$0 \leqslant p < 40$	0
$40 \leqslant p < 80$	44
$80 \leqslant p < 120$	54
$120 \leqslant p < 160$	102

  a Which is the modal class of passengers for
    i Airline A   **ii** Airline B?
  b Calculate an estimate of the mean number of passengers for each airline.
  c Estimate the range for each airline.
  d On the same set of axes construct two frequency polygons to show both airlines.
  e Write two sentences comparing the data for each airline.

Challenge

9 The way in which data is grouped can change the estimated mean.
Investigate how you might raise the estimated mean by grouping the data in Q8 differently.

10 Reflect
  a Write down three ways in which it helps to have good numeracy skills when dealing with data.
  b Write down three ways in which it helps to have good literacy skills when dealing with data.
  c How does having good literacy skills help you in other ways with your mathematics learning?

Q10 Literacy hint

Good numeracy skills means being good at working with numbers.
Good literacy skills means being good at reading, writing and communicating.

Reflect

7.1 Direct proportion

You will learn to:
- Recognise data sets that are in proportion.
- Set up equations that show direct proportion.

Why learn this?
Knowing the relationship between quantities can help you to make predictions.

Fluency
Which of these graphs show direct proportion?

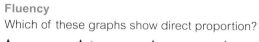
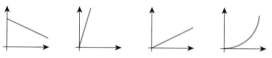

Explore
Are a clothes store's profits in direct proportion to its sales?

Exercise 7.1

1 Which of these are in direct proportion?
a The exchange rate of pounds (£) and Czech koruna (Kč)
b Earnings of a plumber who charges a flat fee and then an hourly rate
c The exchange rate at a bank that charges a £5 flat fee for changing money
d Distance in miles and distance in kilometres

2 The price of eggs varies in direct proportion to the number sold. The price of 6 eggs is $1.98. How much will
a 12 eggs cost **b** 15 eggs cost?

> **Q2b hint**
> Work out the cost of 1 egg.

3 **Real** Two friends compare their mobile phone bills.
Arhan's bill is £2.80 for 80 text messages.
Majed's bill is £5.10 for 150 text messages.
Who has the better deal?

> **Q3 hint**
> The cost of text messages is in direct proportion to the number sent.

4 **STEM** A laboratory takes these readings for variables x and y in one experiment.

x	0.6	1.7	2.4
y	5.4	15.3	21.6

a Plot the points for x and y.
b Does the graph show that the variables are in direct proportion?
c Work out $\frac{y}{x}$ for each pair. What do you notice?
d Copy and complete this arrow diagram.
e Copy and complete this formula linking x and y: $y = \square x$
Discussion How does the formula relate to the graph?

> **Key point**
> When two quantities x and y are in direct proportion, $\frac{y}{x}$ is **constant**.

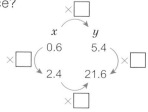

Warm up

5 The table shows the cost of hiring a car.

Number of days	2	5	9
Cost (£)	27	67.50	121.50

a Work out
  cost ÷ number of days
  for each pair of values.
b Is the cost of hiring a car in direct proportion to the number of days?
c Check your answer to part b by drawing a graph, with Number of days on the horizontal axis.
d Copy and complete: cost = ☐ × number of days
e What is the cost of hiring a car for 15 days?

6 **Real** Russell records the temperature of five cities in Celsius (°C) and Fahrenheit (°F).

City	Cape Town	Chicago	Manchester	Rio de Janeiro	Port Stanley
Temperature C(°C)	16	22	21	26	9
Temperature F(°F)	61	72	70	79	48

a Is the temperature in Fahrenheit proportional to the temperature in Celsius? Explain.
b Check your answer to part a by drawing a graph, with °C on the horizontal axis.

Q6a hint

Work out $F ÷ C$ for each city.

7 The values of p and x are in direct proportion.
Work out the missing numbers a, b, c and d.

p	x
8	25
12	a
b	50
c	62.5
20	d

Q7 hint

You could use ratios to find the missing numbers.

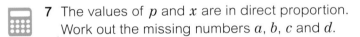

8 **Real** The table below shows the distances (in metres and yards) that a golfer hits a ball with different clubs.
Calculate the missing distances x, y and z.
Give your answers to the nearest integer.

Club	Distance (yards)	Distance (metres)
9-iron	140	128
7-iron	162	x
4-iron	y	194
Driver	z	306

Q8 hint

Are metres and yards in direct proportion?

Discussion How did you find the missing distances?

9 **Modelling** The circumference of Safa's head is 48 cm.
Her height is 162 cm.
a Write Safa's head circumference to height as a ratio.
Safa assumes that head circumference and height are in direct proportion.
Use this model to predict
b the height of a person with head circumference 35 cm
c the head circumference of a person 185 cm tall.
Discussion Is this a reasonable model?

10 **Explore** Are a clothes store's profits in direct proportion to its sales?
Is it easier to explore this question now that you have completed the lesson?
What further information do you need to be able to answer this?

11 **Reflect** The relationship between two variables can be shown on a graph or using a table of values. Do you prefer one method over the other? Why?

7.2 Solving problems using direct proportion

You will learn to:
- Set up equations to show direct proportion.
- Use algebra to solve problems involving proportion.

Why learn this?
Scientists use direct proportion to study the relationship between temperature, volume and pressure of gases.

Fluency
$y = 4x$
Work out y when
- $x = 2$
- $x = 3.5$
- $x = 44$

Explore
How much does a 10 kg mass weigh on Mars?

Exercise 7.2

1 Write down the equation of each line on the right.

2 Solve
 a $15 = 30k$
 b $12 = 8k$

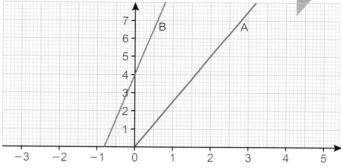

3 **STEM** In a school science experiment, students apply a force to a model car and then measure the acceleration. The table shows some results.

Force, F (newtons)	10	12	25
Acceleration, a (m/s²)	0.5	0.6	1.25

 a Plot a graph of this data.
 b Are force and acceleration in direct proportion? Explain.
 c Write a formula connecting force and acceleration.

4 **Real / Finance** Write a formula linking each pair of quantities.
 a The cost, C, in pence of sending t text messages at 5p per text.

$$C = \square t$$

 b The cost, C, in dollars of x plants at $4 per plant.
 c Yearly earnings, E, in pounds of a footballer who earns £x per week.
 d The number of miles, m, travelled in 2.5 hours at a speed of x miles per hour.
 e The cost, C, in dollars of n biscuits at 35 cents each.
 Discussion What is the same about all of these formulae?

Key point

When
- y varies as x
- y varies directly as x
- y is in direct proportion to x
you can write $y \propto x$.
- $y \propto x$ means 'y is proportional to x'.
When $y \propto x$, then $y = kx$, where k is the **constant of proportionality**.

Q4 Literacy hint

In the formula $C = 5t$, 5 is the **constant of proportionality**. Its value is constant (stays the same) when t and C vary.

Warm up

5 Which of these equations show direct proportion?

  a $P = 5s$

  b $C = 5h + 40$

  c $y = \frac{1}{2}x$

  d $A = d^2$

Worked example

The number of centimetres, C, varies in direct proportion to the number of inches, I.

a 12 inches is equal to 30 centimetres. Write a formula linking C and I.

b How many centimetres are equal to 70 inches?

a $C \propto I$

  $C = kI$ ───── Write the relationship in the form $y \propto x$ and the equation $y = kx$.

  When $I = 12$, $C = 30$

  $30 = k \times 12$ ───── Substitute the values given for I and C into $C = kI$.

  $k = \frac{30}{12} = 2.5$

  $C = 2.5I$ ───── Solve the equation to find k. Rewrite the equation using the value of k.

b When $I = 70$

  $C = 2.5 \times 70$

  $C = 175$ ───── Use your formula to answer the question.

  70 inches = 175 cm

---

6 The price of potatoes, P, varies in direct proportion to the mass, m, sold.
The price of 2.5 kg of potatoes is $6.05.

  a Write a formula linking P and m.

  b Use your formula to work out the price of 4.2 kg of potatoes.

7 **Finance** The South African rand, R, varies in direct proportion with the UK pound, P.
One day 801 South African rand = £45.

  a Write a formula for converting pounds to rand.

  b How many South African rand can you buy with £250?

  c How many UK pounds can you buy with 650 South African rand?

  Discussion What level of accuracy should you use for your answer to part **c**?

Q7 hint

Write a formula: $R =$

8 **Finance** Sarka's commission is in direct proportion to the value of goods sold.
Commission, C, is £51 when £1700 worth of goods, G, is sold.

  a Work out the commission on £2500 of goods sold.

  b Sarka receives £180 commission. What value of goods has she sold?

Q8 hint

Write a formula: $C =$

Subject links: Science (Q3, Q10, Q11 and Explore)

9 Problem-solving x and y are in direct proportion.

x	0.7	t	3.5
y	4.2	14.4	21

  a Write a formula for y.

  b Work out the missing value, t.

Q9 hint

$y = kx$
Use a pair of values from the table to find k.

10 STEM The weight, W, of an object is in direct proportion to the mass, m, of the object.

On Earth, a 14 kg object weighs 137.2 N.

  a Work out the weight of an 18 kg object on Earth.

  b The formula connecting mass and weight is
     $W = m \times$ acceleration due to gravity.
    What is the value of the acceleration due to gravity on Earth?

  c On the Moon, the acceleration due to gravity is 1.6 m/s^2.
    i What is the formula connecting the weight and mass of objects on the Moon?
    ii Work out the weight of the 14 kg object on the Moon.

Q10 Literacy hint

Mass is measured in kg.
Weight is a force and is measured in N (newtons).

Q12b hint

The units for the acceleration due to gravity are m/s^2.

11 Modelling An aeroplane travels 720 miles in 90 minutes.
The distance travelled, d, is in direct proportion to the time, t.

  a Work out how far the aeroplane travels at this speed
    i in 140 minutes
    ii in 1 hour 15 minutes.
  The formula connecting distance and time is $d = s \times t$.

  b What is the speed of the plane in miles per hour?

  c The distance from London to New York is 3450 miles.
    Use your formula and your answer to part **b** to work out the journey time when flying from London to New York.

  Discussion Why does this model not give an exact answer?

Q11b hint

90 minutes = □.□ hours.

12 Explore How much does a 10 kg mass weigh on Mars?
Is it easier to explore this question now that you have completed the lesson?
What further information do you need to be able to answer this?

13 Reflect In this lesson, you met the symbol $\propto$ meaning 'proportional to'.
Write down three advantages of using symbols in mathematics.
Are there any disadvantages?

Explore

Reflect

7.3 Translations and enlargements

You will learn to:
- Understand and use column vectors in translations.
- Work out the scale factor of an enlargement.
- Enlarge shapes using positive scale factors, about a centre of enlargement.
- Describe an enlargement on a coordinate grid.

Why learn this?
With 3D modelling software, designers can use transformations to move objects around their screen.

Fluency
How many squares right and how many squares down does triangle A need to move to get to triangle B?

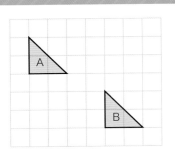

Explore
How can you enlarge a photo using picture tools on a computer?

Exercise 7.3

1 Copy the orange shape onto squared paper. Draw the image of the shape after these translations. Part **a** is done for you.

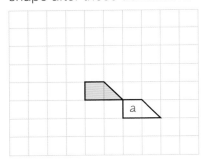

a 2 squares right, 1 square down   **b** 3 squares right, 2 squares up
c 1 square left, 3 squares up   **d** 4 squares left
e 2 squares left, 2 squares down

2 Copy each shape onto squared paper and enlarge it by the scale factor shown.
   a scale factor 3   **b** scale factor 4

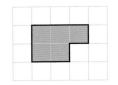

3 Shape B is an enlargement of shape A. What is the scale factor of the enlargement?

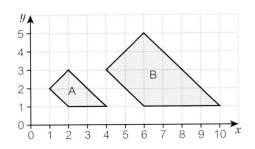

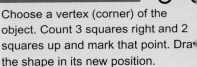

Strategy hint

Choose a vertex (corner) of the object. Count 3 squares right and 2 squares up and mark that point. Draw the shape in its new position.

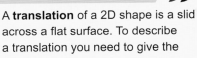

Key point

A **translation** of a 2D shape is a slide across a flat surface. To describe a translation you need to give the movement left or right, followed by the movement up or down.

Confidence

Warm up

4 Reasoning Chen translates shape A 4 squares left and 2 squares down to make shape B, then translates shape B 3 squares right and 4 squares up to make shape C.
Chen says, 'If I translate shape A 1 square left and 2 squares up, I'll end up with shape C.'
Is he correct? Explain your answer.

Q4 Strategy hint

Draw a shape on a grid, label it A, then follow the instructions.

5 Describe how to move from the first point to the second point.
   a (2, 3) to (4, 6)
   b (0, 2) to (1, −3)
   c (3, −1) to (−2, 5)
   d Discussion Can you find a way to work out the answer without drawing a pair of axes?

Strategy hint

Draw a pair of axes from −2 to 6.

Worked example

Translate shape A by the column vector $\begin{pmatrix} 8 \\ -2 \end{pmatrix}$.

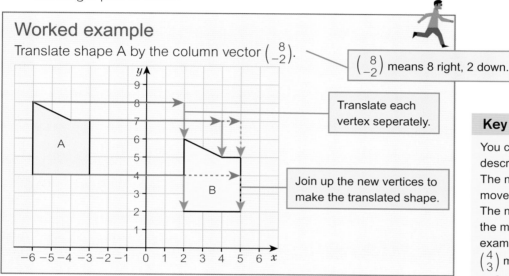

$\begin{pmatrix} 8 \\ -2 \end{pmatrix}$ means 8 right, 2 down.

Translate each vertex seperately.

Join up the new vertices to make the translated shape.

Key point

You can use a column vector to describe a translation.
The number at the top describes the movement to the right or left.
The number at the bottom describes the movement up or down. For example:
$\begin{pmatrix} 4 \\ 3 \end{pmatrix}$ means 4 right, 3 up
$\begin{pmatrix} -2 \\ -1 \end{pmatrix}$ means 2 left, 1 down

6 Copy the diagram.

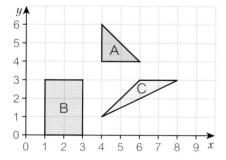

Literacy hint

Vertices is the plural of vertex.

   a Translate shape A by the vector $\begin{pmatrix} 4 \\ -3 \end{pmatrix}$.
   b Translate shape B by the vector $\begin{pmatrix} 8 \\ 3 \end{pmatrix}$.
   c Translate shape C by the vector $\begin{pmatrix} -4 \\ 2 \end{pmatrix}$.

Worked example

Enlarge this triangle using scale factor 2 and the marked centre of enlargement.

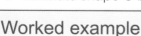

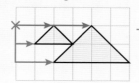

Multiply all the distances from the centre by the scale factor. Count the squares from the centre of enlargement:
• The top vertex of the triangle changes from 2 right to 4 right.
• The bottom left vertex changes from 1 down and 1 right to 2 down and 2 right.

7 Copy these shapes and the centres of enlargement onto squared paper.
Enlarge them by the scale factors given.
   a scale factor 2   **b** scale factor 3   **c** scale factor 3

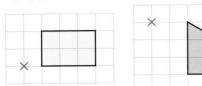 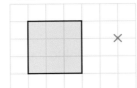

Key point

When you enlarge a shape by a scale factor from a **centre of enlargement**, the distance from the centre to each point on the shape is also multiplied by the scale factor.

8 Copy this diagram onto squared paper. Enlarge the rectangle by scale factor 2, with centre of enlargement (9, 5).

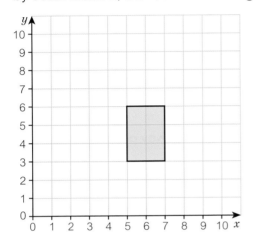

9 **Problem-solving / Reasoning** Draw a pair of axes from 0 to 10.
Draw a triangle A with vertices at (3, 2), (5, 2) and (3, 4).
Draw a triangle B with vertices at (8, 6), (9, 6) and (8, 7).
   a Draw an enlargement of triangle A with scale factor 2 and centre of enlargement (1, 1).
   b Draw an enlargement of triangle B with scale factor 4 and centre of enlargement (9, 7).
   c What do you notice about your answers to parts **a** and **b**?
   d Triangle C has vertices at (3, 6), (4, 6) and (3, 7).
      Draw triangle C on the grid.
   e Salim says, 'If I enlarge triangle C by a scale factor of 3 and centre of enlargement (2, 7), it will give exactly the same triangle as my answers to parts **a** and **b**.'
      Is Salim correct? Explain your answer.

10 Copy these shapes and the centres of enlargement onto squared paper and then enlarge them, using these scale factors.
   a scale factor 2   **b** scale factor 3

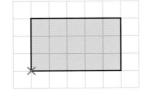 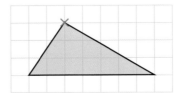

Q10 hint

When the centre of enlargement lies on the edge of the shape, the distance from the centre of enlargement to the shape is 0. This point is in the same place on the grid in the enlarged shape.
You could use dynamic software to check that your enlargements are correct.

Investigation

Shape A has been enlarged to give shape B.

1 What is the scale factor of the enlargement?
2 What do you think the coordinates of the centre of enlargement are?
   Try some different values.
3 Copy the diagram and use straight lines to join together
   corresponding corners of the two shapes. Extend these lines
   across the whole grid. The first one is shown in red on the diagram.
   These lines are called **rays**.
4 What are the coordinates of the centre of enlargement? Use the rays
   you drew in part 3.
5 Draw a shape on a coordinate grid and enlarge it using your own
   scale factor and centre of enlargement. Don't mark the centre
   of enlargement on the diagram. Swap with a partner and ask them
   to work out the scale factor and centre of enlargement, using rays.

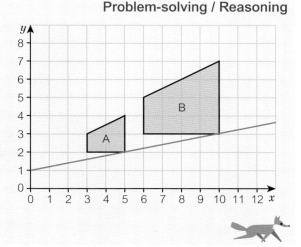

11 **a** Copy this shape onto a coordinate grid. Enlarge it by scale factor 2,
        with centre of enlargement (4, 1).

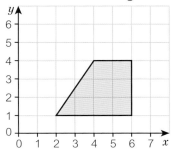

   b Measure the angles in the shape and in the enlargement.
        What do you notice?
   c Measure the sides in the shape and in the enlargement.
        What do you notice?
   Discussion Is this true for all enlargements?

12 Copy these shapes onto a coordinate grid and then enlarge them,
    using the marked centres of enlargement and these scale factors.
    a scale factor 2   **b** scale factor 3

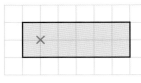
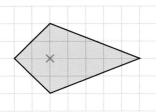

> **Q12 hint**
>
> Follow the same method. Multiply
> the distance from the centre of
> enlargement to each vertex by the
> scale factor.

13 **Explore** How can you enlarge a photo using picture tools on
    a computer?
    Is it easier to explore this question now that you have completed
    the lesson?
    What further information do you need to be able to answer this?

14 **Reflect** This unit is called 'Multiplicative reasoning'.
    How is enlargement multiplicative?
    Why is it good to use reasoning in mathematics?

> **Q14 Literacy hint**
>
> 'Multiplicative' means 'involving
> multiplication and/or division'.
> Reasoning is being able to explain
> why you have done some maths a
> certain way.

Explore

Reflect

7.4 Negative and fractional scale factors

Confidence

You will learn to:
- Enlarge 2D shapes using a negative whole number scale factor.
- Enlarge 2D shapes using a fractional scale factor.
- Understand that the scale factor is the ratio of the lengths of corresponding sides.

Why learn this?
Artists use fractional scale factors to produce micro-sculptures of objects that are in the same proportion as the real-life objects.

Fluency
Write these ratios as unit ratios in the form 1 : m.
- 5 : 10
- 2 : 3
- 4 : 5
- 5 : 4

Explore
How high is a table in a doll's house?

Exercise 7.4

Warm up

1 Copy these shapes and centres of enlargement onto a coordinate grid and then enlarge them, using the scale factors given.

a scale factor 3

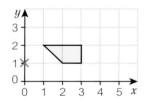

b scale factor 2

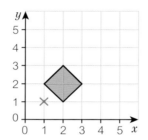

Worked example

Enlarge this triangle using scale factor −2 and centre of enlargement (3, 2).

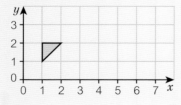
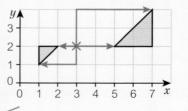

Count the squares from the centre of enlargement:
- The top right vertex of the small triangle changes to the bottom left vertex of the enlarged triangle, from 1 left to 2 right.
- The bottom vertex of the triangle changes to the top vertex of the enlarged triangle, from 1 down and 2 left to 2 up and 4 right.

Key point

A **negative scale factor** has the same effect as a positive scale factor except that it takes the image to the opposite side of the centre of enlargement.

2 Copy these diagrams. Enlarge the shapes using the marked centres of enlargement and the given **negative scale factors**.

a scale factor −3

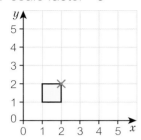

b scale factor −2

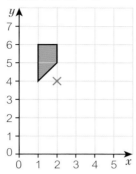

c scale factor −3

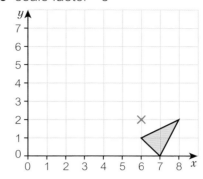

Discussion What is the effect on the side lengths and angles of enlarging a shape by scale factor −1?

3 **Reasoning** Draw a pair of axes from 0 to 12. Draw shape A with vertices at (3, 3), (4, 3), (5, 4), (5, 5) and (3, 5).

a Enlarge shape A using scale factor −2 and centre of enlargement (6, 6).

b Enlarge shape A using scale factor 2 and centre of enlargement (6, 6), then rotate the enlarged shape 180° about the point (6, 6).

c What do you notice about your answers to parts **a** and **b**?

4 Copy each shape onto squared paper.
Enlarge each shape by the scale factor given.

a scale factor $\frac{1}{2}$

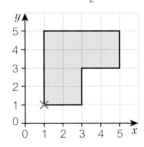

b scale factor $\frac{1}{4}$

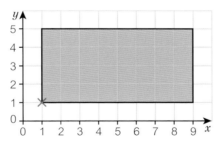

Discussion What happens to the side lengths and angles of a shape when you enlarge it by a positive number less than 1?

5 For each of these diagrams work out the scale factor for

a enlarging shape A to give shape B

b enlarging shape B to give shape A.

i

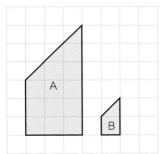

ii

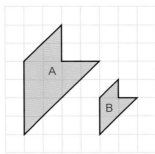

Q2 hint

Use dynamic software to check that your enlargements are correct.

Key point

You can enlarge a shape using a **fractional scale factor**. Use the same method of multiplying the length of each side by the scale factor.

Q4 Literacy hint

We still use the term 'enlarge' for fractional scale factors, even though they make the shape smaller!

6 Reasoning The diagram shows two rectangles.

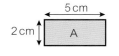 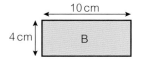

   a What is the scale factor for enlarging rectangle A to give rectangle B?

   b Write the ratio, in its simplest form, of
   i the height of rectangle A to rectangle B
   ii the length of rectangle A to rectangle B.

   c What do you notice about your answers to parts **a** and **b**?

   Discussion What is the ratio of corresponding sides in a shape and its image, where the shape has been enlarged by scale factor 3?

7 Real A model lifeboat is made using a ratio of 1 : 72.
The length of the model is 236 mm.
What is the length of the real lifeboat?
Give your answer in metres to one decimal place.

Q7 hint

The lifeboat and the model are enlargements of each other.

8 Copy this diagram.

   a Enlarge shape A using scale factor $\frac{1}{3}$ and centre of enlargement (7, 1). Label the shape B.

   b Write the ratio of the lengths of the sides of shape A to shape B.

   c Write the enlargement that will take shape B back to shape A.

Q8c hint

Remember to include the scale factor and the centre of enlargement.

9 Make three copies of this diagram.

   a Carry out each of the following combined transformations.
   i Translate the shape 4 squares left and 1 square down, then enlarge it by scale factor 2, centre of enlargement (0, 12).
   ii Rotate the shape 180° about the point (6, 8), then enlarge it by scale factor $\frac{1}{2}$, centre of enlargement (0, 0).
   iii Reflect the shape in the line $x = 9$, then enlarge it by scale factor $\frac{1}{2}$, centre of enlargement (10, 8).

   b Describe a combined transformation that will take the image in part **a ii** to the position of the image in part **a iii**.

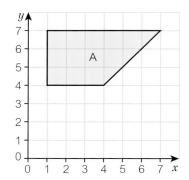

10 Explore How high is a table in a doll's house?
Is it easier to explore this question now that you have completed the lesson?
What further information do you need to be able to answer this?

11 Reflect Look back at Q7 and Q8.
Write a sentence about what the ratios tell you.
What kinds of jobs might involve the use of ratios for enlargement?

7.5 Percentage change

You will learn to:
- Find an original value using inverse operations.
- Calculate percentage change.

Why learn this?
Shop managers calculate percentage change in order to compare the profit or loss they have made on different items.

Fluency
Match each percentage to its equivalent decimal.

70% 35% 7% 3.5% 700% 0.35%

0.035 7 0.7 0.0035 0.07 0.35

Explore
Did the countries in Asia have similar increases in their Gross Domestic Product (GDP) between 2018 and 2019?

Exercise 7.5

1 Work out the percentage $\frac{A}{B} \times 100$, when

  a $A = \$27$ and $B = \$50$
  b $A = \$54.99$ and $B = \$85.99$

2 a Increase $23 by 25%.
  b Decrease $576 by 35%.

Q1 hint
Round your answer to the nearest whole number.

Worked example

In a year the value of a car dropped by 15% to $4760. How much was the car worth at the start of the year?

$100\% - 15\% = 85\% = 0.85$

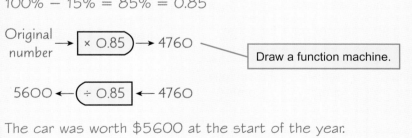

Draw a function machine.

The car was worth $5600 at the start of the year.

Key point

You can use **inverse operations** to find the original amount after a percentage increase or decrease.

3 **Finance** There was a 20% discount in a sale.
A coat had a sale price of $38.
What was the original selling price?

Warm up

4 Finance A shop has three items on sale.
The table shows the discount of each item and the sale price.

	Original price	Discount	Sale price
Item 1		10%	$63.00
Item 2		35%	$53.30
Item 3		65%	$99.75

Work out the original price of each item.

5 Finance / Problem-solving Juanita bought a computer for $420.
It had been reduced by 25%.

a What was the original price of the computer before the reduction?

Sachita bought a computer for $483. It had been reduced by 30%.

b Who saved the most money?

6 Finance The value of a house increased by 30% to $156 000.
What was the original value of the house?

Q6 hint

? → ×1.3 → 156 000

7 Real / Finance Between 2008 and 2012, average weekly earnings
in Wales increased by 5% to £522.90.   Source: StatsWales

What was the average weekly pay in Wales in 2008?

Key point

You can calculate a **percentage change** using the formula

$$\text{percentage change} = \frac{\text{actual change}}{\text{original amount}} \times 100$$

8 Finance Maya invests $2400. When her investment matures she
receives $2592.

Copy and complete the working to calculate the percentage
increase in her investment.

actual change = $2592 − $2400 = $☐

$$\text{percentage change} = \frac{\text{actual change}}{\text{original amount}} \times 100 = \frac{☐}{2400} \times 100$$

$$= ☐\%$$

Q8 Literacy hint

An investment 'matures' when the investment period (e.g. 5 years) ends.

9 Finance Sim invests $3500. When his investment matures he
receives $3430.
Calculate the percentage decrease in his investment.

Q9 hint

Use the same formula

$$\text{percentage change} = \frac{\text{actual change}}{\text{original amount}} \times 100$$

10 Finance The table shows the price a shopkeeper pays for some
items (cost price) and the price he sells them for (selling price).

Item	Cost price	Selling price	Actual profit	Percentage profit
Hoody	$12	$21		
T-shirt	$5	$8		
Fleece	$30	$45		
Polo shirt	$8	$18		

Work out the percentage profit (percentage change) on each item
he sells.

Discussion Is the item with the greatest actual profit the item with
the greatest percentage profit?

Q10 Literacy hint

Percentage profit is the percentage change between cost price and selling price.

11 Finance Hannie bought a flat for $125000. She sells it for $110000. What percentage loss has she made on the flat?

12 Real / Finance The estimated UK cost of the HS2 high speed rail link increased from $32.7 billion to $42.6 billion.

What is the percentage increase in the estimated cost?
Give your answer to the nearest whole number.

Q12 hint

You don't need to write the billions.
42.6 − 32.7 = ☐

13 Problem-solving / Reasoning The table shows information on visitor numbers to a theme park in 2018 and 2019.

Year	Total number of visitors	Ratio of children to adults	Price of child ticket	Price of adult ticket
2018	12460	3 : 2	£8	£15
2019	11220	2 : 1	£10	£18

a Work out the percentage change in the total number of visitors from 2018 and 2019.
Give your answer to one decimal place.

b Does your answer to part **a** show a percentage increase or decrease?

c Work out the percentage change in the amount of money taken in ticket sales from 2018 to 2019.
Give your answer to one decimal place.

Q13c Strategy hint

What information do you need? How can you use the figures in the table?

14 Explore Did the countries in Asia have similar increases in their Gross Domestic Product (GDP) between 2018 and 2019?
Is it easier to explore this question now that you have completed the lesson?
What further information do you need to be able to answer this?

15 Reflect Mara says, 'I find it difficult to remember the percentage change formula. Is it actual change divided by original amount or the other way round?'
Aqeil says, 'I know that if I invest $2 and get $3 in return, I've made $1, which is 50% of $2 or a 50% change.
That helps me to remember the formula.'
Aqeil writes

Try both of Mara's formulae suggestions using Aqeil's numbers.
Which is the correct formula?
What do you think of Aqeil's strategy? Do you have another way of remembering the formula? If so, what is it?

7 Check up

Direct proportion

1 The cost of petrol varies in direct proportion to the number of litres sold. The cost of 5 litres of petrol is $6.75. What is the cost of
   a 15 litres   b 12 litres?

2 The table shows the price and volume of three different bottles of the same shampoo.

Volume (ml)	25	90	150
Cost	$0.90	$3.24	$5.40

   a Draw a graph of the data.
   b Are volume and cost in direct proportion?
   c Write a formula connecting volume and cost.

3 Six toilet rolls cost $1.99. Nine toilet rolls cost $2.69. Is cost directly proportional to number of toilet rolls?

4 The values of A and B are in direct proportion. Work out the missing numbers w, x and z.

A	B
6	20
9	w
x	60
z	2.5

Proportion and problems

5 The value of y is directly proportional to the value of x. When $y = 6$, $x = 32$.
   a Write a formula connecting x and y.
   b What is the value of y when x is 46?

Translation

6 Draw a pair of axes from -7 to 8. Draw a shape A with vertices at $(-5, 3)$, $(-2, 3)$ and $(-3, 5)$.
   Translate shape A by each of these column vectors.

   a $\binom{6}{1}$ Label the image B.   b $\binom{-2}{-3}$ Label the image C.

   c $\binom{0}{-6}$ Label the image D.   d $\binom{8}{-2}$ Label the image E.   e $\binom{10}{0}$ Label the image F.

Enlargement

7 Copy these shapes and centres of enlargement on coordinate grids and then enlarge them, using the scale factors given.
   a scale factor 3   b scale factor -2

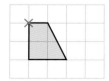

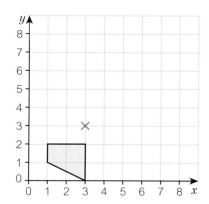

8 Describe the enlargement that takes shape A to shape B.

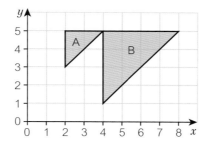

9 Copy the diagram and enlarge the triangle using scale factor $\frac{1}{2}$.

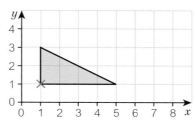

10 A model helicopter is made using a ratio of 1 : 48.
The width of the real helicopter is 18.72 m.
What is the width of the model? Give your answer in millimetres.

Percentage change

11 There was a 30% discount in a sale. A bag had a sale price of $28.
What was the original selling price?

12 Ela invests $3200. When her investment matures she receives $3584.
Work out
   a the actual increase in her investment
   b the percentage increase in her investment.

13 **How sure are you of your answers? Were you mostly**
   😞 **Just guessing**   😐 **Feeling doubtful**   🙂 **Confident**
   What next? Use your results to decide whether to strengthen or extend your learning.

14 In this spider diagram, the four calculations give the amount in the middle.
Work out three possible sets of missing values.

15 Jon has to go to a meeting that starts at 10.30 am. He plans to drive the 150 miles from home to the meeting. Most of the journey is on the motorway. The speed limit on the motorway is 70 mph.
Use an average speed of your choice to work out how long the journey will take and what time he should leave home when
   a there is not much traffic on the roads
   b there is a lot of traffic on the roads.

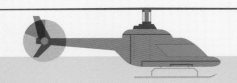

7 Strengthen

You will:
* Strengthen your understanding with practice.

Direct proportion

1 Which graph shows data in direct proportion?

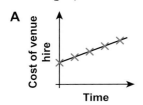
A

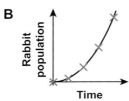
B

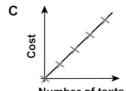
C

Q1 hint

Graphs showing direct proportion are straight lines through the origin.

2 The table shows data from a school science experiment.

p	2	3	5
q	7	10.5	17.5

   a Draw a graph of the data with p on the horizontal axis and q on the vertical axis.
   b Does the graph show that p and q are in direct proportion?
   c Write a formula connecting p and q.

Q2c hint

The formula is the equation of the line.

3 **Real / Finance** Write each statement as an equation showing direct proportion.
   a The cost, C, of making a phone call for x minutes at 3p per minute.
   b The mass, M, of x boxes at 2.3 kg per box.
   c The distance travelled, d, by a swimmer with a speed of 1.4 m/s in n seconds.

Q3a hint

1 minute:	$C = 1 \times 3$ pence
2 minutes:	$C = 2 \times 3$ pence
x minutes:	$C = x \times 3$ pence

$C = \square\, x$ pence

4 The depth of water in a paddling pool is in direct proportion to the length of time the water runs into it.
   After 3 minutes, the water is 48 cm deep.
   a How deep is the water after 4 minutes?
   b How long does it take to fill the pool to a depth of 80 cm?

Q4b hint

5 X and Y are in direct proportion. Find the missing values a and b in this table.

x	y
7	12
21	a
b	60

Q5 hint

Use equivalent ratios.

6 An electrician charges £54 for 3 hours' work and £126 for 7 hours' work. Are his charges in direct proportion to the length of time worked?

Q6 hint

How much for 1 hour?
Multiply it by 7.
Does this equal £126?

7 The distances between pairs of cities are shown in miles, M, and kilometres, K.
The distance in kilometres is directly proportional to the distance in miles.

Distance, M (miles)	Distance, K (km)
12.5	20
19	30.4
24	38.4

  a Copy and complete.

miles : km

12.5 : 20

$\div \square \Big(\quad \Big) \div \square$

$\square : \square$

  b Write a formula that shows the relationship between miles, M, and kilometres, K.

  c Check that your formula works for the last pair of distances.

Q10b hint

1 mile = $\square$ km

$M = \square \times K$

8 **Finance** The Mongolian tughrik, T, varies in direct proportion with the UK pound, P.
One day, £60 is worth 192 000 tughrik.

  a How many Mongolian tughrik can you buy with £1?

  b Copy and complete this formula relating the Mongolian tughrik, T, to the UK pound, P.

$$T = \square P$$

  c How many Mongolian tughrik can you buy with £80?

Q11c hint

Substitute $P = 80$ into your formula.

Proportion and problems

1 Write these using algebra.

  a y is proportional to x

  b c is proportional to r

  c m varies as t

  d p is proportional to q^2

  e n varies as the square of x

Q1 hint

$\propto$ means 'is proportional to',
so $y \propto x$ is another way of writing
$y = kx$.

2 y is directly proportional to x.

  a Write this as a formula using algebra.

When $x = 4.5$, $y = 11.25$.

  b Substitute the values into your '$y = k\square$' formula from part **a**.

  c Solve to find k.

  d Rewrite the formula as $y = \square k$.

  e Use your formula from part **d** to find the value of y when $x = 10$.

Q2a hint

$y \propto \square$
$y = k\square$

3 r varies directly as t. When $t = 3$, $r = 3.6$.

  a Write a formula connecting t and r.

  b Find the value of r when $t = 7$.

4 p is proportional to the square of q.

  a Copy and complete.

$p \propto \square$

$p = \square \square$

When $q = 4$, $p = 30$.

  b Substitute these values into your formula.

  c Solve to find k.

  d Write the formula $p = \square q^2$.

  e Use your formula to find the value of p when $q = 6$.

Translation

1 Write the column vector that maps shape
   a A onto shape B
   b B onto shape A.

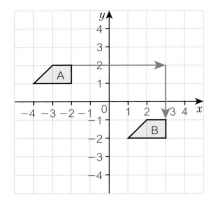

2 Copy the grid and shape A.
   Translate shape A by each of these column vectors.

   a $\begin{pmatrix} -2 \\ 4 \end{pmatrix}$ Label the image B.

   b $\begin{pmatrix} -5 \\ -3 \end{pmatrix}$ Label the image C.

   c $\begin{pmatrix} 3 \\ 5 \end{pmatrix}$ Label the image D.

   d $\begin{pmatrix} 0 \\ 2 \end{pmatrix}$ Label the image E.

   e $\begin{pmatrix} -4 \\ 0 \end{pmatrix}$ Label the image F.

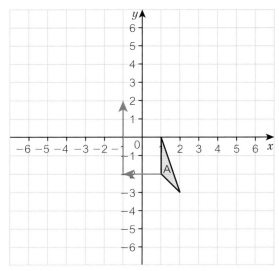

Enlargement

1 Copy these shapes onto coordinate grids. Complete the
   enlargements using these centres and scale factors.

   a scale factor 2

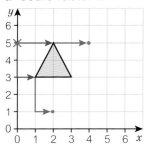

   b scale factor 3

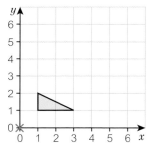

   c scale factor 3

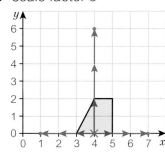

   d scale factor 2

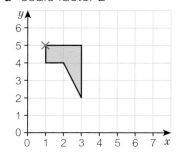

Q1b hint

Draw an arrow from the centre to a
vertex. Multiply the arrow length by
the scale factor. Repeat for other
vertices.

2 In each of these diagrams shape A has been enlarged to shape B. Write down the scale factor and the coordinates of the centre of enlargement.

a
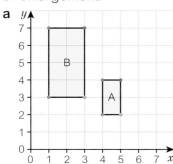

b
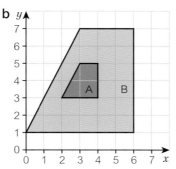

Q2a hint

Join the corresponding corners of the shapes (the coloured dots on the diagram) with straight lines. Make sure the lines are long enough to cross each other.

3 Copy these shapes onto coordinate grids. Complete the enlargements using the marked centres and given scale factors.

a scale factor −2
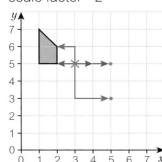

b scale factor −3
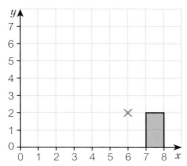

Q3 hint

Draw an arrow from the centre to a vertex. Multiply the arrow length by the scale factor. Draw arrows to the new vertex in the opposite direction. Repeat for other vertices.

4 Copy each shape onto squared paper. Enlarge each shape by the scale factor shown.

a scale factor $\frac{1}{2}$
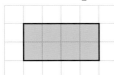

b scale factor $\frac{1}{3}$
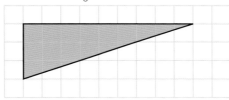

Q4a hint

length = 4 and $\frac{1}{2} \times 4 = \square$

width = 2 and $\frac{1}{2} \times 2 = \square$

5 **Real** A model farmhouse is made using a ratio of 1 : 76.
The height of the model is 85 mm.
What is the height of the real farmhouse? Give your answer in
a millimetres   **b** metres.

Q5 hint

Model : Real

$\times 85 \left(\begin{array}{c} 1 : 76 \\ 85 : \square \end{array} \right) \times 85$

Percentage change

1 There was a 10% discount in a sale. A jacket had a sale price of $36. Complete the working to find the original selling price.

$\div 90 \left(\begin{array}{c} 90\% = \$36 \\ 1\% = \$0.40 \\ 100\% = \square \end{array} \right) \div 90$
$\times 100 \qquad \qquad \qquad \times 100$

2 Work out the original price for each of these items.
   a Discount 20%, sale price $48
   b Discount 40%, sale price $72
   c Discount 15%, sale price $68

Q2a hint

$\div ? \left(\begin{array}{c} \square\% = £48 \\ 1\% = \square \end{array} \right) \div ?$

3 After a 25% increase in membership, the number of members in a surf club went up to 20.

Complete the working to find the original number of members in the club.

100% + 25% = 125%

÷125 (125% = 20) ÷125

1% = 0.16

×100 (100% = ☐) ×100

4 Work out the original number of members in each of these clubs.
  a Increase of 10%, up to 66 members
  b Increase of 30%, up to 195 members
  c Increase of 45%, up to 174 members

Q4a hint

÷? (☐% = 66) ÷?

1% = ☐

5 Anil invests $6000. When his investment matures he receives $6240.
  a Copy and complete the working to calculate his percentage increase.
    original amount = 6000
    actual change = 6240 − 6000 = 240
    percentage change = $\dfrac{\text{actual change}}{\text{original amount}}$ × 100 = $\dfrac{240}{6000}$ × 100 = ☐%
  b Check your answer by increasing $6000 by the percentage you calculated. Do you get $6240?

Q5 hint

Draw this information as a bar model.

$6000 $☐

$6240

6 Work out the percentage profit made on each of the items. For each part, copy and complete the following working. Check your answers.
  original amount = ☐
  actual change = ☐
  percentage profit = $\dfrac{\text{actual change}}{\text{original amount}}$ × 100 = $\dfrac{☐}{☐}$ × 100 = ☐%
  a Bought for $6, sold for $7.50   **b** Bought for $15, sold for $19.50
  c Bought for $120, sold for $222

7 Work out the percentage loss made on each of these items. Check your answers.
  a Bought for $12, sold for $9   **b** Bought for $360, sold for $306
  c Bought for $42, sold for $26.46

Q7a hint

original amount = 12
actual change = 12 − 9 = ☐

percentage change = $\dfrac{\text{actual change}}{\text{original amount}}$ × 100

Enrichment

1 The area of the yellow rectangle is 60% of the area of the blue rectangle.

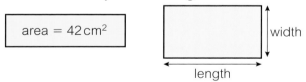

area = 42 cm²   width / length

  a Work out the area of the blue rectangle.
  b Work out a possible length and width of the blue rectangle.

2 Reflect Look back at the questions where you used arrows or bars.
  a Did the arrows help you? Explain why.
  b Did the bars help you? Explain why.

7 Extend

You will:
- Extend your understanding with problem-solving.

 1 Real The distance on a map is directly proportional to the corresponding distance on the ground.
On a map, the distance between two places is 5.3 cm. The scale of the map is 1 : 25 000.
a What is the actual distance between the places in
   i centimetres   **ii** kilometres?
b Two places are 9.8 km apart. How far apart will they be on the map?

 2 a GPS data showed that a footballer ran 26.4 km in the first 3 matches of the season. There are 38 matches in the full season.
Predict how many kilometres he will run in the full season.
b Another player ran 3.57 km in the 42 minutes she appeared as a substitute. How many kilometres would she run in a full 90-minute game?

3 Real / Modelling Write a formula for
a the perimeter, P, of a square with side length s
b the circumference, C, of a circle with radius r
c the area, A, of a square with side length s
d the perimeter, P, of a rectangle with length l and width w.
Discussion Which of these formulae show direct proportion?

4 Real / STEM The table shows measurements of force and extension of a spring made during a science experiment.

Force, F (newtons)	0.2	0.3	0.5	0.6	1	1.2
Extension, E (mm)	5	7.5	12.5	22	25	30

a Draw a graph of the data.
b Identify an outlier in the data.
c Ignoring the outlier, is the force proportional to the extension?
Discussion Can the scientist say that, based on her results, the force is proportional to the extension? Explain your answer.

 5 Real / Problem-solving The table shows the decrease in temperature at different heights on a mountain.

Height above sea level (m)	0	300	700	1200
Temperature decrease (°C)	0	1.2	2.8	4.8

a Are height and temperature decrease in direct proportion?
b Write a formula that shows the relationship between height, h, and temperature decrease, T.
The summit of the mountain is 1344 m above sea level.
One day the temperature at sea level is 15.7°C.
c What is the temperature at the summit?

> **Q5c hint**
> Work out the temperature decrease at 1344 m, then subtract it from 15.7°C.

6 Copy the grid and shape A.

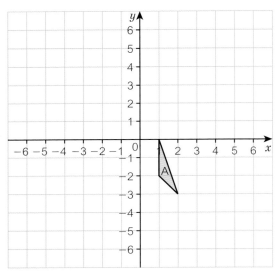

a Translate shape A by the column vector $\begin{pmatrix} -4 \\ 3 \end{pmatrix}$. Label the image B.

b Translate shape B by the column vector $\begin{pmatrix} 7 \\ 2 \end{pmatrix}$. Label the image C.

c Write the column vector that maps shape A onto shape C.

d Shape C is the image of shape A after two column vector translations. How can you use the first two column vectors to find the answer to part **c**?

7 Problem-solving Triangles B and C are enlargements of triangle A.

Q7 hint

Work out the height of triangle B first, from its area. Then use the ratio of the lengths.

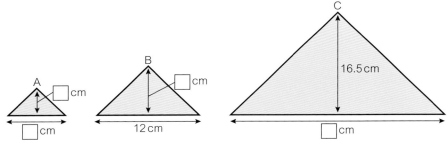

Triangle B has an area of 54 cm².
The scale factor of enlargement of the lengths of triangle A to triangle C is 2 : 11.
Work out the missing lengths.

8 Problem-solving

a Shape A is translated to shape B by the column vector $\begin{pmatrix} x \\ y \end{pmatrix}$.

Write down the column vector that translates shape B to shape A.

b Shape A is translated to shape C by the column vector $\begin{pmatrix} a \\ b \end{pmatrix}$.

Shape C is translated to shape D by the column vector $\begin{pmatrix} c \\ d \end{pmatrix}$.

Write down the column vector that translates shape A to shape D.

9 Copy this diagram.

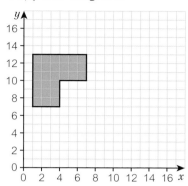

a Work out the perimeter of the shape.

b Transform the shape using an enlargement with scale factor $-\frac{1}{3}$ and centre of enlargement (10, 4). Then reflect the enlargement in the line $x = 7$.

c Use your answer to part **a**, and the scale factor of the enlargement, to work out the perimeter of the final shape. Use the diagram to check that your answer is correct.

10 Real / Reasoning The pie charts show the proportion of oil used for different energy needs in the UK in 1970 and 2012.

Oil used for energy in UK in 1970

13%
42%
25%
20%

Key
▦ Industry
▦ Transport
▦ Domestic
▦ Other

Oil used for energy in UK in 2012

13% 18%
31%
38%

Source: DECC

- In 1970 the total amount of oil used for energy in the UK was 146 million tonnes.
- In 2012 the total amount of oil used for energy in the UK was 140 million tonnes.

a How many tonnes of oil were used by transport in 1970?

b How many tonnes of oil were used by transport in 2012?

c Work out the percentage increase in the amount of oil used by transport from 1970 to 2012.

d Work out the percentage decrease in the amount of oil used by industry from 1970 to 2012.

e 'Other' accounted for 13% in both 1970 and 2012. Does this mean that the same amount of oil was used for 'Other' purposes in 1970 and 2012? Explain your answer.

11 Copy this diagram.

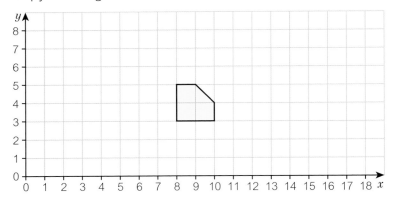

a Transform the shape by rotating it 180° about (10, 5), then enlarge it by scale factor −2 with centre of enlargement (13, 5).

b Describe the single enlargement that will take the final shape back to the original shape.

12 y is proportional to the square of x.
When $y = 5$, $x = 16$.
a What is the value of y when $x = 40$?
b What is the value of x when $y = 3$?

13 y varies as the square of x.
When $y = 4$, $x = 25$.
a What is the value of y when $x = 50$?
b What is the value of x when $y = 6.5$?
Give your answers to 2 decimal places.

14 Finance The interest, I, earned on an investment is directly proportional to the amount invested, A, and the time, t, of the investment in years.
When $4000 is invested for 3 years, the interest earned is $720.
a Work out the value of k, the constant of proportionality.
b Work out the interest earned when $3000 is invested for
  i 7 years
  ii 6 months.

15 Reflect Look back at the questions in these Extend lessons.
a Write down the question that you found easiest to answer. What made it easiest?
b Write down the question that you found most difficult to answer. What made it most difficult?
c Look again at the question that you wrote down for part **b**. What could you do to make this type of question easier to answer?

Q12b hint

Work out the scale factor.
Use rays to work out where the centre of enlargement is.

Q13b hint

x will have two possible values.

Q16c hint

Ask your classmates how they answered this question. Do they have any hints for you?

Reflect

7 Unit test

 1 The distance an aeroplane travels is proportional to the journey time.
An aeroplane travels 240 km in 30 minutes.
How far does it travel in 55 minutes?

2 For each statement
    i write down whether the two quantities are in direct proportion
    ii write a formula to model each situation.
  a The cost, C, in cents of x cereal bars at 59 cents each
  b The cost, C, of hiring a van for x hours at \$12 per hour and a
    \$14 hiring fee

3 The table shows the results of a science experiment.
  a Draw a graph of this data, with d on the horizontal axis.
  b Is d directly proportional to h?

d	2	3	5.5
h	9	13.5	24.75

4 The values of x and y are in direct proportion.
Work out the values of a and b.

x	y
15	90
a	75
23	b

 5 The table shows the extension of a spring when
different masses are added.
  a Are mass and extension in direct proportion?
  b Write a formula that shows the relationship between
    mass, m and extension, e.

Extension, e (mm)	8	12	28
Mass, m (g)	200	300	700

6 Copy this shape onto squared paper and then enlarge it,
using the marked centre of enlargement and scale factor 3.

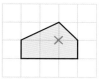

7 For each of these diagrams, describe the enlargement from A
to B.

a
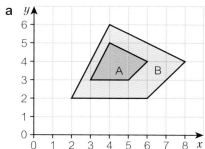

b
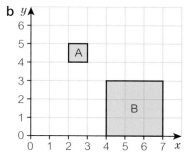

8 Copy this shape onto squared paper and then enlarge it, using
the marked centre of enlargement and scale factor −3.

9 Copy the diagram.

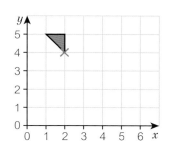

a Translate shape A by the column vector $\begin{pmatrix} 5 \\ -6 \end{pmatrix}$.
Label the new shape B.

b Translate shape B by the column vector $\begin{pmatrix} -7 \\ 9 \end{pmatrix}$.
Label the new shape C.

c Write down the column vector for the translation that maps shape A onto shape C.

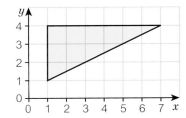

 10 x is proportional to y. When $x = 5$, $y = 2.85$.
   a Write a formula connecting x and y.
   b What is the value of y when $x = 13$?
   c What is the value of x when $y = 16.53$?

 11 A car salesman's commission is in direct proportion to the value of the sales he makes. He is paid $7840 commission because he makes sales of $196 000.
   a Work out the commission on $325 000 of sales.
   b He earns $17 500 commission. Work out the value of his sales.

12 Chan invests $2800. When his investment matures he receives $2968.
Work out
   a how much his investment increased by
   b the percentage change in his investment.

13 Copy this diagram and enlarge the triangle, using scale factor $\frac{1}{3}$ and centre of enlargement (7, 1).

14 A model of a building is 40 cm high. The real building is 6.4 m high.
Work out the scale factor of the model to the building.
Write your answer as
   a a number   **b** a ratio, in the form 1 : n.

15 Jan bought a camper van for $28 000. She sells it for $16 800.
Work out her percentage loss.

Challenge

16 The diagram shows a triangle, some scale factor cards and some area cards.

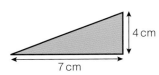 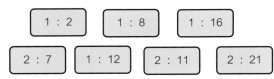 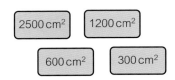

Choose one of the area cards.
Then work out which scale factor card, if used to enlarge the triangle, would give the closest possible area to the one on your card.
Try again with a different card.

17 Reflect Make a list of all the topics you have worked on in this unit where you have used multiplicative reasoning.
Look back at other units you have studied in this book.
List some other mathematics topics that use multiplicative reasoning.
Compare your list with those of your classmates.

> **Q17 hint**
>
> Remember that 'multiplicative' means 'involving multiplication or division'.
> Reasoning is being able to explain why.

Reflect

8.1   Maps and scales

You will learn to:
- Use scales in maps and plans.
- Use and interpret maps.

Why learn this?
Scales on maps help you to work out the real distances between places.

Fluency
What is the scale factor of enlargement from the small rectangle to the large rectangle?

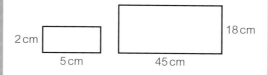

2 cm   5 cm   45 cm   18 cm

Explore
What scale would you use to fit a map of your town on a piece of paper?

Exercise 8.1

1 Copy and complete.
  a 2 m = ☐ cm
  b 620 cm = ☐ m
  c 1350 m = ☐ km

2 On a scale drawing, 1 cm represents 5 cm. What do these lengths on the drawing represent in real life?
  a 5 cm   **b** 6 cm   **c** 15 cm   **d** 4.5 cm
  e How would you represent a real-life length of 35 cm on the scale drawing?

3 This diagram shows the plan of a garden. 1 cm represents 2 m. Sketch the plan and label the real-life lengths in metres.

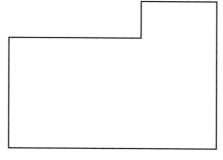

4 On a map, 1 cm represents 120 m. Work out the real-life distance of
  a 15 cm   **b** 12 cm   **c** 45 cm   **d** 6 cm.

Q4a hint

Map   Real life
1 cm   :   120 m
×15   ×15
15 cm   :   ☐ m

5 On a map, 1 cm represents 20 m. Work out the lengths on the map for these real-life distances.
  a 400 m   **b** 6000 m   **c** 900 m
  d 1 km   **e** 5 km   **f** 9 km

Q5a hint

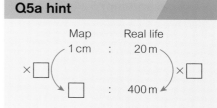

Map   Real life
1 cm   :   20 m
×☐   ×☐
☐   :   400 m

Warm up

6 Real / Problem-solving Here is a map of a village. 1 cm on the map represents 50 m in real life.

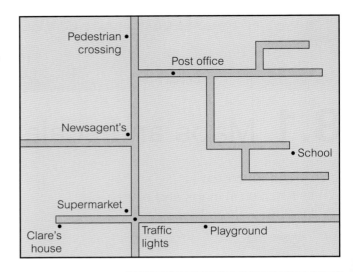

a From the map, estimate the distance as the crow flies (in a straight line) between
  i the traffic lights and the pedestrian crossing
  ii the school and the playground
  iii the post office and the newsagent's.

b Clare can walk 500 m in 5 minutes. How long will it take her to walk from her house to the school?

7 Real / Problem-solving Here is a map of Spain.

a Copy and complete:
  ☐ cm on the map is ☐ km in real life

b Estimate the distance in km between
  i Barcelona and Pamplona
  ii Salamanca and Valencia
  iii Granada and La Coruña.

8 Real A ladder leans against a wall. Its base is 75 cm from the bottom of the wall. It reaches 3.5 m up the wall. Make a scale drawing of the ladder. What angle does the ladder make with the ground?
Discussion Why is the angle the same on the scale drawing as in real life?

9 Explore What scale would you use to fit a map of your town on a piece of paper?
Look back at the maths you have learned in this lesson.
How can you use it to answer this question?

10 Reflect Mika says, 'When working with scales on maps and diagrams, one of the most important things is multiplying by the correct scale factor'.
Do you agree with Mika? Explain.
What else is important when working with scales on maps and diagrams?

Q6 hint

Claire needs to walk along the roads.

Q10 hint

Look back at some of the things you did to answer the questions in this lesson.

8.2 Bearings

You will learn to:
- Measure and use bearings.
- Draw diagrams to scale using bearings.

Why learn this?
Bearings are used in navigation. Ships and planes use them to plan their journeys.

Fluency
What is the angle when you turn
- north to south, clockwise
- north to west, clockwise
- north to south east, anticlockwise
- north to north west, anticlockwise?

Explore
How are bearings the same as angles? How are they different?

Exercise 8.2

1 Draw these angles accurately using a ruler and a protractor.
- **a** 75°
- **b** 130°
- **c** 245°
- **d** 192°

2 Work out the missing angles. Give reasons for your answers.

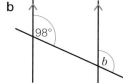

3 A map has a scale of 1 cm to 20 km.
- **a** What is 6 cm on the map in real life?
- **b** What is 120 km in real life on the map?

4 Write each compass direction as a bearing.
- **a** east
- **b** south
- **d** west
- **e** south east
- **f** south west
- **g** north west

5 a Measure the bearing of Village Green from Castle Rock.
 b Measure the bearing of Castle Rock from Village Green.

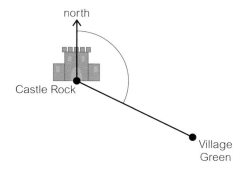

> **Key point**
>
>
>
> A **bearing** is an angle in degrees, measured clockwise from north. A bearing is always written using three digits.
>
>
>
> This bearing is 025°.

> **Q5 hint**
>
> Always measure clockwise from north.

Worked example

Geneva Airport is 400 km from Paris Orly Airport on a bearing of 135°. Draw this bearing accurately using a scale of 1 cm to 50 km.

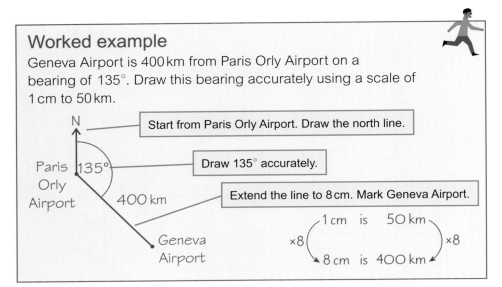

Start from Paris Orly Airport. Draw the north line.

Draw 135° accurately.

Extend the line to 8 cm. Mark Geneva Airport.

1 cm is 50 km
×8 ( ) ×8
8 cm is 400 km

6 **Real** Draw these bearings accurately. Use the scale 1 cm to 50 km.
   a St Symphorien airport is 380 km from Salatos airport on a bearing of 302°.
   b Bellegarde airport is 172 km from St Symphorien airport on a bearing of 170°.

7 A ship is 120 km west of a lighthouse. The ship sails on a bearing of 060° for 18 km.
   a Make an accurate drawing with 1 cm representing 10 km.
   b What are the bearing and distance of the lighthouse from the ship?

Q7 hint

Make a sketch first. Start with:

Ship

8 A ship sails 8 km from port on a bearing of 040°. It then turns and sails for 14 km on a bearing of 200°.
   a Use a scale of 1 cm to 2 km to draw an accurate scale drawing of the journey of the ship.
   b How far away is the ship from its starting point?

9 A plane leaves the airport and flies on a bearing of 070° for 60 miles and then on a bearing of 240° for a further 100 miles.
   a Use a scale of 1 cm to 10 miles to show the plane's journey.
   b How far away is the plane from its starting point?
   c What bearing should the plane use to fly directly back to the airport?

10 **Problem-solving**
   a The bearing of B from A is 120°. Work out the bearing of A from B.
   b The bearing of C from D is 240°. Work out the bearing of D from C.
   c The bearing of E from F is 320°. Work out the bearing of F from E.

Q10 Strategy hint

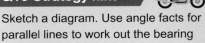

Sketch a diagram. Use angle facts for parallel lines to work out the bearing of A from B.

N

N

Diagram not drawn accurately

120°

A

?

B

11 **Explore** How are bearings the same as angles?
   How are they different?
   Look back at the maths you have learned in this lesson.
   How can you use it to answer this question?

12 **Reflect** Sian says, 'To work out a bearing you just measure the angle between two paths.'
   Look back at the questions in this lesson.
   In what way is Sian correct?
   In what way is she incorrect?

Q12 hint

Does it matter which path you place the 0 line on?

Explore

Reflect

8.3 Scales and ratios

You will learn to:
- Draw diagrams to scale.
- Use and interpret scale drawings.

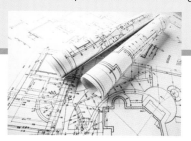

Why learn this?
Architects use scale diagrams to draw plans of buildings before they are constructed.

Fluency
The scale of a map is 1 cm to 50 m.
What distance is represented by
- 2 cm
- 5 cm on the map?

How long on the map would a real-life distance of
- 350 m
- 1000 m be?

Explore
Why is it difficult to draw an accurate world map?

Exercise 8.3

1 Copy and complete.
a $25\,000\,\text{cm} = \square\,\text{m}$
b $40\,000\,\text{cm} = \square\,\text{m}$
c $100\,000\,\text{cm} = \square\,\text{km}$
d $150\,000\,\text{cm} = \square\,\text{km}$

2 Write these ratios in the form $1 : n$.
a $2 : 10$
b $4 : 12$
c $20 : 300$
d $40 : 400$

Q2a hint

3 Copy and complete these equivalent ratios.
a $1 : 100 = 3 : \square$
b $1 : 30 = 5 : \square$
c $1 : 250 = 4 : \square$
d $1 : 500 = 3 : \square$

Worked example
A map has a **scale** of $1 : 25\,000$.
What is the real-life distance in metres for 4 cm on the map?

```
        map        real life
       1 cm       25 000 cm
  ×4  (                    ) ×4
       4 cm     100 000 cm
```

1 cm represents 25 000 cm, so 4 cm represents ——— Work out how much 4 cm represents, in real life, in centimetres.
$4 \times 25\,000 = 100\,000\,\text{cm}$
$100\,000\,\text{cm} \div 100 = 1000\,\text{m}$ ——— Convert the distance to metres.

4 James is using a map with a scale of $1 : 20\,000$.
He measures these distances.
What are the distances in real life?
Write your answers in metres.
a 4 cm
b 6 cm
c 4.5 cm
d 0.5 cm

Key point
The **scale** on a map is given as a ratio $1 : n$. For example, $1 : 25\,000$ means that 1 cm on the map represents 25 000 cm in real life.

Warm up

Topic links: Area, Ratio and proportion, Metric measures

Subject links: Geography (Q6), Design and technology (Q7)

5 Problem-solving Match the scales **A** to **D** with **i** to **iv**.

A 1:10 000   **i** 1 cm to 2.5 km

B 1:250 000   **ii** 1 cm to 250 m

C 1:50 000   **iii** 1 cm to 500 m

D 1:25 000   **iv** 1 cm to 100 m

6 Real Here is a map of the area surrounding Liechtenstein. The scale is 1:500 000.

  a **i** Measure the distance in centimetres between Ruggell and Buchs.

     ii Calculate the real-life distance in kilometres.

  b Calculate the real-life distance in kilometres between

    i Balzers and Planken

    ii Triesen and Vaduz

    iii Trübbach and Mauren.

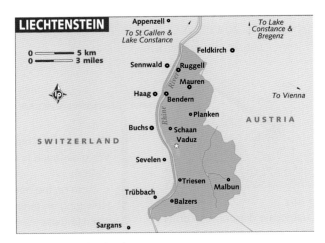

7 Problem-solving Here is a rough sketch (undetailed drawing) of a house.

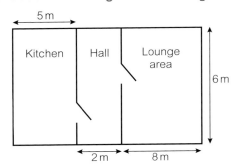

Q7 hint

Convert m on the rough sketch to cm.

  a Make an accurate scale drawing using a scale of 1:200.

  b Divide the lounge area into two rooms, one with an area of 30 m².

  c What is the area of the other room?

8 Problem-solving Write each scale as a map ratio.

  a 1 cm to 1 m   **b** 1 cm to 5 km

  c 5 cm to 1 km   **d** 2 cm to 1.5 km

Q8 hint

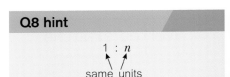

9 a What real-life distance does 4 cm represent on maps with these scales?

    i 1:10 000   **ii** 1:50 000   **iii** 1:250 000

  b For each scale, work out the length on the map that represents a real-life distance of 10 km.

    i 1:10 000   **ii** 1:50 000   **iii** 1:250 000

10 Explore Why is it difficult to draw an accurate world map?

Look back at the maths you have learned in this lesson.

How can you use it to answer this question?

11 Reflect Jaime says, 'To write 1 cm to 50 km as a map ratio, I first multiply 1 by 100 because 1 km = 100 cm. Then I multiply that by 1000, because 1 km = 1000 m. Then I multiply by 50.'

Look back at the questions you answered in this lesson.

Did you use a method similar to Jaime's?

Compare methods with others in your class.

8.4 Congruent and similar shapes

You will learn to:

* Identify congruent and similar shapes.
* Use congruence to solve problems in triangles and quadrilaterals.

Why learn this?
Car manufacturers produce car parts which are congruent so that they fit into all cars in the production line.

Fluency
Which transformations give
* congruent shapes
* similar shapes?
Find the missing angle in this triangle.

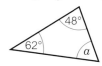

Explore
How do artists making special effects for film use similar shapes?

Exercise 8.4

1 What is the scale factor of the enlargement from
  a A to B
  b B to A?

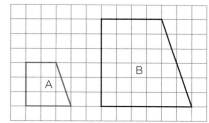

2 Which angles are equal?
Give reasons.

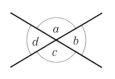

3 Which of these shapes are congruent?
Which shapes are similar?

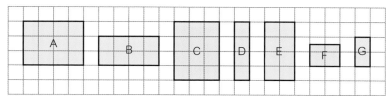

4 **Reasoning** Draw accurately two different triangles ABC where angle A = 30°, side AB = 6 cm, side BC = 4 cm.
Discussion If two triangles have two sides and one angle the same, are they congruent?

Q4 Strategy hint
Sketch the triangle ABC first.

Warm up

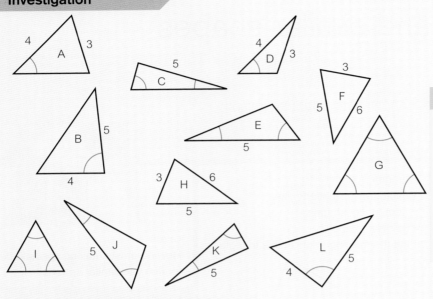

Key point

Triangles are congruent if they have equivalent
- SSS (all three sides)
- SAS (two sides and the included angle)
- ASA (two angles and the included side)
- AAS (two angles and another side).

Triangles where all the angles are the same (AAA) are similar, but might not be congruent.

1 Sort these triangles into congruent pairs.
2 Which triangles are left over? Are there any similar triangles?
3 Which of these rules define whether two triangles will be congruent or similar?
   Triangles with three sides the same (SSS)
   Triangles with two sides and the angle between them the same (SAS)
   Triangles with two angles and the included side the same (ASA)
   Triangles with all angles the same (AAA)
4 Does having two sides and an angle the same always give congruent triangles?

5 Each pair of triangles is congruent. Explain why.

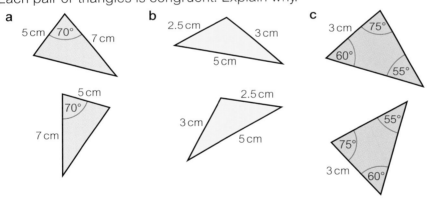

Q5 hint

Choose reasons from SSS, SAS, ASA or AAA.

6 **Reasoning** Which of these triangles are congruent to triangle ABC? Give reasons.

Q6 hint

You may need to work out missing angles.

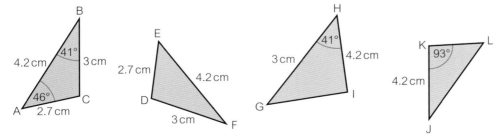

7 **Reasoning** Are all right-angled triangles with one side 6 cm and hypotenuse 11 cm congruent?

8 Reasoning AB and CD are parallel lines, AB = CD.
  a What can you say about angles x and y?
  b Copy the diagram. Mark pairs of equal angles.
  c Show that triangle AEB and triangle CED
    are congruent.

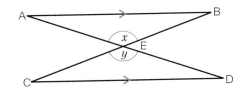

9 Reasoning Explain why triangle ABC is similar to triangle DEF.

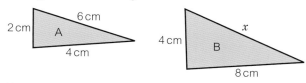

> **Key point**
>
> To show that two shapes are similar,
> show that corresponding angles are
> equal, or find the scale factor for
> corresponding sides.
>
>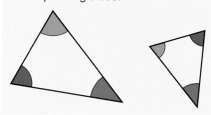

Discussion Are all squares similar? Are all regular pentagons
similar?

10 Triangle A and triangle B are similar.

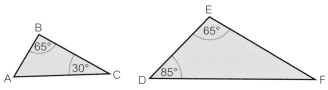

Work out the missing length in triangle B.

> **Q10 hint**
>
> What is the scale factor of the
> enlargement from A to B?

11 Each set shows three similar triangles.
  Calculate the lengths labelled with letters.
  a

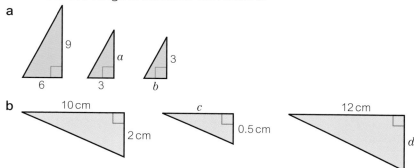

  b

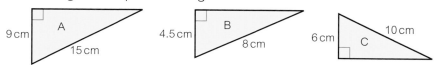

12 Reasoning Which pair of triangles is similar?

13 Explore How do artists making special effects for film use
similar shapes?
  Look back at the maths you have learned in this lesson.
  How can you use it to answer this question?

14 Reflect Ed says, 'Two triangles have equal length sides, so they
must be congruent.'
  Raquel says, 'Two triangles have equal angles, so they must be
congruent.'
  Who is right and who is wrong?
  Explain and correct the mistake that person has made.

8.5 Solving geometrical problems

You will learn to:
- Use similarity to solve problems involving 2D shapes.

Why learn this?
Surveyors use similar triangles to find out the heights of tall structures.

Fluency
Find the missing numbers in each equivalent ratio.
- $4:6 = 8:\square$
- $3:2 = \square:8$
- $5:7 = \square:21$
- $2:5 = 9:\square$

Explore
Can you use triangles to find the height of a tree?

Confidence

Exercise 8.5

Warm up

1 Are these triangles similar? Explain.

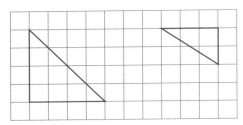

2 These shapes are similar. Find the missing side, x.

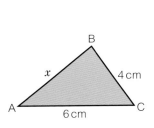

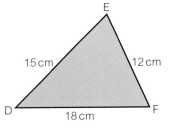

3 Reasoning
  a Explain why angle a = angle e.

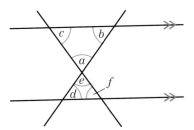

  b Which angle is equal to angle b? Explain.
  c Which angle is equal to angle f? Explain.

4 Reasoning

  a Find the angles in triangle CDE.
     Give reasons.

  b Are triangles ABC and CDE similar?
     Explain.

  c Sketch the triangles the same way up.
     Label the vertices and angles.

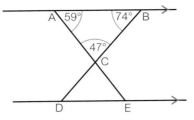

Q4c hint

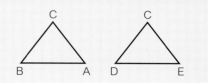

5 Reasoning

  a Show that triangles MNP and PQR are similar.

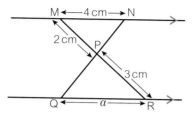

  b Find the missing length, a.

Q5a hint

Follow the method in Q4 parts **a**
and **b**.

Worked example

a Explain why triangles ABD and ACE are similar.

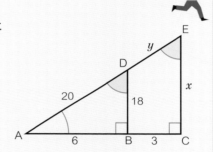

Triangle ABD	Triangle ACE
$\angle A$	$\angle A$
$\angle B = 90°$	$\angle C = 90°$
$\angle D\ =$	$\angle E$ (corresponding angles)

The triangles have the same
angles (AAA).

b Work out length x.

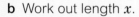

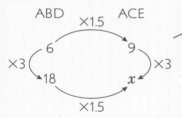

> 9×3 is easier to work out than 18×1.5,
> but they give the same answer.

$x = 9 \times 3 = 27$

c Find the length of AE.

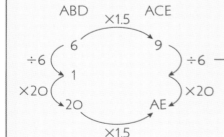

> It is easier to work out 20×1.5 than $9 \div 6 \times 20$,
> but they give the same answer.

$AE = 20 \times 1.5 = 30\,cm$

d Find the length of y.

$y = 30 - 20 = 10\,cm$

Topic links: Angles in triangles, Ratio and proportion

6 Reasoning

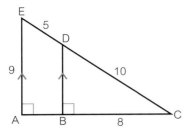

a Explain why triangles ACE and BCD are similar triangles.
b Calculate the length BD.
c Calculate the length AB.

Q6c hint

Find the length AC first.

7 Reasoning

a Explain why triangles ABC and ADE are similar triangles.

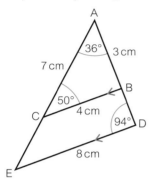

b Find the length of AE.
c Find the length of CE.
d Find the length of BD.

 8 Real / Problem-solving Calculate the height of the Eiffel Tower using similar triangles.

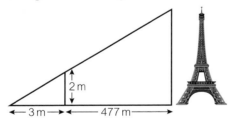

9 Explore Can you use triangles to find the height of a tree?
Look back at the maths you have learned in this lesson.
How can you use it to answer this question?

10 Reflect Look back at Q6. To answer this question you had to:
 • show that triangles are similar
 • identify corresponding lengths
 • solve equations.
Which of these tasks was easiest? Explain.
Which of these tasks was hardest? Explain.

Explore

Reflect

8 Check up

Maps and scales

1 A diagram uses a scale of 1 cm to 12 cm.
Calculate the real-life length represented by 4 cm.

2 A map uses this scale: 1 cm to 30 m.
What distance on the map represents 15 m?

3 This map of a town has a scale of 1 cm to 50 m.

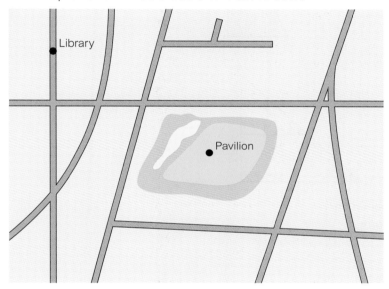

   a Find the distance in metres between the Library and the Pavilion as the crow flies.
   b The distance between the Library and the Town Hall is 400 m.
      What is the distance on the map?

4 A map has a scale of 1 : 25 000.
What distance in metres does 4 cm on the map represent?

Bearings

5 The diagram shows the location of
two airports in London.
Measure the bearing of Stansted airport
from London City airport.

6 A ship sails 12 km from a port on a bearing of 080°.
It then turns and sails for 9 km on a bearing of 140°.
   a Use a scale of 1 cm to 3 km to draw an accurate scale drawing of
the journey of the ship.
   b How far away is the ship from its starting point?
   c On what bearing should the ship sail to return to the port?

Congruence and similarity

7 Which two of these triangles are congruent? Give a reason.

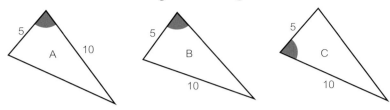

8 All three triangles are similar. Find the missing lengths.

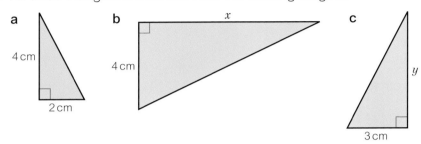

9 Explain why triangles ABC and ADE are similar.

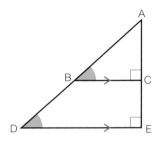

10 a Show that triangles ABC and ADE are similar.
   b Work out the lengths marked with letters.

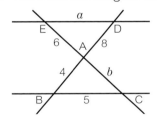

11 How sure are you of your answers? Were you mostly
   ☹ **Just guessing**   😐 **Feeling doubtful**   🙂 **Confident**
   What next? Use your results to decide whether to strengthen or extend your learning.

Challenge

12 Draw three different right-angled triangles with an angle of 45°.
   a Are they all similar? Explain your reasoning.
   b Repeat for right-angled triangles with an angle of 30°.

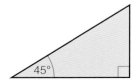

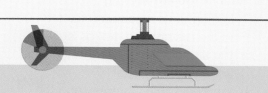

8 Strengthen

You will:
• Strengthen your understanding with practice.

Maps and scales

1 Naima designed this logo. Make an accurate scale drawing of the logo, using 1 cm to represent 3 cm.

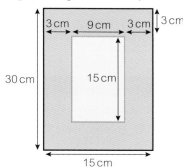

2 A map has a scale of 1 cm to 50 m.
What distance on the map represents a real-life distance of
a 100 m
b 300 m
c 1000 m
d 2000 m
e 1 km?

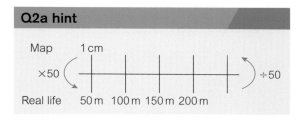

Q2a hint

3 This plan shows Adrian's garden. The scale is 1 cm to 4 m.

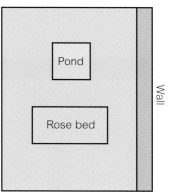

In real life
a how long is the wall
b how long is one side of the square pond
c what are the length and width of the rose bed?

4 A diagram has a scale of 1 cm to 20 cm.
Calculate the real-life length of
a 5 cm   **b** 10 cm   **c** 23 cm   **d** 42 cm.

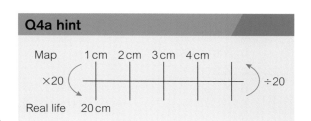

Q4a hint

5 Real / Problem-solving

This map uses a scale of 1 cm to 500 m. Find the distance in metres between

a the Lincoln Memorial and the Jefferson Memorial

b the Watergate Complex and the White House

c the Lincoln Memorial and the Federal Bureau of Investigation.

Q5 Strategy hint

Measure the distance on the map. Use the scale to work out the real-life distance.

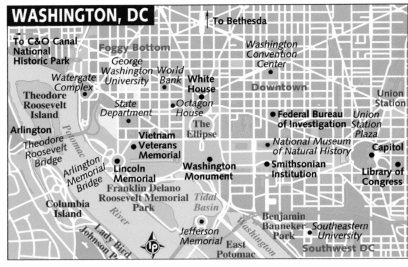

6 Write each scale as a ratio.
a 1 cm to 100 cm
b 1 cm to 20 cm
c 1 cm to 1 m
d 1 cm to 3 m
e 1 cm to 1 km

Q6 hint

In a ratio, both numbers must be in the same units. Convert m and km to cm.

Bearings

1 Write the bearing of B from A in each of these diagrams.

a   **b** 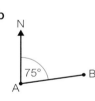   **c** 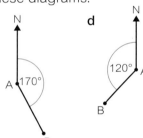   **d**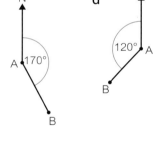

Q1 hint

A bearing is measured clockwise from north. It is always written with 3 digits. A 48° bearing is 048°.

2 a Mark a point, P, on a piece of paper.
   b Draw an accurate bearing of 075° from P.

Q2b hint

Draw a north line at P first.

3 a Mark a point, Q, on a piece of paper.
   b Draw a bearing of 330° from Q.

4 Trace these points. Measure and write down the bearing of
   a Y from X
   b X from X
   c Z from Y
   d X from Y.

Z

Y

X

Q4a hint

Draw the north line at X. Join XY.

5 A ship sails 10 km from a port, P, on a bearing of 060°.
It then turns and sails for 8 km on a bearing of 140°.

　a Copy and complete this sketch of the ship's journey.

　b Draw an accurate scale drawing using 1 cm to 2 km.

　c Use your diagram to work out

　　i how far the ship is from the port

　　ii the bearing on which the ship needs to sail to get back to the port.

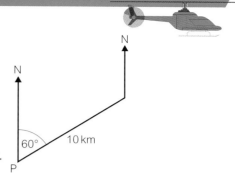

Congruence and similarity

1 Reasoning Which of these triangles is not congruent to A?

Q1 hint

If you rotated triangles B, C and D
which one would not fit exactly on A?

2 a Copy each pair of diagrams accurately. Then draw, or continue, the
lines to make two triangles.

　i 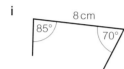　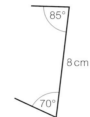　**ii** 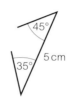　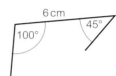

　iii 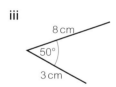　

　b Use the diagrams to help you decide whether two triangles are
congruent if

　　i two corresponding angles and the length of the side between
them are equal (ASA)

　　ii three angles are equal (AAA)

　　iii the lengths of two corresponding sides and the angle between
them are equal (SAS).

3 Triangles P and Q are similar.

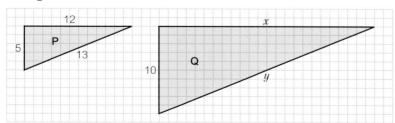

　a Copy and complete the table showing the
pairs of corresponding sides.

　b Use a pair of corresponding sides to work
out the scale factor from P to Q.

　c Use the scale factor to work out x and y.

P	Q
5	10
	x
13	

Q3c hint

P × scale factor = Q

☐ × ☐ = ☐

Topic links: Ratio and proportion, Angles in triangles　　　　**Subject links:** Geography (Maps and scales Q5, Enrichment Q9)

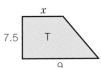

4 Reasoning Find the missing length x in these similar shapes.

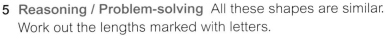

Q4 Strategy hint

Draw a table for S and T like the one in Q3.

5 Reasoning / Problem-solving All these shapes are similar. Work out the lengths marked with letters.

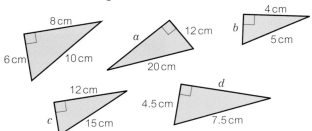

Q5 Strategy hint

Sketch the triangles the same way up.

6 Which of these triangles are similar to triangle A?

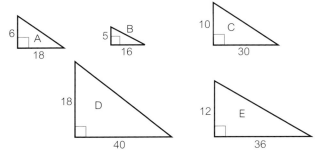

7 Reasoning The diagram shows two triangles.
a Explain why
  i $a = b$ ii $c = d$ iii $e = f$.
b When three pairs of angles are equal, what does this tell you about the two triangles?
c Trace each triangle and then sketch them the same way up. Label the measurements you know. Find the missing lengths.

8 Reasoning
a What can you say about BC and DE? Explain how you know.
b Why does angle ABC = angle ADE?
c What is the scale factor of enlargement from triangle ABC to ADE?
d Work out the length DE.

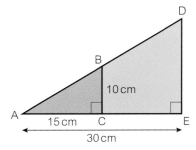

Enrichment

9 a Find a map of your local area.
b Use the map to find the distance from your school to your home.
c Make a list of the landmarks (important buildings or places) that are within 5 km of your school.

10 Reflect Look back at the strategy hints in these strengthen lessons. Did they help you to answer the questions?
Think about a question you found difficult. Describe a strategy you used to help solve the problem.

8 Extend

You will:
- Extend your understanding through problem-solving.

1 Use a scale of 1 cm : 1 km to draw each bearing accurately.

a Caltown is 8 km from Mayville on a bearing of 050°

b Georgetown is 4 km from Caltown on a bearing of 210°

c What is the real-life distance between Georgetown and Mayville?

2 Write each map scale as a ratio.

a 2 cm to 1 km　　　　**b** 4 cm to 20 km　　　　**c** 6 cm to 4 km

3 Real / Modelling This map of Wales has a scale of 1 : 2 500 000.

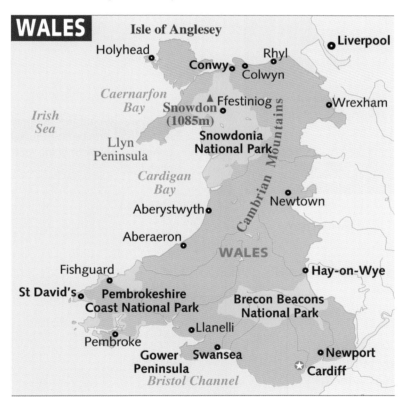

a Calculate the real-life distance between
   i Newport and Pembroke
   ii Swansea and Aberaeron
   iii Hay-on-Wye and Conwy.

b Estimate how long it takes to travel by car at 60 km/h between Liverpool and Swansea.

c Why is your answer to part **b** an estimate?

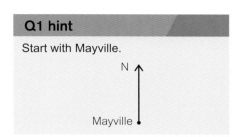

Q1 hint

Start with Mayville.

N

Mayville

Q2 hint

1 : ☐

Q3a hint

Give your answers in km.

4 **Real / STEM** In a Sankey diagram the widths of the arrows are drawn to scale to show how much each part represents.

Q4 hint

Measure the arrows.

a This Sankey diagram shows how the energy is used in an old-fashioned light bulb.
  i How many joules does 1 cm represent?
  ii How much energy is transferred by heat?
  iii How much energy is transferred by light?

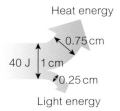

Heat energy

40 J 1 cm 0.75 cm 0.25 cm

Light energy

b Using squared paper, and a suitable scale, draw a Sankey diagram for these bulbs:
  i an energy-saving lamp with an input of 100 J, 75 J light energy and 25 J heat energy
  ii a filament lamp with input of 60 J, 20 J light energy and 40 J heat energy.

5 **Real / Problem-solving / Reasoning**
The real-life length of the football pitch is 100 m.
Use this plan of a sports field to answer these questions.

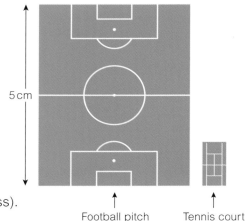

a Work out the scale used in the plan.

b Calculate the area of the football pitch.

c Calculate the area of the tennis court.

Q5b hint

Calculate the width of the football pitch first.

d It costs £22.50 per square metre to lay artificial turf (grass). How much will it cost to turf three tennis courts?

5 cm

Football pitch   Tennis court

6 **Problem-solving** This sketch shows the plan for Mr Jones's garden.

a Choose an appropriate scale and make an accurate scale drawing.

b Calculate the area of the patio in m².

c Mr Jones wants to lay paving stones on his patio. Each paving stone measures 50 cm by 50 cm. How many paving stones does Mr Jones need?

d Each paving stone costs £5. Calculate the cost of the paving stones.

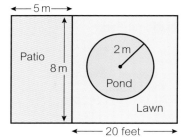

←5 m→

Patio   8 m   2 m

Pond

Lawn

←— 20 feet —→

7 **Reasoning** In this arrowhead, angle BAD = 35° and angle ABD = 40°.
Calculate

a angle BDA

b angle BDC

c angle DCB.

d Explain why triangles ABD and BCD are congruent.

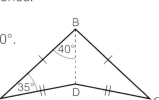

B
40°
35°
A   D   C

8 Reasoning These triangles are all congruent.
Work out the missing sides and angles.

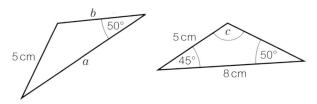

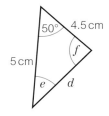

Q8 hint

Sketch them all facing the same way.
For example, like this:

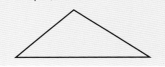

9 Reasoning

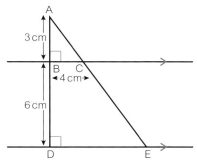

Q9 hint

You can use Pythagoras' theorem
to find the lengths of sides in a
right-angled triangle.

a Find the length AC.   **b** Find the length AE.

10 Real / Problem-solving This map shows some airports in Germany.

A plane leaves Hanover airport and travels for 200 km on a bearing of
120°. It then travels for 400 km on a bearing of 200°.
At which airport does it land?

11 Three radio masts are at the vertices of an equilateral triangle with side
30 km. Each has a range of 10 km.
a Draw a scale diagram to show the areas the radio signal can reach.
b Would you get a signal if you stood in the middle of the triangle?

12 Sketch each of these situations. Use angle facts to answer the questions.
a A ship sails from a port on a bearing of 050° for 10 km.
On what bearing must it travel to return to the port?
b A plane flies from an airport on a bearing of 230° for 100 km.
On what bearing must it travel to return to the airport?

Topic links: Ratio and proportion, Angles in triangles   **Subject links:** Geography (Q3, Q10) Science (Q4)

13 Reasoning Find the lengths marked x and y on these diagrams.

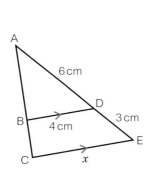 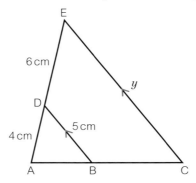

Q13 hint

First show that the two triangles ABD and ACE are similar.

14 Reasoning AC is a diagonal of the rectangle ABCD.
Explain why triangle ABC is congruent to triangle ADC.

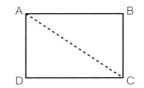

15 Reasoning The centre of this circle is O.
Prove that triangle OBC and triangle OAC are congruent.

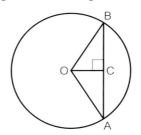

Investigation   Reasoning

1 Are these rectangles similar?

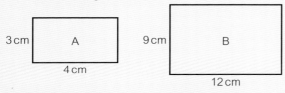

2 Write the ratio of their lengths and their areas.
3 What is the length scale factor?
4 What is the area scale factor?

Lengths   A   ×☐   B   Areas   A   ×☐   B

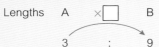   

  3   :   9   12   :   ☐

5 Draw five pairs of other similar rectangles. Copy and complete this table.

Length	Width	Ratio of lengths	Length scale factor	Ratio of areas	Area scale factor

6 Can you see a pattern between the area scale factor and the length scale factor?
7 Repeat the investigation for right-angled triangles.

16 Reflect Copy and complete this paragraph with at least three sentences:
When I am given a mathematics problem to solve, this is what I do ...
Compare your paragraph with others in your class.
What did you learn from your classmates?

8 Unit test

1 This is a map of some Greek islands.
  a Measure the bearing of Lipsi from Patmos.
  b Measure the bearing of Kalimnos from Lipsi.
  c Which island is on a bearing of 143° from Ag. Marina?

2 The scale on a diagram is 1 cm to 25 m.
  Calculate the real-life length of
  a 4 cm
  b 10 cm
  c 0.5 cm.

3 A map uses a scale of 1 cm to 25 m.
  What length on the map represents
  a real-life distance of
  a 75 m
  b 200 m
  c 500 m
  d 5 m?

4 The scale of this map is 1 : 25 000.

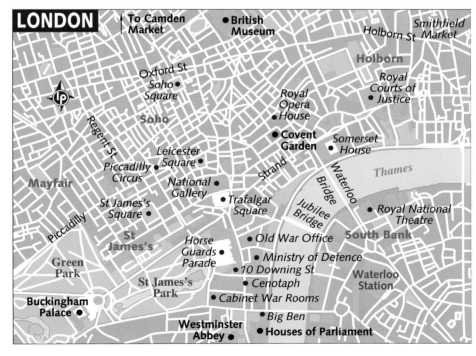

Use the map to find the distances, in metres, from
a Trafalgar Square to Somerset House
b Piccadilly Circus to St James's Square.

5 A ship sails 30 km from a port on a bearing of 040°.
   It then turns and sails for 20 km on a bearing of 150°.
   a Use a scale of 1 cm to 5 km to draw an accurate scale
      drawing of the journey of the ship.
   b How far away is the ship from its starting point?
   c On what bearing should the ship sail to return to the port?

6 Triangles A, B and C are all congruent.

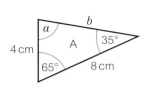 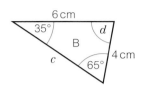 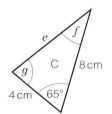 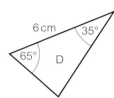

   a Work out the missing sides and angles.
   b Explain why triangle D is not congruent to the others.

7 These triangles are similar. Find the missing lengths.

   a   b   c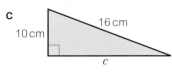

8 These trapeziums are similar. Find the missing sides.

   a 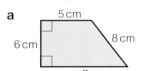   b 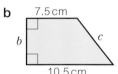   c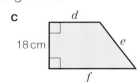

9 a Explain why triangles ACE and BCD are similar.
   b Calculate the length BD.
   c Calculate the length AB.

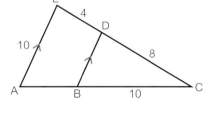

10 SU and TV are the diagonals of parallelogram STUV.
    Prove that there are two pairs of congruent triangles.

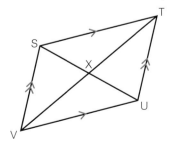

Challenge

11 Are all right-angled triangles similar? Explain.

12 **Reflect** Make a list of all the topics you have worked on in this
    unit where you have used multiplicative reasoning.
    List some other mathematics topics that use multiplicative reasoning.
    Compare your list with those of your classmates.

Reflect

9.1 Rates of change

You will learn to:
- Solve problems involving rates of change.
- Convert units with compound measures.

Why learn this?
British speed limits are given in miles per hour (mph) but many countries use kilometres per hour (km/h). Converting between them is useful when travelling abroad.

Fluency
Rearrange the formula $s = \dfrac{d}{t}$ to make
- d the subject
- t the subject.

Explore
What is the speed limit on French motorways in mph?

Exercise 9.1

1 This distance–time graph shows a hiker's journey.

Calculate the hiker's average speed in miles per hour (mph) from
- **a** A to B
- **b** B to C
- **c** C to D.

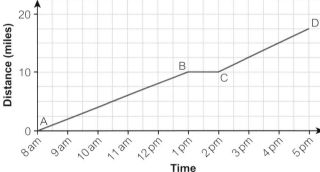

Hiker's journey

(Distance (miles) on vertical axis, Time on horizontal axis from 8am to 5pm. Points A, B, C, D shown.)

> **Key point**
>
> When compound measures involve dividing by a unit of time, they are called **rates of change**. Speed is the rate of change of distance with time.

2 Write these times in hours and minutes.
- **a** $2\frac{1}{4}$ hours
- **b** 0.75 hours
- **c** 1.5 hours
- **d** 3.2 hours

3 Work out the average speed for each journey.
- **a** A car travels 200 km in 5 hours.
- **b** An athlete runs 400 m in 64 seconds.
- **c** An aeroplane travels 2475 miles in $4\frac{1}{2}$ hours.
- **d** A swimmer completes a 50 m length in 40 seconds.

> **Q3 hint**
>
> Most objects do not travel at a constant speed. You usually calculate **average speed** over a whole journey.
>
> average speed = $\dfrac{\text{distance travelled}}{\text{time taken}}$

4 An arrow flies 15 m to a target at an average speed of 60 m/s. Find the time taken for it to reach the target.

> **Q4 Literacy hint**
>
>
>
> **m/s** means 'metres per second'.

5 A horse jockey completes a 2.4-mile course at an average speed of 32 mph. Calculate the length of time it takes him
- **a** in hours as a decimal
- **b** in minutes and seconds.

6 **Real** An aeroplane descends at a constant rate of 200 feet per minute. How long does it take the aircraft to descend from an altitude of 18 000 feet to an altitude of 10 000 feet?

7 **Real / Problem-solving** Johanna drives 90 miles to visit friends. She plans to travel at an average speed of 55 mph and wants to arrive by 1 pm. Calculate the latest time Johanna should leave.

8 **Problem-solving** The Channel Tunnel is 31.4 miles long. The speed limit for trains in the tunnel is 160 km/h. Work out the time taken for a train travelling at the speed limit to complete its journey through the tunnel.

Q8 hint

Use 5 miles = 8 km.

Key point

To convert between compound measures, convert each unit one at a time.

Worked example

Convert 72 km/h to m/s.

72 × 1000 = 72 000
72 km/h = 72 000 m/h

Start by converting 72 km into m. You now have the speed in metres per hour.

72 000 ÷ 3600 = 20
72 000 m/h = 20 m/s

There are 60 × 60 = 3600 seconds in 1 hour. Divide the speed in metres per hour by 3600 to find the speed in metres per second.

---

9 Convert 45 km/h into m/s.

10 The peregrine falcon can reach speeds of up to 90 m/s when diving. Convert this speed into km/h.

11 **Problem-solving / Reasoning** Amir's remote-controlled car has a maximum speed of 32 km/h. A world-class athlete can run 200 m in 19.6 seconds. Amir says his car could beat the sprinter in a 200 m race. Is he correct? Show your working to explain.

12 This distance–time graph shows trips taken by three different cyclists.
   a Which cyclist travelled at the fastest speed?
   b Which cyclist had the highest average speed for the entire journey?
   A fourth cyclist completes the same trip as cyclist C, starting and finishing at the same time. She travels at a constant speed for the whole journey.
   c Calculate her constant speed, giving your answer correct to 1 decimal place.

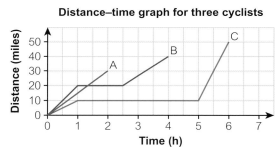

Distance–time graph for three cyclists

13 **Explore** What is the speed limit on French motorways in mph? What have you learned in this lesson to help you to explore this question? What further information do you need?

14 **Reflect** Saz says, 'When I'm converting between compound measures I look at the units to help decide whether to multiply or divide. m/s (metres per second) is a bit like a fraction $\frac{m}{s}$ so I multiply by the length measure and divide by the time measure.'
Did you use a method similar to Saz's to help?
What other methods do you use when working with compound measures?

9.2 Density and pressure

You will learn to:
- Calculate density and pressure.
- Solve problems involving compound measures.

Why learn this?
Meteorologists examine air pressure so that they can predict a storm.

Fluency
$v = u + at$
- Calculate v when $u = 5$, $a = 2$ and $t = 10$.
- Calculate u when $v = 100$, $a = 5$ and $t = 4$.

Explore
How do snow shoes reduce your chance of sinking into deep snow?

Exercise 9.2

1 Work out the volume of this triangular prism.

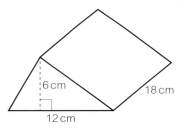

6 cm
18 cm
12 cm

2 Convert
   a 4 cm² into mm²
   b 600 cm² into m²
   c 0.3 m³ into cm³
   d 750 ml into cm³

Q2 hint

1 cm
1 cm   10 mm
10 mm

3 Make x the subject of each formula.
   a $y = 10x$
   b $3y = 2 - x$
   c $y = \dfrac{5}{x}$
   d $2(x + 1) = 4y$

4 **Real / STEM** As part of a science experiment, Kiki measures the mass and volume of samples of four different metals. She records her results in this table.

Metal	Volume (cm³)	Mass (g)
Titanium	16	72
Zinc	200	1427
Silver	42	441
Tin	1500	10 920

Calculate the **density** of each substance, giving your answers in g/cm³ correct to 1 decimal place.

Key point

Density is a compound measure. Density measures the mass per unit volume. Density is often measured in grams per cubic centimetre (g/cm³) and kilograms per cubic metre (kg/m³). The Greek letter ρ (rho) is used to represent density.

$$\text{density } (\rho) = \frac{\text{mass}}{\text{volume}}$$

Warm up

Worked example

Sandalwood has a density of $900 \, kg/m^3$. Calculate the volume of a piece of sandalwood with a mass of $7560 \, kg$.

$\text{volume} = \dfrac{\text{mass}}{\text{density}}$ — Rearrange the formula density = $\dfrac{\text{mass}}{\text{volume}}$ to make volume the subject.

$= \dfrac{7560}{900}$

$= 8.4 \, m^3$ — The unit of density is kg/m^3 and the unit of mass is kg, so the unit of volume is m^3.

5 STEM The table shows the densities of three common metal alloys.

Metal alloy	Density, ρ (kg/m^3)
Brass	8400
Steel	7820
Sterling silver	10400

Calculate

a the volume of 50 kg of brass

b the mass of $1.3 \, m^3$ of steel

c the mass of $4 \, cm^3$ of sterling silver

d the volume of 75 g of brass.

Q5c hint

The density is given in kg/m^3 so you need to convert cm^3 to m^3.

6 Problem-solving 250 ml of cooking oil has a mass of 230 g. Calculate the density of cooking oil in g/cm^3.

7 Problem-solving / Modelling The floor of this room is covered with rubber tiles with a density of $1200 \, kg/m^3$. The tiles are 5 mm thick. Estimate the total mass of the rubber tiles.

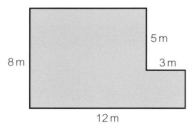

8 STEM / Problem-solving An electrical solder is made by combining 15 g of tin with 85 g of lead. Tin has a density of $7.3 \, g/cm^3$ and lead has a density of $11.3 \, g/cm^3$. Calculate the density of the solder.

9 STEM The density of the metal mercury is $13500 \, kg/m^3$. Convert this density into g/cm^3.

10 A force of 65 N is applied to an area of $12 \, cm^2$. Calculate the **pressure**. Give your answer to 1 decimal place.

11 Real At a depth of 10 m, water has a pressure of $9.8 \, N/cm^2$. Calculate the force applied to a diving mask with a surface area of $320 \, cm^2$ at this depth.

Key point

Pressure is a compound measure. Pressure is the force applied over a given area. The most common units of pressure are newtons per square centimetre (N/cm^2) and newtons per square metre (N/m^2).

$\text{pressure} = \dfrac{\text{force}}{\text{area}}$ or $P = \dfrac{F}{A}$

12 Problem-solving Calculate the force needed to produce a pressure of $520\,N/m^2$ on an area of $250\,cm^2$.

Q12 Strategy hint
Make sure that all the area measures are in the same units.

13 Modelling / Real A roofer (person who builds/repairs roofs) uses a board to reduce the pressure applied to a roof he is working on. The roofer has a weight of $880\,N$, and wants the maximum pressure applied to the roof to be $500\,N/m^2$. Calculate the minimum area of board he should use to distribute his weight.

14 STEM / Problem-solving Objects that are less dense than their surroundings float. The density of water at $4°C$ is $1\,g/cm^3$.

a Decide which of these objects will float in a bowl of water with a temperature of $4°C$.

	Object	Mass
A	Wood 1cm 5cm 2cm	7g
B	Plutonium 1cm 1cm 1cm	19.8g
C	Polystyrene 5cm 20cm 2cm	2g
D	Iron 2cm 5cm 2cm	160g

b The density of mercury is $13.6\,g/cm^3$. Which of the objects will float in mercury?

Discussion Do your answers change when the volume of the object is increased?

15 Explore How do snow shoes reduce your chance of sinking into deep snow?
Look back at the maths you have learned in this lesson. How can you use it to answer this question?

16 Reflect Dale says, 'A compound measure combines two different measures. A rate of change is a type of compound measure that describes exactly how one quantity changes in relation to time.'
Dale begins this table to explain:

Compound measure	Example
Speed: measure of distance and time	20 miles per hour

Copy Dale's table and add more examples of compound measures. Highlight those that are rates of change.

9.3 Upper and lower bounds

Confidence

You will learn to:
- Understand the effect of rounding.
- Find upper and lower bounds.

Why learn this?
You need to know the margin of error in your measurements if you are ordering new windows for a house.

Fluency
Work out
- 7000 − 50
- 0.9 + 0.05
- 20 − 0.5
- 0.036 − 0.0005

Explore
How accurate should measures be when
- cooking
- building a house
- calculating a country's GDP?

Exercise 9.3

Warm up

1 Round 253.0992 to
  a the nearest 100
  b the nearest 10
  c 1 decimal place
  d 2 decimal places.

2 The length of this roll of tape has been rounded to 1 decimal place. Which of the lengths in the cloud could be the actual length of the tape?

Length 4.2 m

4.1 m   4.13 m   4.22 m
4 m   4.17 m
4.25 m   4.209 m

Worked example

A piece of paper is 21 cm wide, correct to the nearest cm. Calculate the **upper bound** and **lower bound** for the width of the piece of paper.

Upper bound = 21.5 cm ——— Any number less than 21.5 is rounded to 21.

Lower bound = 20.5 cm ——— Any number greater than or equal to 20.5 is rounded to 21.

> **Key point**
> When a measurement is rounded, the actual value could be bigger or smaller than the rounded value. The biggest possible actual value is called the **upper bound**.
> The smallest possible actual value is called the **lower bound**.

Discussion If you round 21.5 cm to the nearest whole number you get 22 cm. Why is this value still used as the upper bound?

3 Write down the upper and lower bounds for each measurement.
  a The Mariana Trench in the Pacific Ocean is 11 km deep, to the nearest km.
  b The Moon orbits the Earth every 27 days, to the nearest day.
  c The mass of a tennis ball is 56.7 g, to 1 decimal place.
  d The height of the Eiffel Tower is 300 metres, to the nearest 10 m.

4 There were 65 000 people at a football match, rounded to the nearest thousand. Write down the upper and lower bounds for the number of people at the football match.

> **Key point**
> The upper bound is half a measure greater than the rounded value. The lower bound is half a measure less than the rounded value.

> **Q4 hint**
> The number of people is a discrete measurement. This means it must be a whole number. Work out the largest possible whole number that rounds to 65 000, to the nearest thousand.

5 Problem-solving A carton contains 500 ml of smoothie drink, correct to the nearest 10 ml. The carton costs £3.20. Calculate
   a the greatest possible cost per ml
   b the least possible cost per ml.
   Give your answers in pence.

6 Nisha uses a computer program to record her reaction time. She measures it as 0.26 seconds, to 2 decimal places. Copy and complete this inequality to show the upper and lower bounds of her reaction time.
   $\square \leqslant t < \square$
   Discussion Why do you need to use different inequality signs for the lower and upper bounds?

Key point

You can use inequalities to show upper and lower bounds for continuous measurements like time, length or mass.

7 STEM Pau measures the duration, t seconds, of a chemical reaction and records his result as
   $70.05 \leqslant t < 70.15$
   What degree of accuracy was Pau using for his measurement?

8 Copy and complete this table.

Measurement	Degree of accuracy	Actual value
6.3 seconds	1 decimal place	6.3 ± 0.05 seconds
5800 m	nearest 100 m	5800 ± □ m
0.09 km	2 decimal places	0.09 ± □ km
8.0 kg	1 decimal place	□ ± □ kg

Q8 Literacy hint

The symbol ± means 'plus or minus'. You can use it to show the **absolute error** in a measurement.

9 A box of nails contains between 115 and 125 nails.
   Write this in the form $\square \pm \square$

Key point

The **absolute error** is the maximum difference between the measured value and the actual value.

10 Problem-solving A recipe makes 800 g of cake mix, correct to the nearest 10 g. The mixture is divided equally between 4 cake tins. Calculate the maximum **absolute error** for the amount of cake mix in each tin.

11 Real A section of fencing is 180 cm long, to the nearest 10 cm. 8 sections of fencing are joined together.
   a Write down the upper and lower bounds for one piece of the fencing.
   b Work out the upper and lower bounds for the total length of the fencing.
   c Work out the absolute error for the total length of the fencing.
   Discussion What effect does multiplying or dividing a measurement by a whole number have on upper and lower bounds and absolute error?

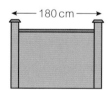

12 Explore How accurate should measures be when
   • cooking
   • building a house
   • calculating a country's GDP?
   Choose some sensible numbers to help you explore this situation. Then use what you've learned in this lesson to help you answer the question.

13 Reflect In this lesson you have shown rounding errors in lots of different ways. Make a list of the different ways you can show the actual values of a rounded number. What are the advantages and disadvantages of each method?

Topic links:
Rounding, Decimals, Inequalities

Subject links:
Science (Q6, Q7), Cookery (Q10)

Active Learn   Homework, Year 9, Unit 9

Unit 9 Accuracy and measures   202

Explore

Reflect

9 Check up

Rates of change

1 The distance–time graph shows a cyclist's journey.

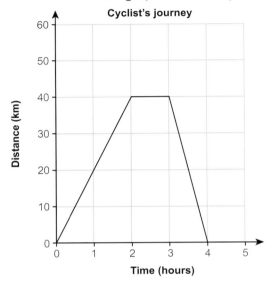

Calculate the cyclist's average speed, in km/h, between

a 0 and 2 hours

b 2 and 3 hours

c 3 and 4 hours.

2 A car completes a 225-mile journey in 6 hours.
Calculate its average speed in mph.

3 A marathon runner completes a 42 km course at an average speed of 7 km/h. Calculate the time taken to complete the course.

4 Convert 36 km/h into m/s.

5 Convert 12 m/s into km/h.

6 Duhr and his friend Taariq live 12 km apart along the same road.
It take Duhr 10 minutes to drive to Taariq's home.
The speed limit for the road is 50 mph.
Does Duhr stay within the speed limit when he drives to Taariq's home?
Use calculations to explain your answer.

Density and pressure

7 The diagram shows a gold bar.

7.2 cm   2.5 cm   4.0 cm

    a Calculate the volume of the gold bar.
Gold has a density of 19.3 g/cm^3.
    b Calculate the mass of the gold bar in kg.

8 A ruby has a volume of 6.5 cm^3 and a mass of 25.2 g.
Calculate the density of the ruby.

9 A cube-shaped box with side length 0.2 m and weight 60 N sits on a level surface.
Calculate the pressure acting on the base of the box.

10 A broach is made by mixing 15 g of gold with 5 g of copper.
The gold has a density of 19.3 g/cm^3 and the copper has a density of 8.9 g/cm^3.
What is the density of the metal in the broach?

Upper and lower bounds

11 An egg weighs 60 g correct to the nearest gram.
Write down the upper and lower bounds for the mass of the egg.

12 A statue is 20 m tall, to the nearest metre.
Copy and complete this inequality for the height of the statue.
    □ ⩽ height < □

13 A plant seedling is 11.9 cm tall, to 1 decimal place.
Write the absolute error of its height in the form 11.9 ± □ cm.

14 A £1 coin has a thickness of 3.15 mm, correct to 2 decimal places.
State the upper and lower bounds for the thickness of the coin.

15 A steel bar is 110 cm to the nearest 10 cm.
5 of these bars are to be welded together to make one long steel pole.
    a Write down the upper and lower bounds of one steel bar.
    b Write down the upper and lower bounds of the finished pole.
    c Write down the absolute error for the length of the pole.

16 **How sure are you of your answers? Were you mostly**
    🙁 **Just guessing**   😐 **Feeling doubtful**   🙂 **Confident**
What next? Use your results to decide whether to strengthen or extend your learning.

Challenge

17 An old-fashioned shower has a flow rate of 9.5 litres per minute.
A water-saving shower has a flow rate of 6.1 litres per minute.
Estimate how much water a person will save in one year using the water-saving shower.
What assumptions have you made?

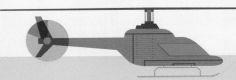

9 Strengthen

You will:
• Strengthen your understanding with practice.

Rates of change

1 Find the average speed for each journey.
  Give units with your answers.
  a A runner finishing a 12-mile course in 4 hours.
  b A train travelling 360 miles in 5 hours.
  c A pedestrian walking 4 miles in 1 hour and 20 minutes.

> **Q1 hint**
>
> You can use the formula triangle for speed. The position of the variables tells you whether to multiply or divide.
>
> $d = s \times t$
> $s = \dfrac{d}{t}$
> $t = \dfrac{d}{s}$

2 A swimmer completes a 400-m race at an average speed of 0.8 m/s.
  Calculate the time taken in minutes and seconds.

3 A car travels 100 miles at a constant speed of 40 miles per hour.
  Calculate the time taken in hours and minutes.

4 The distance–time graph shows the journey of a car.

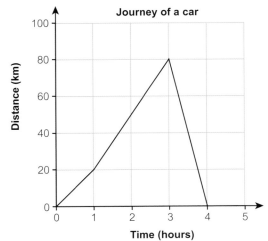

Calculate the maximum speed of the car. Give your answer in km/h.

5 A satellite moving at a constant speed travels 480 km in 1 minute.
  Calculate its speed in km/h.

> **Q5 hint**
>
> Work out how far the satellite travels in 1 hour.

Density and pressure

1 Calculate the density of each material.
Give units with your answers.
  a An iron girder (beam) with a volume of 0.6 m³ and mass of 4188 kg.
  b A platinum bracelet with a volume of 3.5 cm³ and a mass of 74.9 g.

2 **Problem-solving** This diagram shows a skateboard ramp.
It is made of solid concrete with a density of 2400 kg/m³.
Calculate the mass of the skateboard ramp.

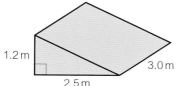

1.2 m
3.0 m
2.5 m

3 **STEM** The density of lead is 11.3 g/cm³.
Convert this density into kg/cm³.

4 **STEM** An aeroplane window has an area of 990 cm².
The force acting on the window due to the pressurised air in the cabin is 5148 N.
Calculate the pressure on the window in N/cm².

5 **STEM** A force of 200 N is applied to an area of A cm².
Given that the pressure acting on the area is 25 N/cm², calculate the value of A.

6 **STEM** A piece of metal has a density of 5 600 kg/m³ and a mass of 38 kg.
What is the volume of the piece of metal?
Give your answer correct to 3 significant figures.

Q1 hint

You can use the formula triangle for density.

mass = density × volume

density = $\dfrac{\text{mass}}{\text{volume}}$

volume = $\dfrac{\text{mass}}{\text{density}}$

Q2 hint

Start by working out the volume of the prism using the formula
volume of prism = length × area of cross-section

Q4 hint

This is the formula triangle for pressure.

Upper and lower bounds

1 There were 86 000 people at a rugby match, rounded to the nearest thousand.
Write down the upper and lower bounds for the number of people at the rugby match.

85 000   85 500   86 000   86 500   87 000

2 A bucket contains 3 litres of water, correct to the nearest litre.
Which of the following statements are true?
Give reasons for your answers.
  A The actual amount of water in the bucket could be 3.2 litres.
  B The upper bound for the amount of water in the bucket is 3.4 litres.
  C The lower bound for the amount of water in the bucket is 2.5 litres.

3 Write down the upper and lower bounds for each measurement.
  a The London Eye is 135 m high, correct to the nearest metre.

134   135   136

  b The age of the Earth is 4.54 billion years, to 2 decimal places.
  c A cheetah can run at 70 mph, correct to the nearest 10 mph.
  d The radioactive isotope radon-222 has a half-life of 3.8 days, to 1 decimal place.

Q3a hint

All of the highlighted values round to 135 to the nearest whole number:

4 The population of the UK in 2014 was 64.1 million, to 1 decimal place. Write down the upper and lower bounds for the population of the UK in 2014.

5 Samantha measured the capacity of a glass as 250 ml to the nearest 10 ml.
Copy and complete this statement showing the absolute error in her measurement.
Actual capacity = 250 ± □ ml

Q4 hint

The number given is to 1 decimal place, so the upper and lower bounds will have 2 decimal places.

Q5 hint

How much bigger or smaller could the capacity be?

Enrichment

1 STEM / Problem-solving This table shows the densities of six different metals.

Metal or alloy	Density, ρ (g/cm³)
Aluminium	2.7
Cadmium	8.6
Lead	11.3
Magnesium	1.7
Tin	7.4
Tungsten	19.2

Each of these solid cuboids is made from one of the six metals.
Work out which metal is used for each cuboid.

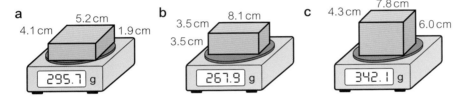

a 5.2 cm 4.1 cm 1.9 cm 295.7 g
b 8.1 cm 3.5 cm 3.5 cm 267.9 g
c 7.8 cm 4.3 cm 6.0 cm 342.1 g

2 STEM The weight of an object is the force due to gravity.
On Earth, weight is calculated by the formula
weight = mass × 9.8
A backpack has a mass of 20 kg.
a Work out the weight of the backpack on Earth.
On Mars, weight is given by the formula
weight = mass × 3.7
b Work out the weight of the backpack on Mars.

Q2b Literacy hint

Weight is a force, so it is measured in newtons.

3 Reflect These Strengthen lessons suggested using number lines and formula triangles to help you to answer the questions.
Look back at the questions with a number line. Did they help you? Explain why.
Look back at the questions with formula triangles. Did they help you? Explain why.
In what other subjects have you used triangles to help with formulae?

Reflect

9 Extend

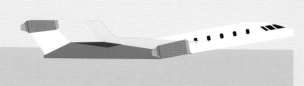

You will:
- Extend your understanding with problem-solving.

1 A football pitch must be between 100 yards and 130 yards long, and between 50 yards and 100 yards wide.
Write both of these measurements in the form $\square \pm \square$ yards.

Q1 hint

The first number is half-way between the minimum and maximum values.

2 The upper and lower bounds for the mass, x kg, of an elephant are given as $4950 \leqslant x < 5050$.
Work out the degree of accuracy that the elephant was weighed to.

3 **Reasoning** An oven thermometer records the temperature as 177°C, correct to the nearest °C.
Jamie says that the actual temperature, T °C, must be in the range $176.5 \leqslant T \leqslant 177.49$.
Is Jamie correct?
Give a reason for your answer.

4 **Real** A skydiver falls at a constant speed of 55 m/s from an altitude of 3700 m.
She must open her parachute at least 500 m above the ground.
How long can she wait before opening her parachute?

5 **Modelling / Problem-solving**
This bathtub is filled from a tap with a flow rate of 18 litres per minute.
Model the bathtub as a cuboid and estimate the length of time it will take to fill three-quarters of the bathtub.

152 cm
76 cm
36 cm

Q5 hint

1 litre = $\square$ cm³

6 **Modelling** This bowling ball weighs 16 lb and has a radius of 10.8 cm.
Estimate the density of the resin used to make the bowling ball.
Give your answer in g/cm³ to 1 decimal place.
Discussion What assumptions do you have to make as part of your estimate?

10.8 cm

Q6 hint

2.2 lb ≈ 1 kg

7 On its outward journey a ship sails 144 km in 8 hours.
The return journey takes 2 hours longer.
How much faster, on average, does the ship travel on its outward journey.

8 **Problem-solving** The diagram shows a running track made up of two straight 100-m sections and two semicircular sections with diameter 64 m.

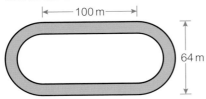

Emma runs around the track at an average speed of 7.2 m/s.
Calculate the length of time she take to complete 4 laps.

9 **Problem-solving / Reasoning** The diagram shows a 900 ml flask containing 350 ml of oil.
An iron bar of mass 4.2 kg is placed into the flask.
The density of iron is 7.9 g/cm³.
Will the flask overflow?
Explain your answer.

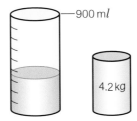

Q9 Strategy hint

Work out the volume of the iron bar. It will displace the same volume of oil when placed in the flask.

10 A 25 litre tank, measured to the nearest litre, is filled with water using a jug that holds 500 ml, to the nearest 10 ml.
Work out
   a the minimum number of jugs required to fill the tank
   b the maximum number of jugs required to fill the tank.

11 **STEM / Problem-solving** This solid metal block has a density of 8500 kg/m³.
   a Calculate the mass of the block.
   b Calculate the weight of the block in newtons.
   c The block is upright. Calculate the pressure exerted by the block on the ground.
   The block is rotated so that one of its longer faces rests on the ground.
   d Calculate the pressure exerted by the block on the ground in this position.

Q11 Literacy hint

The weight of an object is the force due to gravity.
On Earth, weight = mass × 9.8.

12 **Problem-solving** Blackpool Tower is 158 m tall to the nearest metre.
Baked bean tins are 11 cm tall to the nearest cm.
If you stacked 1500 baked bean tins on top of each other, would they definitely reach the top of the tower?

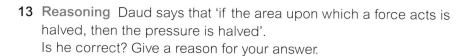

13 Reasoning Daud says that 'if the area upon which a force acts is halved, then the pressure is halved'.
Is he correct? Give a reason for your answer.

14 Reasoning Identical boxes are loaded onto a lorry.
Padma says that if the mass of each box is correct to the nearest kg, then the total mass of the loaded boxes will be correct to the nearest kg.
Explain why she is incorrect.

Q14 Strategy hint
Choose some numbers to help with your explanation.

15 A bag of sugar has a mass of 500 g, to the nearest 10 g.
   a Write the absolute error for the mass of the bag in the form
      500 g ± ☐
   b Calculate the absolute error for the mass of 8 bags of sugar.
   One bag of sugar is divided equally between 8 bowls.
   c Calculate the absolute error for the mass of sugar in each bowl.

Investigation

Problem-solving / Reasoning

Amrita and Ben want to work out the thickness of a 2p coin. They are both going to measure thicknesses to the nearest mm. Amrita measures one 2p coin and records a thickness of 2 mm. Ben measures a stack of fifteen 2p coins and records a thickness of 28 mm.
1 Write down the upper and lower bounds for the actual thickness of Amrita's coin.
2 Use Ben's measurement to estimate the thickness of one 2p coin.
3 Show working to explain why Ben's method of measuring thickness is more accurate than Amrita's.
4 What could you do to get a more accurate measurement? Try it.

16 Reasoning Metal A has a density of 8300 kg/m³.
Metal B has a density of 3800 kg/m³.
20 kg of metal A is mixed with 10 kg of metal B.
Work out
   a the volume of the mixture
   b the density of the mixture.
Give your answers to 3 significant figures.

17 Problem-solving A box of mass 20 kg exerts a pressure of 392 N/m² on the surface on which it rests.
Find the increase in pressure when Aisha, who has a mass of 60 kg, sits on top of the box.

Q17 hint
Use $F = mg$ where g is 9.8 m/s².

18 A cube-shaped piece of wood has a density of 740 kg/m³.
It exerts a pressure of 1813 kg/m² on the surface on which it sits.
By taking the acceleration due to gravity to be 9.8 m/s², find the length of the sides of the cube.

Q18 hint
Use density $= \dfrac{\text{mass}}{\text{volume}}$ and
pressure $= \dfrac{\text{force}}{\text{area}}$

19 Reflect Look back at the questions in these extend lessons.
Write down the question that was the easiest to answer.
What made it easy?
Write down the question that was the most difficult to answer.
What made it difficult?
Look again at the question you found most difficult. What could you do to make this type of question easier to answer?

Q19 hint
Ask your classmates how they answered this question. Do they have some hints for you?

Q19 hint
density $= \dfrac{\text{mass}}{\text{volume}}$ and pressure $= \dfrac{\text{force}}{\text{area}}$

Reflect

9 Unit test

1 The mass of a letter is 52 g to the nearest gram.
Write down
  a the upper bound for the mass of the letter
  b the lower bound for the mass of the letter.

2 The mass of a block of cheese is 400 g, to the nearest 10 g.
Write this in the form
  $\square$ g $\leqslant$ mass $<$ $\square$ g

3 A box of matches contains between 46 and 56 matches.
Write this in the form
  $\square \pm \square$

4 A runner completes a 12-mile course in 1 hour and 36 minutes.
Calculate his average speed in miles per hour.

5 A speedboat travels 75 km at an average speed of 30 km/h.
Calculate the time taken in hours and minutes.

6 Convert 5 m/s into km/h.

7 This triangular prism has a mass of 5.2 kg.

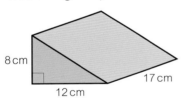

8 cm
12 cm
17 cm

Calculate the density of the material
used to make the triangular prism.
Give your answer in g/cm³ correct
to 1 decimal place.

8 The point of a nail is a circle with radius 0.5 mm.
The nail is hit with a force of 150 N.
Calculate the pressure exerted by the point of the nail. Give your
answer in N/cm², correct to the nearest 1000 N/cm².

9 A length of bunting is made by joining together 6 identical flags.
Each flag has a length of 40 cm, correct to the nearest 10 cm.

Calculate the lower bound for the length of the bunting.

10 A carton contains 600 ml of juice, correct to the nearest 10 ml.
The juice is divided equally between 5 glasses.
Calculate the maximum absolute error for the amount of juice in each glass.

Challenge

11 The diagram shows the dimensions of the Statue of Liberty in New York. All the dimensions are correct to the nearest metre.
Work out the maximum possible value of
a the height of the whole statue from A to D
b the distance BC from the head of the statue to its feet
c the distance CD from the top of the head to the top of the torch
d the ratio of the height of the statue BD to the height of the plinth AB.

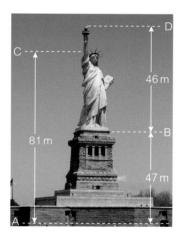

12 **Reflect** The title of this unit is 'Accuracy and measures'.
Look back at the questions in this unit.
Make a list of all the ways you have used accuracy.
Make a list of all the different types of measures you have used.
Compare your list with those of your classmates.

10.1 Drawing-straight line graphs

Confidence

You will learn to:
- Draw graphs with equation $y = mx + c$.
- Draw graphs with equation $ax + by = c$.
- Identify parallel lines.

Why learn this?
Computer games designers specify how a character moves across the screen by giving the equations of the lines they follow.

Fluency
- Which graph has a positive gradient? Which has a negative gradient?
- What are the x- and y-intercepts of each graph?

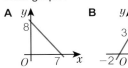

Explore
How can a video game character move around an obstacle?

Warm up

Exercise 10.1

1 For each line
  a work out the gradient
  b write down the y-intercept
  c write down the equation.

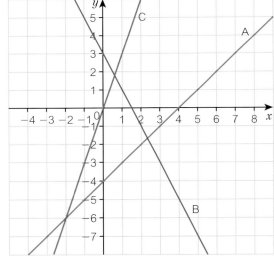

2 **a** What is the value of x at any point on the y-axis?
  b What is the value of y at any point on the x-axis?
  c Copy and complete.
    i The y-intercept of a graph has x-coordinate ☐.
    ii The x-intercept of a graph has y-coordinate ☐.

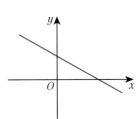

3 Draw these graphs from their equations.
  Use a coordinate grid from −10 to +10 on both axes.
  a $y = 2x + 3$
  b $y = 2x - 2$
  c $y = 3x$
  d $y = \frac{1}{2}x + 1$
  e $y = -2x + 1$
  f $y = -3x + 4$

Q3a hint

Plot the y-intercept and then draw a line from the y-intercept with the correct gradient.

4 Which of these lines are parallel to $y = -x + 1$?

A $y = -x + 2$ **B** $y = x + 3$ **C** $y = 3x + 1$ **D** $y = -2x + 6$ **E** $y = 4 - x$

Discussion What other lines are parallel to $y = -x + 1$?

5 Write the equation of a line parallel to
a $y = 3x - 5$
b $y = -2x + 7$
c $y = 3x$, with y-intercept (0, 4)
d $y = -2x$, that crosses the y-axis at -5.

6 a Without drawing the graphs, sort these equations into pairs of parallel lines.

A $y = -2x + 3$

B $y = \frac{1}{2}x + 3$

C $y = 2x - 3$

D $y = -2x - 23$

E $y = 2x + 3$

F $y = 0.5x - 3$

b Which of the equations in part **a** give lines that intersect the y-axis at the same place?

Discussion What is the same about the equations of two lines that are parallel? What is different?

7 a Copy and complete the table for the graph of $3x + 4y = 6$.

x	0	
y		0

b Use the values from the table to plot the graph of $3x + 4y = 6$.

8 Plot the graphs with these equations.
a $2x - y = -4$
b $3x - y = 2$
c $y + 3x = 1$
d $2y - x = 2$
e $x - y = 3$
f $x + y = 5$

Discussion Look at the equation and graph in part **f**. Where do you think the graph of $x + y = 7$ will cross the axes? What about $x + y = -2$?

Key point

Lines that are **parallel** have the same gradient.

Q5a, b hint

c can be any number.

Q6a hint

What do you know about the gradients of parallel lines?

Q8 hint

You could use a graph-plotting package to plot the graphs.

Investigation

You can write the equation of a line as a function machine.

$y = 3x + 2$

$$x \longrightarrow \boxed{\times 3} \longrightarrow \boxed{+2} \longrightarrow y$$

The function gives an output value y for every input value x.
You can reverse the function machines to find the **inverse function**.

$$y = \frac{x-2}{3} = \frac{x}{3} - \frac{2}{3}$$

$$y \longleftarrow \boxed{\div 3} \longleftarrow \boxed{-2} \longleftarrow x$$

1 Find the inverse function of
   a $y = 2x$ **b** $y = 3x$ **c** $y = x$

2 Plot the graph of $y = 2x$ and of its inverse function on the same axes.

3 Do the same for $y = 3x$ and its inverse function, and for $y = x$ and its inverse function.
   a What do you notice about the graph of a function and its inverse function?
   b Write a rule connecting the graph of a function and its inverse function.
   c Test your rule for a more complex function.
   d Plot the graph of $y = 3x + 2$ and its inverse function on the same axes.
   e Does this graph obey your rule?

4 **a** Draw the graph of $y = 4x - 1$.
   b Use your rule to draw the graph of the inverse function.
   c Work out the equation of this line.
   d Check that your graph is correct by finding the inverse function of $y = 4x - 1$.

> **Part 2 hint**
>
> You could use a graph-plotting package.

> **Part 3 hint**
>
> What transformation takes the graph onto the graph of its inverse function?

9 **Explore** How can a video game character move around an obstacle?
   Look back at the maths you have learned in this lesson.
   How can you use it to answer the question?

10 **Reflect** There are two ways of drawing graphs of linear functions. In Q5 you plotted the y-intercept and then drew a line from the y-intercept with the correct gradient. In Q7 you completed a table like this

x	0	
y		0

and then plotted the points and joined them with a straight line. Which method is better for each of these equations?
   a $y = 4x + 1$ **b** $2x + 3y = 5$
   Explain why.

> **Key point**
>
> To compare the gradients and y-intercepts of two straight lines, their equations need to be in the form $y = mx + c$.

> **Key point**
>
> To find the y-intercept of a graph, find the y-coordinate where $x = 0$.
> To find the x-intercept of a graph, find the x-coordinate where $y = 0$.

10.2 Graphs of quadratic functions

You will learn to:
- Understand and draw graphs of quadratic functions.
- Identify quadratic graphs and their features.
- Solve problems using quadratic graphs.

Why learn this?
The path of a basketball can be modelled using a quadratic function.

Fluency
Describe the transformation that maps A to B.

Explore
What is the best way to throw a basketball into the net?

Exercise 10.2

1 Copy and complete this table of values for $y = x^2$.

x	-4	-3	-2	-1	0	1	2	3	4
y									

2 Work out the value of $2x^2$ when
   a $x = 4$ **b** $x = -3$ **c** $x = -1$

3 Work out the value of $x^2 - 5$ when
   a $x = 4$ **b** $x = -2$ **c** $x = 0$

4 a Draw an x-axis from -4 to 4 and a y-axis from -30 to 30. Plot the coordinates from your table of values for $y = x^2$ in Q1. Join the points with a smooth curve.
Label your graph $y = x^2$.
   b Describe the symmetry of your graph.

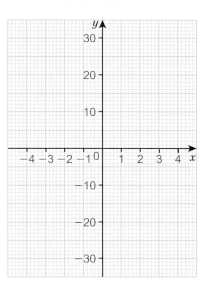

> **Key point**
>
> A **quadratic function** contains a term in x^2 but no higher power of x. $y = x^2$, $y = 5x^2$, $y = x^2 + 5$ and $y = x^2 + 3x + 2$ are all quadratic. The graph of a quadratic function is called a **parabola**.

Warm up

> **Q4b hint**
>
> What is the equation of the line of symmetry?

5 Reasoning

a Copy and complete this table of values for the quadratic function
$y = x^2 + 10$.

x	−4	−3	−2	−1	0	1	2	3	4
y									

b Plot the graph of $y = x^2 + 10$ on the same axes as Q4.
Label your graph with its equation.

c What is the same about the two graphs?

d What is different about the two graphs?

e Predict what the graph of $y = x^2 - 10$ will look like. Plot the graph on the same axes as Q4 to test your prediction.

Discussion What will the graphs of $y = x^2 + 5$ and $y = x^2 - 5$ look like?
How does the graph of $y = x^2$ change when you add or subtract a **constant**?

Q5e hint

You could use a graph-plotting package.

Q5 Literacy hint

A **constant** is a value that doesn't change.

6 Reasoning

a Draw an x-axis from −4 to 4 and a y-axis from 0 to 50.

b Copy and complete this table of values for the quadratic function $y = 2x^2$.

x	−4	−3	−2	−1	0	1	2	3	4
y									

c Plot the graphs of these quadratic functions on the same axes.

  i $y = x^2$ **ii** $y = 2x^2$ **iii** $y = \frac{1}{2}x^2$

d What is the same about the three graphs?

e What is different about the three graphs?

Discussion How does the graph of $y = x^2$ change when you multiply x^2 by a number greater than 1? Less than 1?

7 Reasoning

a Copy and complete this table of values for the quadratic function $y = 2x^2 + 10$.

x	−4	−3	−2	−1	0	1	2	3	4
$2x^2$		18							
+10	+ 10	+ 10	+ 10	+ 10	+ 10	+ 10	+ 10	+ 10	+ 10
y		28							

b Plot the graph of $y = 2x^2 + 10$.

c Describe how adding 10 changes the graph of the function $y = 2x^2$.

d Describe how multiplying x^2 by 2 and adding 10 changes the graph of the function $y = x^2$.

Discussion What will the graph of $y = 2x^2 - 10$ look like?
What will the graph of $y = 3x^2 + 10$ look like?

Q7 Strategy hint

Don't draw the axes until you know the largest and smallest values of y.

Investigation   Reasoning

a Plot the graphs of $y = x^2$ and $y = -x^2$ on the same axes. What do you notice?

b Plot the graphs of $y = 3x^2$ and $y = -3x^2$ on the same axes. What do you notice?

c **i** Predict the shape of the graph of $y = -2x^2$. (Look at the graph of $y = 2x^2$ that you drew in Q6.)

   ii Plot the graphs of $y = -2x^2$ and $y = 2x^2$ on the same axes to check your prediction.

8 Look at your graphs in this lesson.
Write the coordinates of their **turning points** and say if they are **maxima** or **minima**.

Discussion For a quadratic graph how can you tell what the coordinates of the turning point are by looking at its equation?

9 Match each graph to its function.

i $y = x^2$ **ii** $y = -x^2 + 10$ **iii** $y = 2x^2$
iv $y = 2x^2 - 10$ **v** $y = -x^2$ **vi** $y = -2x^2$

A 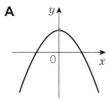   **B** 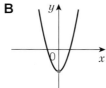   **C**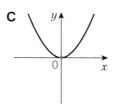

D 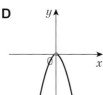   **E** 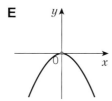   **F**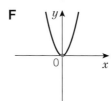

10 **Real / Modelling / Problem-solving** A machine launches (shoots into the air) tennis balls at a speed of 50 ft/s at an angle of between 19° and 45° to the ground.
The graphs show the paths of a ball launched at the minimum and maximum angles.

a What is the maximum height of a ball launched at 45°?

b A ball is launched at 19°. How far from the machine will it be at a height of 2 ft?

c Giovanni can reach a ball at a height of 8 ft. A ball is launched at 45°. How close can he be to the machine to hit the ball?

d A tennis court net has a height of 3 ft in the middle. What is the furthest the tennis ball machine can be from the net so that all of the balls clear the net?

11 **Explore** What is the best way to throw a basketball into the net? Is it easier to explore this question now that you have completed the lesson?
What further information do you need to be able to answer this?

12 **Reflect** Ferenc and Zoe are discussing Q9. Ferenc says, 'First I looked at the shape of the parabola and decided whether the **coefficient** of x^2 would be positive or negative.'
Zoe says, 'First I looked at the y-intercept of the parabola so I knew whether there would be a constant term.'
Did you use Ferenc or Zoe's method to answer Q9?
What other information did you need to think about?

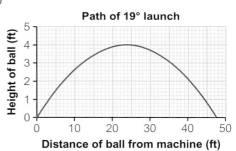
Path of 19° launch

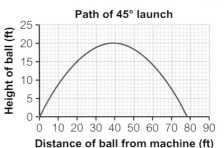
Path of 45° launch

Explore

Reflect

10.3 Simultaneous equations

Confidence

You will learn to:
- Solve a pair of simultaneous equations.

Why learn this?
You can solve two equations together to work out the cheapest phone deal.

Fluency
Write an expression for the cost of
- 3 cups of tea at £x each
- 4 cups of coffee at £y each
- 3 teas and 4 coffees.

Explore
Is it better for a business to pay $55 per callout for computer repairs or pay $100 per year and then $38 per callout?

Exercise 10.3

Warm up

1 **Modelling** Write an equation for each of these.
  a 3 bags of soil and 1 plant weigh 75 kg altogether.
    Use x for the weight of a bag of soil and y for the weight of a plant.
  b It costs $44 for 2 adults and 2 children to attend a football game.
    Use x for the price of an adult ticket and y for the price of a child ticket.
  c 3 boxes of cereal and 2 litres of milk cost £10.49.
    Use x for the cost of a box of cereal and y for the price of a litre of milk.

2 For the equation $2x - 5y = 25$, work out
  a x, when $y = 1$ **b** x, when $y = 4$
  c y, when $x = 5$ **d** y, when $x = 12$

Literacy hint
Solve means work out the values for x and y.

Worked example

Solve the **simultaneous equations** $y = 3x$ and $5x + y = 46$.

$$5x + y = 46 \quad (1)$$
$$y = 3x \quad (2)$$

> Write one equation above the other with the equals signs lined up. Number them (1) and (2).

$$5x + 3x = 46 \quad (1)$$
$$8x = 46$$
$$x = 5.75$$

> Substitute $y = 3x$ into equation (1).

$$y = 3 \times 5.75$$
$$y = 17.25$$

> Simplify and solve.

> Substitute the value of x into one equation. Choose the simpler one to solve.

Check:
$$5x + y = 46 \quad (1)$$
$$5 \times 5.75 + 17.25 = 46 \checkmark$$

> Check the values in the other equation.

Key point
You can solve two **simultaneous equations** to find the values of two variables.

3 Solve these pairs of simultaneous equations.

a $3x + y = 15$
$y = 2x$

b $5x + y = 60$
$y = 3x$

c $2x + y = 17$
$y = 2x$

d $x + 3y = 22$
$\frac{1}{2}x = y$

e $2x + y = 32$
$y = 4x$

Q3e hint

Leave your answer as a simplified fraction.

4 **Problem-solving / Modelling** 4 oranges and 1 watermelon cost $6.30. The cost of 1 watermelon is 5 times the cost of 1 orange.
a How much does 1 orange cost?
b How much does 1 watermelon cost?

5 **Problem-solving / Modelling** A sports venue holds 720 people with 15 standing rows and 10 seated rows. Each standing row holds twice the number of people as a seated row.
a How many people are in each standing row?
b How many people are in each seated row?

6 **Problem-solving / Modelling** It costs 1 adult and 3 children $17.50 to go to the cinema. A child ticket costs half the price of an adult ticket.
a What is the price of a child ticket?
b What is the price of an adult ticket?

 7 At the school play, students sold programmes for $4.50 and ice creams for $1.50. They sold twice as many ice creams as programmes. Altogether they made $322.50.
How many programmes and how many ice creams did the students sell?

Worked example

Solve the simultaneous equations $5x + y = 43$ and $x - y = 5$.

$5x + y = 43$ (1)
$x - y = 5$ (2)

> Write one equation above the other with equals signs lined up. Number them.

$6x + 0 = 48$ (1) + (2)
$x = 8$

> Add equations (1) and (2) together to cancel y. Solve for x.

$8 - y = 5$
$y = 3$

> Substitute $x = 8$ into one equation to work out y.

Check:

$5x + y = 43$ (1)
$5 \times 8 + 3 = 43$ ✓

> Substitute both values into the other equation to check.

---

8 Solve these pairs of simultaneous equations.

a $4x + y = 17$
$3x - y = 11$

b $3x + y = 20$
$2x - y = 0$

c $4x - y = 19$
$5x + y = 53$

d $5y - x = 16$
$3y + x = 12$

e $6x + 2y = 51$
$x - 2y = 5$

f $2x - 5y = 0$
$2x + 5y = 20$

Discussion This method of solving simultaneous equations is called the elimination method. Why do you think this is?

9 **Real / Modelling** A boat travels downstream at 6.5 miles per hour.
The same boat travels back upstream at 3.5 miles per hour.
The speed of the boat in still water is x mph. The speed of the
current is y mph.
Downstream: Speed of boat = $x + y$
Upstream: Speed of boat = $x - y$
 a Work out the speed of the boat in still water.
 b Work out the speed of the current.

10 **Problem-solving / Modelling** The sum of two numbers is 19.
The difference between the two numbers is 7.
Use a and b to represent the numbers.
 a Write two equations linking a and b.
 b Solve the simultaneous equations.

11 Solve these pairs of simultaneous equations.

 a $7x + y = 45$ b $5x + 2y = 41$
   $4x + y = 27$ $3x + 2y = 27$
 c $3x + 9y = 66$ d $2x + 7y = 17$
   $3x + 3y = 30$ $6x + 7y = 37$

Q11 Strategy hint

Subtract one equation from the other
to eliminate one of the variables.

12 **Real** A bike rental company charges a **flat fee** plus an hourly rate.
Etsu rented a bike for 4 hours and paid $18. Lanika rented a bike for
7 hours and paid $25.50.
 a How much was the cost per hour to rent a bike?
 b How much was the flat fee to rent a bike?
 c Miku rents a bike for 2 hours.
  How much does it cost?

Q12 Literacy hint

A **flat fee** is a fixed amount that
doesn't change according to the
number of hours rented.

13 **Real** At a water park, 2 adults and 2 children pay $21 for entry.
A different group of 2 adults and 5 children pay $30.
Work out the cost for 1 adult and the cost for 1 child.

14 **Explore** Is it better for a business to pay $55 per callout for
computer repairs or pay $100 per year and then $38 per callout?
Is it easier to explore this question now that you have completed
the lesson?
What further information do you need to be able to answer this?

15 **Reflect** In this lesson you have solved simultaneous equations in two
different ways:
 • substitution
 • elimination.
 a Write, in your own words, the difference between the two methods.
 b Write down a pair of simultaneous equations that can be
  solved using
  • substitution
  • elimination.

Explore

Reflect

10.4 Using $y = mx + c$

You will learn to:
- Rearrange equations of graphs to find the gradient and y-intercept.
- Find the equation of the line between two points.

Why learn this?
The marketing manager of a furniture shop might analyse gradients of graphs of sales figures to predict future trends.

Fluency
What is the equation of this line?

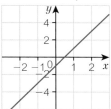

Explore
How do you know which supermarket is increasing their sales the fastest?

Exercise 10.4

1 Draw the graph of $x + 2y = 6$.
  Use a coordinate grid from -10 to $+10$ on both axes.

2 **a** Without drawing the graphs, sort these equations into pairs of parallel lines.

   A $y = \frac{1}{4}x - 1$ **B** $y = -4x + 7$ **C** $y = 4x + 1$

   D $y = -4x + 1$ **E** $y = 4x - 5$ **F** $y = \frac{1}{4}x + 7$

   b Which equations in part **a** give lines that intersect the y-axis at the same place?

3 Make x the subject.
   a $y = x - 9$ **b** $y = 5x$
   c $y = \frac{1}{3}x$ **d** $y = -\frac{3x}{4}$
   e $y = 8 - \frac{2x}{5}$ **f** $y = 2(x - 3)$

4 **a** Draw the graph of $5x + 2y = 10$.
   b Use your graph to write down the gradient and y-intercept.
   c Write the equation of the line as $y = mx + c$.
   d Rearrange $5x + 2y = 10$ to make y the subject.
      What do you notice?

   Discussion How can you find the gradient and y-intercept of the line $3x + y = 7$?

5 Which of these equations are equivalent?

  A $y = 3 - 2x$ **B** $y - 2x = 3$
  C $y + 2x = 3$ **D** $y = 3x - 2$
  E $y = 2x + 3$ **F** $y - 3x = 2$

Q5 hint

Rearrange each equation to make y the subject.

6 a Write each equation in the form $y = mx + c$.

  i $y - 4x = 9$

  ii $2y - 7x = 3$

  iii $3y + 11x = 9$

  iv $\frac{1}{2}y + 4x = 5$

b Which line has the steepest gradient?

Key point

To compare two lines, write their equations in the form $y = mx + c$.

7 Decide whether each pair of lines have the same y-intercept.

  a $y - 4 = 7x$ and $y + 3x = 4$ **b** $4x - 2y = 7$ and $y = 4x + 7$
  c $x + y = -1$ and $3x + 5y = -5$ **d** $-3x + 6y = 12$ and $10 + 7x = 5y$

8 Decide whether each pair of lines is parallel.

  a $y = 3x + 7$ and $3y = 9x - 4$ **b** $y = 2x + 5$ and $y = -\frac{1}{2}x + 7$
  c $2y = 3x + 8$ and $3y = 2x + 9$ **d** $x = y - 7$ and $5x - 5y = 7$
  e $-x = 4 + y$ and $3x - 4y = 1$

9 Which of these lines pass through $(0, -2)$?
Show how you worked it out.

  A $y = -2x + 2$ **B** $2y - 3x = -4$
  C $3x + 2y = 4$ **D** $5x + y = -10$
  E $y = 3x - 2$

Q9 hint

Make y the subject. Write the x-term first on the right-hand side.

Worked example

Find the equation of the line that passes through points A(4, 2) and B(9, 17).

$y = mx + c$

At A, $x = 4$ and $y = 2$

  $2 = m \times 4 + c$

  $2 = 4m + c$

Points A and B lie on the line, so their coordinates satisfy the equation of the line. Substitute the x- and y-values from point A into $y = mx + c$ and write an equation for the line.

At B, $x = 9$ and $y = 17$.

  $17 = m \times 9 + c$

  $17 = 9m + c$

Substitute the x- and y-values from point B into $y = mx + c$.

  $17 = 9m + c$ (2)
  $2 = 4m + c$ (1)
  $15 = 5m$ (2) − (1)
  $m = 3$

Solve the simultaneous equations to find m and c. To eliminate c, subtract equation (1) from equation (2).

  $2 = 4 \times 3 + c$

  $c = -10$

Substitute $m = 3$ into equation (1).

Equation of line is $y = 3x - 10$.

Substitute the values of m and c into $y = mx + c$.

Topic links: Straight-line graphs, Changing the subject

10 Write the equation of the line
   a parallel to $y = 3x + 5$ with y-intercept $(0, -2)$
   b parallel to $y = -4x + 6$ that passes through $(0, 3)$
   c parallel to $y = 2x - 3$ that passes through the origin.

Q8b Strategy hint

Substitute your x-value from part **a** into the equation of the line to get the y-value. Write the x- and y-values as coordinates.

11 Find the equation of the line that passes through points C(3, 2) and D(6, 8).

12 Find the equation of the line that passes through points E(8, 3) and F(1, −4).

13 **a** What is the x-coordinate of every point on the line $x = 4$?
   b Where does the line $y = 2x + 1$ cross the line $x = 4$?

14 **Real / Modelling** There is a linear relationship between the price, P, charged by a cleaning company and the number of hours, h, spent cleaning. The company charges $60 for 2 hours of cleaning and $99 for 5 hours of cleaning.
   a Copy and complete.
      Two points on the graph $P = mh + c$ are (2, ☐) and (☐, 99).
   b Work out the equation of the line.
   c What does the gradient represent?
   d What does the y-intercept represent?

Key point

A linear relationship can be expressed in the form $y = mx + b$ or $P = mh + c$.

15 **Real / Modelling** There is a linear relationship between the value, V, of a car and its age, a.
   A 5-year-old car is worth $14 000.
   The same car is worth $11 400 2 years later.
   a Work out an equation in the form $V = ma + c$.
   b What was the value of the car when it was new?

Q12b hint

What is the age of a new car?

16 **Explore** How do you know which supermarket is increasing their sales the fastest?
   Is it easier to explore this question now that you have completed the lesson?
   What further information do you need to be able to answer this?

17 **Reflect** Write down, in your own words, as many facts about straight-line graphs as you can. Compare your facts with those of your classmates.
   Use these words:

   parallel

   equation

   y-intercept

   gradient

Explore

Reflect

10.5 More simultaneous equations

You will learn to:
- Solve more complex simultaneous equations.

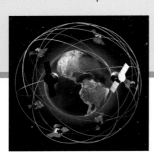

Why learn this?
Most real-life situations require more complex simultaneous equations to model them.

Fluency
Would you add or subtract to solve these pairs of simultaneous equations?
- $2x + y = 21$ and $5x - y = 9$
- $7y + 3x = 15$ and $7y + 2x = 31$
- $4x + y = 16$ and $6x + y = 11$
- $8y - 3x = 42$ and $3y - 3x = 17$

Explore
In what year will the population of India equal the population of China?

Confidence

Exercise 10.5

Warm up

1 Solve these pairs of simultaneous equations.

    a $2x + y = 9$ **b** $4x + 3y = 32$

       $3x - y = 6$ $2x + 3y = 28$

2 Multiply each term in the equation $2x + 3y = 6$

    a by 2   **b** by 3   **c** by −2

> **Q2 hint**
> $\square x + \square y = \square$

> ## Worked example
> Solve the simultaneous equations $3x + y = 18$ and $x + 2y = 11$.
>
> $3x + y = 18$ (1)
>
> $x + 2y = 11$ (2)
>
> $6x + 2y = 36$ (3)
>
> $x + 2y = 11$
>
> $5x + 0 = 25$ (3) − (2)
>
> $x = 5$
>
> $3 \times 5 + y = 18$
>
> $y = 3$
>
> $5 + 2 \times 3 = 11$ ✓
>
> Solution is $x = 5$ and $y = 3$
>
> > First write the equations one under the other and label them (1) and (2).
> > Adding or subtracting will not eliminate either x or y.
>
> > Multiply equation (1) by 2 so that it has the same y-coefficient as equation (2).
>
> > Subtract one equation from the other.
>
> > Substitute $x = 5$ into equation (1).
>
> > Check that $x = 5$ and $y = 3$ work in equation (2).

Discussion Does it matter whether you eliminate x or y first?

3 **Reasoning** Aasif wants to solve this pair of simultaneous equations.

$$7x + y = 53 \qquad (1)$$
$$x + 2y = 28 \qquad (2)$$

  a What could he multiply equation (1) by?

  b What could he multiply equation (2) by?

  c Use your answer to part **a** or part **b** to solve the equations.

4 Solve these pairs of simultaneous equations.

  a $3x + y = 25$
  $x + 5y = 27$

  b $4x - y = 3$
  $x + 2y = 21$

  c $x - 6y = -28$
  $5x - y = 5$

  d $x - 2y = 6$
  $11x + y = 89$

5 **Real / Modelling** Two different groups watch a cricket match.

  Group 1: 5 adults and 1 child pay $117.

  Group 2: 1 adult and 3 children pay $43.

  a Write an equation that models group 1.

  b Write an equation that models group 2.

  c Solve the simultaneous equations to work out the cost for

   i 1 adult

   ii 1 child.

6 **Real / Modelling** At a theme park, Ryu goes on two fairground rides:
  the big dipper once and the dodgems 5 times. This costs him $10.50.
  Jin goes on the big dipper 7 times and the dodgems once. She pays
  $22.50.
  Work out the cost for one ride on

  a the big dipper

  b the dodgems.

7 **Real / Modelling** A job is divided up into day shifts and night shifts.
  The job will take 62 hours in total.
  Workers can choose between two plans.

  Plan A: 9 day shifts and 1 night shift.

  Plan B: 1 day shift and 7 night shifts.

  Both plans have exactly the right amount of time for the job.

  How long is

  a a day shift

  b a night shift?

8 Solve these pairs of simultaneous equations.

  a $5x + y = 15$
  $3x + 4y = 26$

  b $3x - y = 18$
  $4x + 2y = 44$

  c $5x - 3y = -6$
  $x + 2y = 17$

  d $9x + 2y = 31$
  $4x - 4y = -40$

9 **Real / Modelling** Two branches of the same company have the same pay structure. Managers are paid $x annually and staff are paid $y annually.

Branch A has 3 managers and 19 staff.
Their total annual wages come to $513 500.

Branch B has 1 manager and 5 staff.
Their total annual wages come to $142 500.

Work out the annual wage of a manager and a staff member.

10 **Real / Modelling** Jeff is on an exercise plan.
On day 1, he runs for 30 minutes and then cycles for 20 minutes.
He burns 390 calories.
On day 2, he runs for 40 minutes and then cycles for 10 minutes.
He burns 420 calories.
How many calories does Jeff burn by
a running for 1 minute
b cycling for 1 minute?

11 **Finance** Mohana and Amit both own shares in the same two companies.
Mohana owns 7 shares in company A and 16 shares in company B.
The value of her investment is $106.77.
Amit owns 21 shares in company A and 12 shares in company B.
The value of his investment is $118.35.
What is the value of 1 share in company A and 1 share in company B?

12 **Explore** In what year will the population of India equal the population of China?
Is it easier to explore this question now that you have completed the lesson?
What further information do you need to be able to answer this?

13 **Reflect** In this lesson you have solved lots of simultaneous equations from word problems.
What did you find most difficult about these questions?
What did you find easiest?
Write yourself a hint to help you with this sort of problem in the future.

10.6 Graphs and simultaneous equations

You will learn to:

• Solve simultaneous equations by drawing graphs.

best solution

Why learn this?
Businesses use graphs of equations to find the best solution.

Fluency
$y = x^2 - 6x$
Find y when

• $x = 8$
• $x = 2$
• $x = 6$
• $x = \frac{1}{2}$

Explore
How can you throw two balls across a park and make sure they collide?

Exercise 10.6

1 a Copy and complete the table of values for $y = x^2$.

x	−2	−1	0	1	2
y					

b Draw the graph of $y = x^2$ from $x = -2$ to 2.

2 Solve each quadratic equation.

a $x^2 + 6x + 8 = 0$ **b** $x^2 - 3x - 18 = 0$

3 a Plot the graphs of $x - 3y = 4$ and $2x + y = 15$.

    b Write down the coordinates of the **point of intersection**.

> **Key point**
>
> The point where two (or more) lines cross is called the **point of intersection**.

Investigation

Problem-solving

1 Solve this pair of simultaneous equations using algebra.

$2x - y = 7$
$x + 2y = 11$

2 Plot the two lines on a coordinate grid.

3 Write down the coordinates of the point of intersection.

Discussion What do you notice about your answers to parts **1** and **3**?

4 Repeat steps **1**–**3** with these equations.

$4x - y = 5$
$6x + y = 15$

5 Graph this pair of equations.

$3x - 5y = 12$
$3x - 5y = 6$

Discussion What do you notice about the graphs in part **5**?

> **Key point**
>
> You can find the solution to a pair of simultaneous equations by
> • drawing the lines on a coordinate grid
> • finding the point of intersection.

4 Draw graphs to solve these pairs of simultaneous equations.

   a $4x - y = 12$

      $x + y = 8$

   b $2x + y = 14$

      $3x - y = 11$

Q4 hint

You could use a graph-plotting package.

5 **Real / Problem-solving** Suhal buys a total of 24 books from a charity shop. Hardbacks cost £2 and paperbacks cost £1.50. He spends £43.50.

   Let x represent the number of hardbacks.

   Let y represent the number of paperbacks.

   a $x + y = \square$

   b $2x + 1.5\square = \square$

   c On the same set of axes, draw graphs of the equations in parts **a** and **b.**

   d How many of each book does Suhal buy?

6 **Real / Modelling** Two families visit a theme park.

   The entrance costs are:

   Family A: 3 adults and 2 children cost £46.

   Family B: 2 adults and 5 children cost £54.50.

   a Write down two equations to model these situations.

   b Draw a graph to model the simultaneous equations in part **a.**

   c Write down the cost of an adult ticket and the cost of a child ticket.

   Discussion How accurate are your answers?

7 **Real / Problem-solving / Modelling** 20-second advert slots on television cost $\$x$ and 30-second slots cost $\$y$.

   During a commercial break, five 20-second adverts and one 30-second advert cost \$16 500. Two 20-second adverts and three 30-second adverts cost \$17 000.

   a Draw a graph to model these situations.

   b Work out the cost of one 20-second advert and one 30-second advert.

8 **Real / Problem-solving / Modelling** At a barbecue, in the afternoon 15 burgers and 12 drinks are sold for a total of £84.

   In the evening 56 burgers and 48 drinks are sold for a total of £320.

   a Draw a graph to model this situation.

   b Estimate the cost of 1 burger and 1 drink.

9 Here is a graph of two equations.

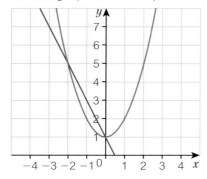

   Solve the equations simultaneously.

Topic links: Straight-line graphs

10 For each pair of equations

  i $y = -3x + 5$ and $y = x^2 + 7$
  ii $y = 2x + 2$ and $y = x^2 - 1$

  a plot their graphs

  b write down the coordinates of the point of intersection.

  Discussion What are the solutions to $x^2 + 7 = -3x + 5$?

Q10 hint

First make a table of values from $x = -5$ to $x = 5$.

11 Work out the point of intersection algebraically.

  a $y = x^2 - 6$ and $y = 5x$

  b $y = x^2 - 5$ and $y = -4x$

  c $y = x^2$ and $y = 2x + 8$

  d $y = x^2 - 8$ and $y = 2x$

Q11a hint

$y = x^2 - 6$ and $y = 2x$
They both equal y so they equal each other.
$x^2 - 6 = 2x$

12 **Reasoning** Adam is trying to solve this pair of simultaneous equations:
$2y - 6x = 2$ and $y - 3x = 8$
Draw graphs to show why there are no solutions.

13 **Problem-solving / Reasoning** This is the graph of $y = x^2 + 2$.

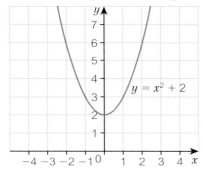

  a Write down the equation of a line that will never intersect $y = x^2 + 2$.

  b Show algebraically that the two graphs will not cross.

14 **Explore** How can you throw two balls across a park and make sure they collide?
Is it easier to explore this question now that you have completed the lesson?
What further information do you need to be able to answer this?

15 **Reflect** In this unit you have solved simultaneous equations using algebra and using graphs. Which do prefer? Why?
Compare your preferences with those of your classmates.

Explore

Reflect

10 Check up

Quadratic graphs

1 a Copy and complete this table of values for $y = x^2 - 4$.

x	−3	−2	−1	0	1	2	3
y							

b Plot the graph of $y = x^2 - 4$.

2 The diagram shows the graph of $y = 2x^2 - 5$.

a Describe the symmetry of the graph.

b Write the coordinates of the turning point. Is it a maximum or a minimum?

Simultaneous equations

3 Solve these equations.

$5x + y = 72$
$y = 3x$

4 On a trip to an ice-skating rink, Wafiza buys 1 adult ticket and 5 child tickets. This costs her $31.50. Adult tickets are twice the price of child tickets.

a Write two equations. Use y for price of adult tickets and x for price of child tickets.

b Work out the cost of

  i 1 adult ticket

  ii 1 child ticket.

5 The sum of two numbers is 21 and their difference is 7. Let x and y represent the numbers.

a Write down two equations to model this situation.

b Solve the equations to find the values of x and y.

6 Solve these equations simultaneously.

$7x + y = 22$ $x + y = 4$

7 Solve these equations simultaneously.

$8x + y = 42$ $x + 5y = 15$

Straight-line graphs

8 a Rearrange each equation in the form $y = mx + c$.

b Write the gradient and the y-intercept.

  i $y - 3x = -7$

  ii $3x + 2y = 6$

  iii $3y + \frac{1}{2}x = 5$

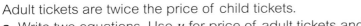

9 Decide whether each pair of lines is parallel.

a $y = 2x - 5$ and $2y = 4x + 9$

b $-x = 8 + 2y$ and $5x - 3y = 7$

c $y = -3x + 6$ and $y = \frac{1}{3}x - 2$

10 Draw graphs to solve these simultaneous equations.

$4x + y = 8$ $\qquad x - y = 2$

11 Work out the equation of the line joining points A(2, 9) and B(6, 1).

12 Match each equation to one of the graphs.

i $y = -2x + 5$

ii $y = 2x - 2$

iii $y = 4x + 5$

iv $y = 2x + 5$

A
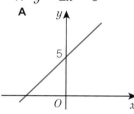

B
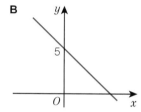

C
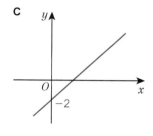

D
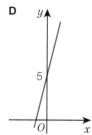

13 Write the equation of the line parallel to $y = -2x + 5$ with y-intercept (0, 3).

14 How sure are you of your answers? Were you mostly

😦 Just guessing 😐 Feeling doubtful 🙂 Confident

What next? Use your results to decide whether to strengthen or extend your learning.

Challenge

15 a Copy and complete the table of values for the quadratic function $y = (x - 3)^2$.

x	0	1	2	3	4	5	6	7	8
y	9								

b Plot the graph of $y = (x - 3)^2$.

c What are the coordinates of the turning point?

d Find the coordinates of the turning point for each quadratic function.

i $y = (x - 1)^2$

ii $y = (x + 6)^2$

e Write a quadratic function whose graph has a turning point at

i (5, 0)

ii (-2, 0).

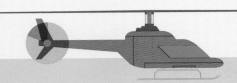

10 Strengthen

You will:
- Strengthen your understanding with practice.

Quadratic graphs

1 a Copy and complete this table of values for the function $y = 3x^2$.

x	−4	−3	−2	−1	0	1	2	3	4
x^2	16								
$y = 3x^2$	48								

b Copy each pair of coordinates and use your table to complete them.
(−4, 48), (−3, ☐), (−2, ☐)

c Draw these axes on graph paper and plot the graph of the function $y = 3x^2$.

d What are the coordinates of the turning point of the graph?

e Is the turning point a minimum or maximum point?

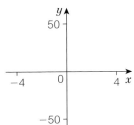

Q1 hint

x	−4
x^2	−4 × −4 = 16
$y = 3x^2$	3 × 16 = 48

Q1d hint

The turning point of the graph is the lowest point.

(☐, ☐)

2 a Use your table in Q1 to complete this table of values for the function $y = -3x^2$.

x	−4	−3	−2	−1	0	1	2	3	4
$3x^2$	48								
$y = -3x^2$	−48								

b Plot the graph of $y = -3x^2$ on the same axes as in Q1.

c What are the coordinates of the turning point of the graph?

d What transformation maps the graph of $y = 3x^2$ to the graph of $y = -3x^2$?

Q2b hint

Use your table to write down pairs of coordinates on the graph of the function $y = -3x^2$.

Q2d hint

Could you
- reflect it
- rotate it about a point
- translate it?

3 The diagram shows the graphs of the functions
  i $y = x^2$ **ii** $y = 2x^2$ **ii** $y = 4x^2$

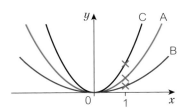

The point where $x = 1$ has been marked on each graph.
a For each function, work out the value of y when $x = 1$.
b Use your answers to match each function to its graph, A, B or C.

4 a **Reasoning** Copy and complete this table of values for the function $y = x^2 + 5$.

x	−4	−3	−2	−1	0	1	2	3	4
x^2	16								
$y = x^2 + 5$	21								

b Copy the axes in Q1. Plot the points and join them with a smooth curve. Label your graph $y = x^2 + 5$.

c **i** What are the coordinates of the minimum point?
   ii How can you tell the coordinates of the minimum point by looking at the function $y = x^2 + 5$?

d What are the coordinates of the minimum points of
   i $y = x^2 + 10$ **ii** $y = x^2 + 15$ **iii** $y = x^2 - 10$?

e Plot the graphs of each function in part **d** on your axes.

f Copy and complete this sentence to describe how you can transform $y = x^2 + 10$ into the graph of $y = x^2 + 15$:
   Translate $y = x^2 + 10$ _____ _____ units.

g Describe the transformation that maps
   i the graph of $y = x^2 + 5$ to the graph of $y = x^2 + 15$
   ii the graph of $y = x^2 + 5$ to the graph of $y = x^2 - 10$.

Q4f hint

Compare the two graphs. Does the graph move up or down? By how many units?

5 a Plot the graph of the function $y = 3x^2 + 10$ for $x = -4$ to 4.

b **i** What are the coordinates of the minimum point of the graph?
   ii How can you tell the coordinates by looking at the function?

c What would be the coordinates of the minimum point of the graphs of **i** $y = 3x^2 + 15$ **ii** $y = 3x^2 - 10$?

Q5a hint

Use a table of values to find some points to plot. Draw a pair of axes on graph paper that reach the largest and smallest values of y.

6 Match each function to its graph.

i $\boxed{y = x^2}$

ii $\boxed{y = 3x^2 + 10}$

iii $\boxed{y = -3x^2}$

iv $\boxed{y = x^2 + 5}$

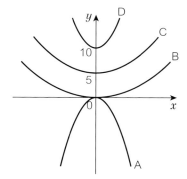

Q6 Strategy hint

Look at the graphs you have already drawn.

Height of arrow

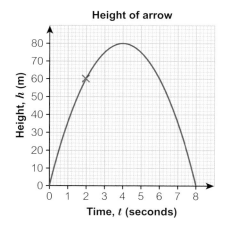

7 **STEM / Reasoning** The graph shows the height, h m, of an arrow t seconds after it was thrown.
The height, h, can be found using the formula
   $h = 40t - 5t^2$.

a **i** What are the coordinates of the maximum point of the graph?
   ii What can you say about the arrow at this point?

b How long was the arrow in the air?

c The point marked with a cross shows when the arrow was 60 m high.
   i Use the graph to read the value of t when $h = 60$.
   ii Check that $h = 60$ and your value of t satisfy the equation $h = 40t - 5t^2$.

d Use your graph to find the other solution of the equation in part **c**.

Q7c ii hint

Substitute your values into the equation.

8 a Copy and complete the table of values for the function $y = x^2 + x - 2$.

x	−4	−3	−2	−1	0	1	2	3	4
x^2	16								
$y = x^2 + x - 2$	10								

b Plot the graph of $y = x^2 + x - 2$.

c Copy and complete this sentence:
The graph crosses the x-axis at $x =$ ___ and $x =$ ___

d Factorise the quadratic expression $x^2 + x - 2$.

e What do you notice about your answers to parts **c** and **d**?

Q8d hint

$x^2 + x - 2 = (x + \square)(x - \square)$

Simultaneous equations

1 Find the values of x and y that satisfy these pairs of equations.

a $4x + y = 24$
  $y = 2x$

b $2x + y = 30$
  $y = 4x$

c $x + 7y = 66$
  $\frac{1}{4}x = y$

d $x + 4y = 18$
  $\frac{1}{4}x = y$

Q1a hint

$4x + y = 24$
$y = 2x$ so $4x + 2x = 24$

Q1c hint

$\frac{1}{4}x = y$, so $x = \square$

 2 Real / Modelling On a trip to the cinema, Yuto buys 1 adult ticket and 5 child tickets. This costs him \$28. Adult tickets cost 3 times as much as child tickets.

a Write an equation that shows what Yuto paid.

b Write an equation that shows the relationship between adult and child tickets.

c Use your equations to find the cost of 1 adult and 1 child ticket.

Q2a hint

Choose two letters to represent the cost of each ticket.

3 Real / Modelling On a trip to the zoo, a group spends \$99 on 3 adult tickets and 5 child tickets.
Adult tickets are twice the price of child tickets.
What is the price of 1 adult ticket and 1 child ticket?

4 $8x + y = 49$ and $3x - y = 6$

a Add the two equations together.

b What happens to the value of y? Explain.

c Solve your equation to work out x.

d Using the value of x, find the value of y.

Q4a hint

$8x + y = 49$
$+ 3x - y = 6$

5 Find the values of x and y that satisfy these pairs of equations.

a $6x + y = 34$ and $4x - y = 16$ **b** $5x + y = 44$ and $3x - y = 12$

Q5 hint

Use the same strategy as in Q4. Remember to add all the like terms together.

6 Modelling Two numbers have a sum of 46 and a difference of 20.

a Write two equations to model this situation.

b Solve the simultaneous equations to work out the two numbers.

Q6 hint

$x + y = \square$
$x - y = \square$

7 $5x + 2y = 58$ and $3x + 2y = 42$ are a pair of simultaneous equations.

a Subtract one equation from the other.

b What happens to the value of y? Explain.

c Solve your equation to work out x.

d Using the value of x, find the value of y.

Q7a hint

$5x + 2y = 58$
$- 3x + 2y = 42$

8 Solve these pairs of simultaneous equations.

a $6x + y = 13$ and $4x + y = 9$ **b** $x + 3y = 8$ and $x + 9y = 20$

9 Solve these pairs of simultaneous equations.
   a $4x + y = 28$ and $2x − y = 2$ **b** $2x + y = 2$ and $y = −3x$
   c $7x + y = 36$ and $2x + y = 11$

10 A plumber charges a flat fee x plus an hourly rate y.
   She charges \$101 for 2 hours and \$193 for 6 hours.
   Work out her flat fee and her hourly rate.

11 This is a pair of simultaneous equations.
   $5x + y = 21$ $x + 4y = 8$
   a Multiply all the terms in the first equation by 4.
      Then subtract one equation from the other and solve.
   b Solve the pair of simultaneous equations again. This time multiply
      all the terms in the second equation by 5. Then subtract one
      equation from the other and solve.

12 Solve these pairs of simultaneous equations.
   a $6x + y = 28$ **b** $5x − y = 4$ **c** $3x + y = 15$
      $x + 3y = 33$ $x + 3y = 4$ $x − 2y = −9$

13 **Real / Problem-solving** Six crates and 5 boxes weigh 38.5 kg.
   Four crates and 1 box weigh 20.3 kg.
   What is the weight of 1 crate and the weight of 1 box?

Straight-line graphs

1 Write each equation in the form $y = mx + c$.
   a $y − 4x = 5$ **b** $y − 3x = 7$ **c** $−2x + y = 9$

2 **a** Write each equation in the form $y = mx + c$.
      i $2y − 6x = 8$ **ii** $2y + 7x = 5$
      iii $7y + 2x = 5$ **iv** $3y − 5x = 7$
      v $\frac{1}{2}y − 2x = 3$
   b Write down the gradient and the y-intercept for each equation.

3 A graph has equation $3x − 4y = 12$.
   a What is the value of x when $y = 0$?
   b Copy and complete: The graph crosses the x-axis at ($\square$, 0).
   c What is the value of y when $x = 0$?
   d Copy and complete: The graph crosses the y-axis at (0, $\square$).
   e Draw suitable axes and plot the points in parts **b** and **d**.
   f Draw the graph of $3x − 4y = 12$.

4 **a** Draw the graph of $y = x + 2$.
   b On the same axes, draw the graph of $y = 5$.
   c Where the two graphs cross, label this the 'point of intersection'.
   d Write down the coordinates of the point of intersection.

5 Draw graphs to solve these simultaneous equations.
   a $y = 2x + 1$ **b** $y = x − 4$ **c** $2x − 3y = 6$
      $x = 3$ $x + y = 2$ $x + y = 8$

6 Which of these lines are parallel?
   A $2x + 3y = 10$
   B $y = 2x + 3$
   C $2x + y = −6$
   D $3y = 6x + 18$

Q9 hint

For each pair of equations, which is
the best method? The method used
in Q1, Q4 or Q7?

Q10 hint

$x + \square y = 101$
$x + \square y = 193$

Q16 hint

Which is the better method? Adding
or subtracting the equations?

Q17 hint

First construct a pair of simultaneous
equations.

Q1 hint

Rearrange each equation to make
y the subject.

Q2b hint

In the form $y = mx + c$, m is the
gradient and c is the y-intercept.

Q3a hint

When $y = 0$, $3x − 4 × 0 = 12$.
So, $3x = 12$, $x = \square$.

Q4a hint

Follow the method in Q2.

Q5 hint

Plot each pair of graphs on the same
coordinate grid.
Then write down the coordinates of
their point of intersection.

7 a Problem-solving Sort these equations of lines into two sets: one set with y-intercept $(0, 1)$ and the other set with y-intercept $(0, -1)$.
   A $y = \frac{1}{2}x + 1$ **B** $y = 2x - 1$ **C** $y = 2x + 1$ **D** $y = -x - 1$

Q7b hint

$-x = -1 \times x$

b For each equation write the gradient and its direction: ╱ or ╲

c Match each graph to an equation from part **a**.

i   ii 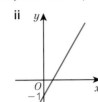   iii 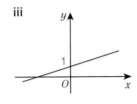   iv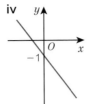

8 A fairground charges an entrance fee and then a fee per ride.
   Esha goes on 18 rides and pays a total of $15.10.
   Nasima goes on 7 rides and pays a total of $10.15.
   What is the entrance fee and what is the fee per ride?

Q11 hint

Write $15.10 as 1510 cents.

9 Mustafa finds the equation of the line joining points $(1, 3)$ and $(7, 15)$.
   a Copy and complete:
   At $(1, 3)$, $x = \square$ and $y = \square$.
      Substitute into $y = mx + c$
            $\square = \square m + c$ (1)
   b Write another equation using the point $(7, 15)$.
   Label the equation (2).
   c Solve the equations simultaneously to work out m and c.
   d Write the equation of the line.

10 Work out the equation of the line joining
   a $(4, 9)$ and $(6, 17)$ **b** $(3, 10)$, and $(6, 1)$.

Q13 hint

Substitute each pair of coordinates into $y = mx + c$.

11 Real / Problem-solving 17 units of electricity cost $8.06 and 23 units of electricity cost $9.14
   Find a linear equation that connects the cost C and the number of units u of electricity.

Q14 hint

Two points on the line would be $(17, \$8.06)$ and $(23, \$9.14)$.
Write $8.06 and $9.14 in pence.

Enrichment

1 a Write three pairs of simultaneous equations with solutions $x = 3$ and $y = 4$.
   Solve them to check that you are correct.
   b Sketch each pair of simultaneous equations on the same axes.

2 Reflect Copy and complete these sentences about these Strengthen lessons.
   I found questions ....easiest. They were on...................
   (list the topics).
   I found questions ....the most difficult. I still need help
   with .... (list the topics).

Reflect

10 Extend

You will:
* Extend your understanding with problem-solving.

 1 The approximate area, A cm², of a circle with radius r cm is given by the formula $A = 3.14r^2$.

a Copy and complete the table of values.

Radius, r (cm)	0	2	4	6	8	10
Area, A (cm²)						

b Use graph paper to plot the graph of $A = 3.14r^2$.

c Use your graph to estimate
   i the area of a circle with radius 7 cm
   ii the radius of a circle with area 100 cm².

2 Real / Problem-solving The length, s ft, of a car skid mark can be estimated using the formula $s = 0.05v^2$, where v mph is the speed of the car when the brakes are applied.

a Make a table of values for $v = 0$ to 60.

b Use graph paper to plot the graph of $s = 0.05v^2$.

c A car driver saw a deer in the road and skidded to a stop. The skid mark was 95 ft long. Estimate the speed of the car when the brakes were applied.

d It takes approximately 1.4 seconds for a driver to react before braking.
   i Estimate the distance the car travelled before the driver applied the brakes in part **c**.
   ii Estimate the distance the car travelled from the time the driver saw the deer.

> **Q2d i hint**
> Convert the speed in miles per hour to feet per second.

3 Find the values of x and y that satisfy these pairs of equations.

a $8x + y = -24$
   $y = -2x$

b $4x - y = -20$
   $y = -x$

> **Q3b Strategy hint**
> Substitute a few values of x into each equation.

> **Q3 hint**
> Be careful when multiplying and dividing with positives and negatives.

4 Work out the equation of the line joining the points $(-7, -4)$ and $(-3, -18)$.

5 Look at this pair of equations.
   $2x + 2y = 20$ (1)
   $5x + 3y = 44$ (2)

a Explain why $x + y = 10$.

b What is the value of $3x + 3y$?

c Use your answer to part **b** to work out the value of $2x$.

d Find the values of x and y that satisfy the pair of equations.

e Use a similar method to solve
   $3x + 3y = 36$ and $2x + 5y = 27$

6 **Real / Modelling** A camp site charges for entrance and then for each night of camping.
The Walter family paid £343 for 9 nights of camping.
The Ali family paid £235 for 6 nights of camping.
Let x represent the entrance fee and y represent the cost per night.
   a Write down an equation to model the Walter family's charge.
   b Write down an equation to model the Ali family's charge.
   c Work out the cost of one night.
   d Work out the entrance fee.

7 a Describe the transformation that maps the graph of $y = x^2$ onto the graph of $y = x^2 + 10$.
   b Describe the transformation that maps the graph of $y = x^2$ onto the graph of $y = -x^2$.
   c Describe the transformation that maps the graph of
      i $y = 2x^2$ onto the graph of $y = 2x^2 - 5$
      ii $y = x^2 + 10$ onto the graph of $y = -x^2 - 10$.

Q7 hint

Use the correct term for the transformations (reflection, rotation, translation or enlargement) and give accurate descriptions.

Q7c hint

Use a graph-plotting package to check your answers.

8 **Problem-solving** The diagram shows a window y m wide and x m high.

The ratio of height to width of a window is $x : 1$,
where x is the positive solution to the equation
$x^2 - x - 1 = 0$.
   a Plot a table of values for $y = x^2 - x - 1$, for x values
      0, 0.5, 1, 1.5, 2, 2.5, 3.
   b Use your answers to plot the graph of $y = x^2 - x - 1$.
   c A window has a height of 2 m. Work out its width.

9 **Problem-solving** Taan catapulted a toy paratrooper from the top of a cliff.
The height, h m, of the toy above sea level after t seconds is given by the formula $h = 25t - 5t^2 + 50$.
   a Make a table of values for $t = 0$ to 8.
   b Plot the graph of h against t.
   c Use your graph to estimate
      i the maximum height of the toy
      ii the time it took to reach the ground.

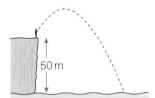

50 m

Q10 Strategy hint

Write an expression for the length of the rectangle.

10 **Problem-solving** The perimeter of this rectangle is 20 cm.

x Perimeter = 20 cm

   a Find a formula for the area A of the rectangle in terms of x.
   b Plot the graph of A for $x = 0$ to 10.
   c Use your graph to estimate
      i the maximum possible area of the rectangle
      ii the dimensions of the rectangle when the area is 15 cm^2.

11 STEM / Problem-solving The diagram shows a lamp with a parabolic mirror.

The bulb is placed at the focal point of the parabolic mirror so that the rays of light leaving the lamp are parallel.

a Draw the mirror by plotting the quadratic function
$y = 0.1x^2 + 2.5$ between $x = -8$ and 8.

b The mirror is 16 cm wide. Work out the depth of the mirror.

c The distance of the focal point, F, from any point, P, on the parabola is the same as the y-coordinate of P.

   i Mark any point P on your parabola.

   ii Find the y-coordinate of P.

   iii Use compasses to mark the position of the focal point F.

   iv How far is the bulb from the bottom of the lamp?

d A ray of light from the bulb bounces off the mirror at the point $Q(x, y)$. Work out the distance the light travels from the bulb to the glass.

12 Solve these pairs of simultaneous equations.

  a $7x - 2y = 22$
     $3x + y = 15$

  b $5x + y = 12$
     $11x - 3y = 16$

13 For this pair of simultaneous equations
    $5x + 4y = 91$ (1)
    $4x - 3y = 48$ (2)

  a solve the equations using method A

  b solve the equations using method B.

  Discussion Which method did you prefer? Why?

Method A
• (1) × 4. Label it (3)
• (2) × 5. Label it (4)
• (3) − (4)

Method B
• (1) × 3. Label it (5)
• (2) × 4. Label it (6)
• (5) + (6)

14 Find the values of x and y that satisfy these pairs of equations.

  a $4x - 3y = 18$
     $3x + 7y = 32$

  b $2x + 3y = 37$
     $5x - 2y = 7$

  c $8x - 3y = 3$
     $5x + 2y = 29$

  d $3x + 5y = -20$
     $2x - 3y = 12$

15 Real / Modelling 3 adults and 2 children attend an exhibition and pay $70.

5 adults and 3 children attend the same exhibition and pay $113.50.

  a Write two equations to model this situation.

  b Solve the equations to find the price of an adult ticket and the price of a child ticket.

  c A family of 2 adults and 5 children go to the same exhbition. How much do they pay?

16 Real / Modelling One week Grace uses her mobile phone to send 17 text messages and make 8 minutes of calls. This costs her $2.07. The next week she sends 28 text messages and makes 24 minutes of calls. This costs her $4.60.

How much does the phone company charge for each text message and each minute of calling?

Q16 hint

First, convert the money from pounds to pence.

17 **Real / Modelling** At a school fair, bottles of water cost 60 cents and cans of fizzy drink cost 80 cents. Sansan sells 45 drinks altogether and makes a total of $31.80.
   a Write down an equation to model the number of drinks sold.
   b Write down an equation to model the total money taken.
   c Draw the graphs on suitable axes.
   d How many bottles of water and how many cans of fizzy drink did Sansan sell?

18 On the same axes draw the graphs of
   a $2y + 3x = 12$ and $4y + 6x = 24$
   b $2x + 5y = 10$ and $2x + 5y = 20$
   Discussion What do you notice about these lines? How many solutions are there to each pair of simultaneous equations? What happens when algebra is used to solve the simultaneous equations?

Key point

Simultaneous equations can have **no solutions**, **one solution** or **infinitely many solutions**.

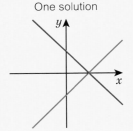
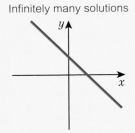

19 **Reasoning** Use algebra to decide whether these pairs of equations have **no solution**, **one solution** or **infinitely many solutions**. If possible, find the values of x and y that satisfy these pairs of equations.
   a $x - y = 3$
     $3x - y = -5$
   b $5x + y = 13$
     $5x - y = 7$
   c $4x + 5y = 20$
     $8x + 10y = 40$
   d $2x - 6y = 4$
     $3x - 9y = 2$
   e $5x + 3y = -9$
     $2x - 4y = 12$

20 **Problem-solving** Use simultaneous equations to work out the values of x and y.
   a
   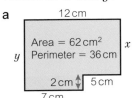
   b
   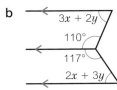

Q20 hint

Use the information to form a pair of simultaneous equations.
Then solve the equations to find x and y.

21 For each of the following questions
   a write down a pair of simultaneous equations that models the situation
   b solve the equations to find the value of each number.
      i The sum of two numbers is 65. One number is 4 times the value of the other number.
      ii Two numbers have a sum of 8 and a difference of 20.
      iii Two numbers have a sum of 51. One of the numbers is 19 more than the other.

22 **Finance** The difference in value between share A and share B is $27.
   Share A increases threefold and share B increases twofold.
   The difference in value is now $119.
   Work out the value of share A and share B.

23 Solve these simultaneous equations using substitution.
   a $3x + y = 14$
      $y = x + 2$
   b $6x - y = 26$
      $y = x + 2$
   c $3y + 2x = 49$
      $x = y + 7$

Q23a hint

Replace the y term in the first equation with $x + 2$.
You are substituting $x + 2$ for y.

24 The sketch shows the graph of $y = x^2 - 8x + 7$.

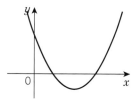

   a Factorise $x^2 - 8x + 7$.
   b Write down the points where the graph crosses the x-axis.

Investigation   Reasoning

1 Show that when $x = 5$ and $y = 0$, $x^2 + y^2 = 25$.
2 Show that when $x = -4$ and $y = 3$, $x^2 + y^2 = 25$.
3 Write down some other pairs of coordinates where $x^2 + y^2 = 25$.
4 Plot the points on coordinate axes and draw the graph of $x^2 + y^2 = 25$.
5 Copy and complete: The graph is a ☐ with a ☐ of 5 and a ☐ at (0, 0).
6 Pick a point within the line. At this point is $x^2 + y^2 < 25$ or is $x^2 + y^2 > 25$?

25 **Reflect** Copy and complete this sentence in at least three different ways:
   'When I am given a mathematics problem to solve, this is what I do …'
   Compare your sentences with those of your classmates.

Reflect

10 Unit test

1 a Copy and complete this table of values for the function
   $y = 2x^2 + 5$.

x	−3	−2	−1	0	1	2	3
y							

   b Plot the graph of $y = 2x^2 + 5$.

2 Write these equations in the form $y = mx + c$.

   a $y - 2x = 11$ b $y + \frac{1}{2}x = 7$

3 For each equation write
   a the gradient   b the y-intercept.
      i $y = 3x + 7$ ii $y = \frac{1}{4}x - 1$

4 Find the values of x and y that satisfy these pairs of equations.
   a $9x + y = 48$ b $x + 5y = 35$
       $y = 3x$ $x = 2y$

5 The sum of two numbers is 9. One of the numbers is 5 times the other.
   Work out the value of both numbers.

6 Draw graphs to solve this pair of simultaneous equations.
   $y = 3x + 2$ $y = 6x - 1$

7 Find the values of x and y that satisfy these pairs of equations.
   a $3x + y = 40$ b $7x + 3y = 63$
       $x - y = 8$ $8x - 3y = 27$

8 Work out the equation of the line joining points (4, 6) and (8, 18).

9 a Write each of these equations in the form $y = mx + c$.
      i $3y = 2x + 9$ ii $4y - 10x = 24$ iii $3y - 2x = 18$
   b Which lines have the same gradient?
   c Which lines have the same y-intercept?

10 The diagram shows the graph of $y = -x^2 + 10$.
   a Describe the symmetry of the graph.
   b What are the coordinates of the turning point?
   c Is it a maximum or a minimum?

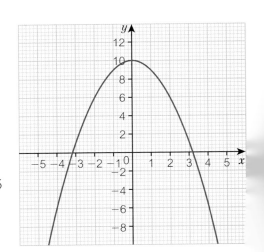

11 Which of these equations
   A $y = 3x - 5$ **B** $2y - 4x = 5$ **C** $3y + 2x = -4$ **D** $y = 2x + 5$
   a gives the steepest graph
   b is a line that passes through (0, 5)
   c are lines that pass through (1, −2)?

12 Find the values of x and y that satisfy these pairs of equations.
   a $x + 7y = 66$ b $6x + 5y = 47$
       $x + 4y = 39$ $2x + 5y = 39$

13 A fairground charges for entrance and then for each ride.
Sabir went on 14 rides and spent a total of $36.
Chika went on 5 rides and spent a total of $22.50.
Let x represent the cost per ride and y represent the entrance fee.
a Write an equation for Sabir.
b Write an equation for Chika.
c Find the values of x and y that satisfy these pairs of equations.

14 Find the values of x and y that satisfy these pairs of equations.
a $4x + y = 41$ **b** $6x - y = 11$
   $x + 6y = 39$ $x + 2y = 17$

15 A shop sells bouncy balls and yo-yos. The bouncy balls cost 40 cents each and
the yo-yos cost 50 cents each.
Asha bought 80 items from the shop. She spent $33.50.
Let x represent the number of bouncy balls and y represent the number of yo-yos.
a Write an equation that models the number of items Asha bought.
b Write an equation that models the amount of money, in cents, that Asha spent.
c Plot these equations on a coordinate grid with x and y from 0 to 100.
d Use your graph to work out how many bouncy balls and how many yo-yos
Asha bought.

16 a Draw the graphs of $y = x^2 - 4$ and $y = -3x$ coordinate axes.
b Write down the coordinates of the points of intersection.

Challenge

17 Each of these points lies on one of the graphs. Match each point with its graph.
$(-2, 2)$ $(-1, 2)$ $(2, 4)$ $(2, 1)$ $(1, -2)$ $(-1, -1)$

A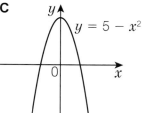
$y = x^2 - 3$

B
$y = (x - 1)^2 - 5$

C
$y = 5 - x^2$

D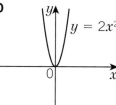
$y = 2x^2$

E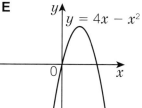
$y = 4x - x^2$

F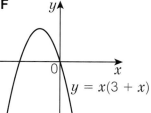
$y = x(3 + x)$

18 Reflect Look back at the questions you answered in this test.
Which one are you most confident that you have answered correctly? What
makes you feel confident?
Which one are you least confident that you have answered correctly? Why?
Discuss the question you feel least confident about with a classmate or your
teacher. How does discussing it make you feel?

11.1 The tangent ratio

Confidence

You will learn to:
- Use conventions for naming sides of a right-angled triangle.
- Work out the tangent of any angle.
- Use the tangent ratio to work out an unknown side of a right-angled triangle.

Why learn this?
Trigonometry is used by engineers to build bridges.

Fluency
In each right-angled triangle, which side is the hypotenuse?

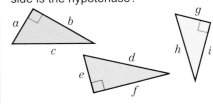

Explore
How does an architect use trigonometry to design the roof of a building?

Exercise 11.1

Warm up

1 Round these numbers to 1 decimal place.
   a 4.56　　　　　　　　　**b** 7.04
   c 8.476　　　　　　　　**d** 0.465

 2 Use your calculator to write each fraction as a decimal.
   Give your answers to 1 decimal place.
   a $\frac{4}{2}$　　　**b** $\frac{2}{11}$　　　**c** $\frac{2}{2}$　　　**d** $\frac{4}{13}$

3 Rearrange each formula to make P the subject.
   a $10 = \frac{P}{2}$　　　　　　**b** $2 = \frac{P}{3}$
   c $3 = \frac{P}{T}$　　　　　　　**d** $2 = \frac{4}{P}$

4 In each triangle, which side is
   a the **hypotenuse**
   b the **opposite** side to angle θ
   c the **adjacent** side to angle θ?

   i 　ii 　iii 　iv 　v

Key point

The side opposite the chosen angle (angle θ in this diagram) is called the **opposite** side. The side next to θ is called the **adjacent** side.

Investigation

1 Draw these triangles accurately using a ruler and protractor.

a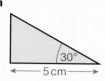

b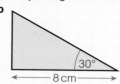

c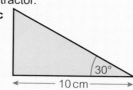

2 Explain why all the triangles are similar.

3 Label the opposite side to 30° 'opp' and the adjacent side to 30° 'adj'.

4 Measure the opposite sides and the adjacent sides.

5 Copy and complete this table.

Triangle	Opposite length	Adjacent length	$\dfrac{\text{opposite}}{\text{adjacent}}$ (1 d.p.)
a			
b			
c			

6 a What patterns do you notice in your table?

  b What do you think will happen for other right-angled triangles with an angle of 30°?

  c Test your hypothesis by drawing some more right-angled triangles with an angle of 30°.

7 Repeat with an angle of 50° instead of 30°.

Discussion What does this tell you about the ratio of the sides of similar triangles?

5 Use your calculator to find these values, correct to 1 d.p.

  a tan 35°   **b** tan 54°   **c** tan 72°

6 Write **tan θ** as a fraction for each triangle.

a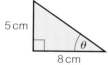

b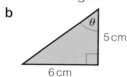

c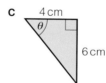

Discussion Use your calculator to find tan 90°.
Draw a diagram to explain why this happens.

Key point

The ratio of the opposite side to the adjacent side is called the **tangent** of the angle.

The tangent of angle θ is written as **tan θ**.

$$\tan\theta = \frac{\text{opposite}}{\text{adjacent}}$$

Worked example

Use the **tangent** ratio to work out the value of x, correct to 1 d.p.

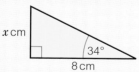

$\tan\theta = \dfrac{\text{opposite}}{\text{adjacent}}$ — Write the tangent ratio.

opposite $= x$
adjacent $= 8$ — Identify the opposite and adjacent sides.

$\theta = 34°$

$\tan 34° = \dfrac{x}{8}$ — Substitute the sides and angle into the equation.

$8 \times \tan 34° = x$ — Rearrange to make x the subject.
Use your calculator to work out $8 \times \tan 34°$.

$x = 5.4\,\text{cm}$ (to 1 d.p.)

7 Work out the value of x, correct to 1 d.p.

a

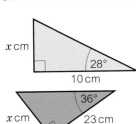

b

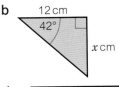

c

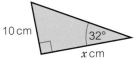

d

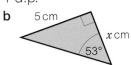

8 Work out the value of x, correct to 1 d.p.

a

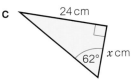

b

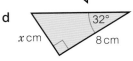

c

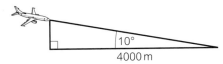

d

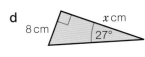

Q8a hint

$\tan \theta = \dfrac{\text{opp}}{\text{adj}}$

$\tan 32° = \dfrac{10}{x}$

Rearrange the formula to make x the subject.

9 Real / Modelling An aircraft is landing.
Its descent makes an angle of 10° with the ground and its horizontal distance from landing is 4000 m.
Calculate the vertical height of the aircraft above the ground.

10 Problem-solving Calculate the height of this isosceles triangle.

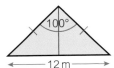

11 Explore How does an architect use trigonometry to design the roof of a building?
Is it easier to explore this question now that you have completed the lesson? What further information do you need to be able to answer this?

12 Reflect Look back at the questions in this lesson.
Which other areas of mathematics do you need to use when working with tangents?

11.2 The sine ratio

You will learn to:
- Work out the sine of any angle.
- Use the sine ratio to work out an unknown side of a right-angled triangle.

Why learn this?
Trigonometry is used in cartography – the making of maps.

Fluency
Write these fractions as decimals.
Round each number to 1 d.p.
- $\frac{5}{12}$
- $\frac{4}{11}$
- $\frac{3}{7}$
- $\frac{9}{17}$

Explore
How can you measure the height of a kite above the ground?

Exercise 11.2

1 Copy these triangles.
Label the hypotenuse and the sides opposite and adjacent to angle θ.

2 Rearrange each formula to make H the subject.

a $5 = \frac{H}{3}$ **b** $9 = \frac{H}{2}$ **c** $6 = \frac{3}{H}$ **d** $3 = \frac{9}{H}$

Investigation

Reasoning

1 Draw these triangles accurately using a ruler and protractor.

  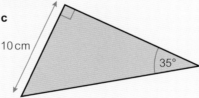

2 Label the hypotenuse of each triangle.
3 Label the opposite side to 35° 'opp' and the adjacent side to 35° 'adj'.
4 Measure the opposite side and the hypotenuse of each triangle.
5 Copy and complete this table.

Triangle	Opposite length	Hypotenuse length	$\frac{\text{opposite}}{\text{hypotenuse}}$ (1 d.p.)
a			
b			
c			

6 a What patterns do you notice in your table?
   b What do you think will happen for other right-angled triangles with an angle of 35°?
   c Test your hypothesis by drawing some more right-angled triangles with an angle of 35°.
7 Repeat with an angle of 70° rather than 35°.
Discussion What does this tell you about the ratio of the sides of similar triangles?

3 Use your calculator to find these values, correct to 1 d.p.

   a sin 43°   **b** sin 84°   **c** sin 17°

4 Write **sin θ** as a fraction for each triangle.

   a 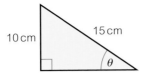   **b**   **c**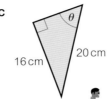

Q3a hint

On your calculator, enter

Key point

The ratio of the opposite side to the hypotenuse is called the **sine** of the angle.
The sine of angle θ is written as **sin θ**.

$$\sin \theta = \frac{\text{opposite}}{\text{hypotenuse}}$$

Worked example

Use the **sine** ratio to work out x, correct to 1 d.p.

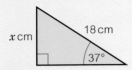

$\sin \theta = \dfrac{\text{opposite}}{\text{hypotenuse}}$ ——— Write the sine ratio.

opposite $= x$ ——— Identify the opposite side and the hypotenuse.

hypotenuse $= 18$

$\theta = 37°$

$\sin 37° = \dfrac{x}{18}$ ——— Substitute the sides and angle into the equation.

$18 \times \sin 37° = x$ ——— Rearrange to make x the subject.
                       Use your calculator to work out $18 \times \sin 37°$.

$x = 10.8$ cm (to 1 d.p.)

---

5 Work out the value of x, correct to 1 d.p.

   a 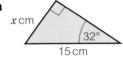   **b**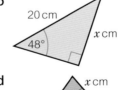

   c   **d**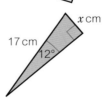

6 Work out the value of x, correct to 1 d.p.

   a 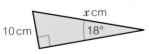   **b**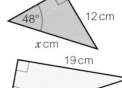

   c   **d**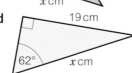

Q6a hint

$\sin \theta = \dfrac{\text{opp}}{\text{hyp}}$

$\sin 18° = \dfrac{10}{x}$

Rearrange the formula to make x the subject.

7 Real / Modelling A skateboard ramp is 50 cm long and makes an angle of 35° with the ground.
Calculate the height of the ramp.

8 Real / Modelling A ladder 6 m long is leaning against a wall.
The angle between the ladder and the ground is 72°.
What height above the ground does the ladder reach?

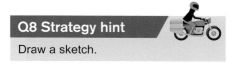

Q8 Strategy hint

Draw a sketch.

9 Problem-solving Work out the perimeter of this right-angled triangle.

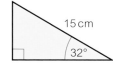

10 Problem-solving / Reasoning For each triangle
  i decide whether you need to use the tangent or the sine ratio
  ii work out the value of y.

a 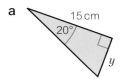   **b** 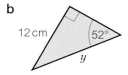   **c**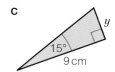

11 Explore How can you measure the height of a kite above the ground?
Is it easier to explore this question now that you have completed the lesson? What further information do you need to be able to answer this?

12 Reflect The hint for Q8 suggested drawing a sketch.
Did the sketch help you?
Explain how.

Explore

Reflect

11.3 The cosine ratio

You will learn to:
- Work out the cosine of any angle.
- Use the cosine ratio to work out an unknown side in a right-angled triangle.

Confidence

Why learn this?
Trigonometry is used by astronomers to find the distance from the Earth to stars.

Fluency
In each right-angled triangle, identify the hypotenuse and the sides adjacent and opposite to the angle θ.

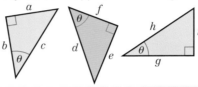

Explore
How can you use the cosine ratio to design a ramp for a skateboard?

Exercise 11.3

Warm up

1 For this triangle, write the fraction
   a $\tan \theta$
   b $\sin \theta$

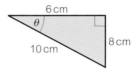

2 Rearrange each formula to make T the subject.

   a $2 = \dfrac{T}{9}$ **b** $3 = \dfrac{T}{4}$ **c** $7 = \dfrac{2}{T}$ **d** $2 = \dfrac{5}{T}$

Investigation

Reasoning

1 Look at the triangles you drew in the Investigation in lesson 11.2.
2 Copy and complete this table.

Triangle	Adjacent length	Hypotenuse length	$\dfrac{\text{adjacent}}{\text{hypotenuse}}$ (1 d.p.)
a			
b			
c			

3 What patterns do you notice in your table?
4 Repeat for the triangles with a 40° angle.
Discussion What does this tell you about the ratio of the sides of similar triangles?

3 Use your calculator to find these values, correct to 1 d.p.
   a $\cos 53°$ **b** $\cos 62°$ **c** $\cos 46°$ **d** $\cos 19°$

4 Write **cos θ** as a fraction for each triangle.

   a
   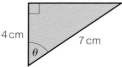

   b
   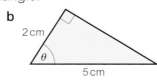

Key point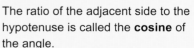

The ratio of the adjacent side to the hypotenuse is called the **cosine** of the angle.
The cosine of angle θ is written as **cos θ**.
$$\cos \theta = \frac{\text{adjacent}}{\text{hypotenuse}}$$

Worked example

Use the **cosine** ratio to work out x, correct to 1 d.p.

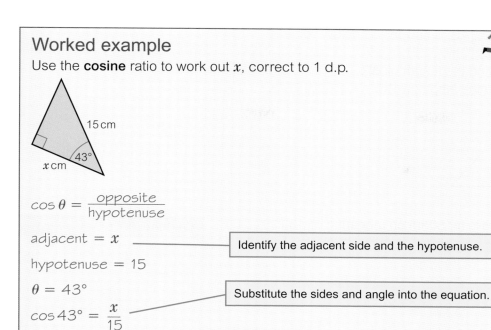

$$\cos \theta = \frac{\text{opposite}}{\text{hypotenuse}}$$

$\text{adjacent} = x$ ———— Identify the adjacent side and the hypotenuse.

$\text{hypotenuse} = 15$

$\theta = 43°$ ———— Substitute the sides and angle into the equation.

$\cos 43° = \dfrac{x}{15}$

$15 \times \cos 43° = x$ ———— Rearrange to make x the subject.
Use your calculator to work out $15 \times \cos 43°$.

$x = 11.0 \text{ cm (to 1 d.p.)}$

5 Work out the length of side x for each triangle, correct to 1 d.p.

a

x cm 36°
12 cm

b

x cm 24° 24 cm

c
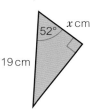
52° x cm
19 cm

d

x cm
68°
6 cm

6 Calculate the length of side x for each triangle, correct to 1 d.p.

a
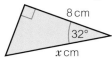
8 cm
32°
x cm

b

x cm 24° 14 m

c
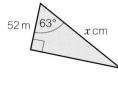
52 m 63°
x cm

> **Q6a hint**
>
> $\cos \theta = \dfrac{\text{adj}}{\text{hyp}}$
>
> $\cos 32° = \dfrac{8}{x}$
>
> Rearrange the formula to make x the subject.

7 **Modelling / Problem-solving** A roof is made from beams that make an isosceles triangle.
The sloping side of the roof is 8 metres.
The roof makes an angle of 30° with the horizontal.
Calculate the width of the roof.

> **Q7 hint**
>
> $\cos \theta = \dfrac{\text{adj}}{\text{hyp}}$ is true only in a right-angled triangle.

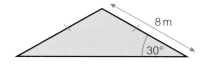
8 m
30°

8 Real / Modelling A flagpole, AB, is supported by two ropes, BD and BC.

   a Use the cosine ratio to find the length of BD.

   b Use the sine ratio to find the length of BC.

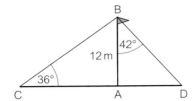

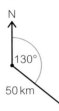

9 Real / Modelling A ship sails for 50 km on a bearing of 130°.

Q9 hint

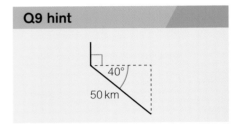

How far east has it travelled?

10 Problem-solving For each triangle

   i decide whether you need to use the tangent, sine or cosine ratio

   ii work out the value of p.

a 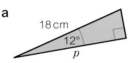   **b** 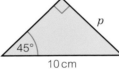   **c**

11 Explore How can you use the cosine ratio to design a ramp for a skateboard?

Is it easier to explore this question now that you have completed the lesson? What further information do you need to be able to answer this?

12 Reflect A mnemonic for remembering sine, cosine and tangent ratios is SOH CAH TOA. Will this help you to remember them? If not, can you think of another memory aid?

11.4 Using trigonometry to find angles

You will learn to:
- Use the trigonometric ratios to work out an unknown angle in a right-angled triangle.

Why learn this?
Trigonometry is used by aeroplane pilots to find the angle of descent when landing.

Fluency
What is the inverse of
- +3
- ×4
- ÷5
- −7
- $x^3 + 1$?

Explore
How do pilots use trigonometry to find the angle of descent?

Exercise 11.4

 1 For this triangle, find
  a $\sin \theta$
  b $\cos \theta$
  c $\tan \theta$

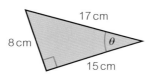

 2 a Use the sine ratio to work out the value of x.

  b Use the cosine ratio to work out the value of y.

  c Use the tangent ratio to work out the value of s.

Investigation

Problem-solving / Reasoning

In this triangle, $\tan \theta = \frac{4}{5}$.

1 Write down possible values for a and b.
2 Make an accurate drawing of the triangle using these values.
3 Measure the angle θ to the nearest degree.
4 Draw two more triangles where $\tan \theta = \frac{4}{5}$, and use them to measure θ.

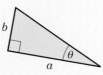

Warm up

Worked example

Use the sine ratio to find the missing angle in this right-angled triangle.

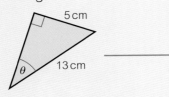

Label the sides.

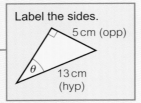

5 cm (opp)

13 cm (hyp)

Using the sine ratio

$$\sin \theta = \frac{opposite}{hypotenuse}$$

$$\sin \theta = \frac{5}{13}$$

$$\theta = 22.6°$$

You need to find $\sin^{-1} \frac{5}{13}$
Use these buttons on your calculator:

SHIFT sin 5 ÷ 1 3 =

3 Use the $\cos^{-1}$ function on your calculator to find θ.

a $\cos \theta = \frac{3}{10}$ **b** $\cos \theta = \frac{3}{7}$ **c** $\cos \theta = 0.42$

4 Use the $\sin^{-1}$ function on your calculator to find θ.

a $\sin \theta = \frac{7}{10}$ **b** $\sin \theta = \frac{3}{4}$ **c** $\sin \theta = 0.12$

5 Use the $\tan^{-1}$ function on your calculator to find θ.

a $\tan \theta = \frac{1}{2}$ **b** $\tan \theta = \frac{5}{8}$ **c** $\tan \theta = 0.8$

6 a Use the sine ratio to work out the missing angles.

i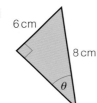
6 cm
8 cm
θ

ii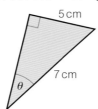
5 cm
7 cm
θ

b Use the cosine ratio to work out the missing angles.

i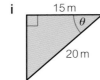
15 m
θ
20 m

ii
4 m
θ
6 m

Q6b hint

Follow the same method as in the worked example but use the cosine ratio.

c Use the tangent ratio to find the missing angles.

i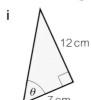
12 cm
θ
7 cm

ii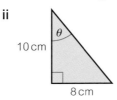
θ
10 cm
8 cm

7 Work out the missing angle in each right-angled triangle.

a
4 cm
10 cm θ

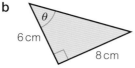
b
θ
6 cm
8 cm

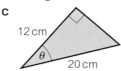
c
12 cm
θ
20 cm

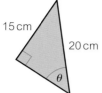
d
15 cm
20 cm
θ

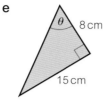
e
θ 8 cm
15 cm

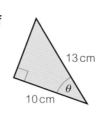
f
13 cm
θ
10 cm

8 **Real / Problem-solving** Jamie builds a skate ramp with 2 metres of wood.
He wants the vertical height of the ramp to be 1 metre.
What angle does the wood need to make with the ground?

Q8 hint

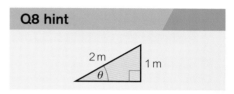
2 m
1 m
θ

9 **Real / Problem-solving** A ship sails 30 km north and 50 km east.
On what bearing has it travelled?

Q9 hint

Write the bearing using three figures.

10 **Problem-solving / Reasoning** Ellie draws this triangle.

Not to scale
θ

She works out that tan θ = 1.
What kind of triangle has Ellie drawn? Explain.

11 **Explore** How do pilots use trigonometry to find the angle of descent?
Is it easier to explore this question now that you have completed the lesson? What further information do you need to be able to answer this?

12 **Reflect** The inverse of sine is expressed as $\sin^{-1}$.
Think about where you have met the notation $^{-1}$ before.
Did it mean the same thing in that situation?

Explore

Reflect

11.5 Solving problems using trigonometry

You will learn to:
• Use trigonometry to solve problems involving missing lengths and angles.

Why learn this?
Oceanography is the study of the ocean. Scientists use trigonometry to calculate the intensity and height of tides in the ocean.

Fluency
Calculate
• cos 56°
• sin⁻¹ $\frac{3}{4}$
• tan⁻¹ 0.3
Round each answer to 1 d.p.

Explore
How can you use trigonometry to calculate the height of a tree?

Confidence

Exercise 11.5

Warm up

1 Work out the length of the missing side of these triangles.

a
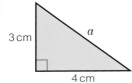
3 cm · a · 4 cm

b
6 cm · 6 cm · b

c
7 m · c · 5 m

d
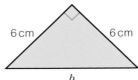
d · 15 mm · 10 mm

2 Work out the value of y.

a
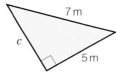
y cm · 21 cm · 48°

b
y cm · 56° · 14 cm

c
18 cm · 51° · y cm

3 Choose the correct trigonometric ratio and work out x.

a
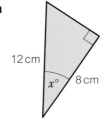
12 cm · $x°$ · 8 cm

b
9 cm · $x°$ · 18 cm

c
20 cm · 27 cm · $x°$

4 Real / Problem-solving A plane flies for 120 km on a bearing of 070°.

N

70° 120 km

a How far east has the plane travelled?
b How far north has it travelled?

5 Real / Problem-solving Fernando is flying a kite.
The string of the kite makes an angle of 25° with the horizontal.
The horizontal distance between Fernando and the kite is 30 metres.
Work out the length of the string of the kite.

Q5 Strategy hint
Sketch a diagram to help.

6 Problem-solving Work out the area of this isosceles triangle.

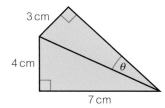

7 cm

37°

Q6 hint
You need to find the height of the triangle first.

7 cm

37°

7 Problem-solving Calculate the size of angle θ in this diagram.

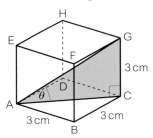

3 cm

4 cm

θ

7 cm

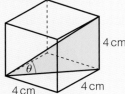

8 Problem-solving Work out the angle between AG and AC.

H
E
G
F
3 cm
θ
D
C
A
3 cm
3 cm
B

Investigation

Reasoning

1 Draw a cube with side length 4 cm.
2 Work out the angle marked θ.
3 Compare your answer with Q8.
4 Repeat for different sized cubes.
5 What do you notice?
6 Explain.

4 cm
θ
4 cm   4 cm

9 Explore How can you use trigonometry to calculate the height of a tree?
Is it easier to explore this question now that you have completed the lesson? What further information do you need to be able to answer this?

10 Reflect Look again at the work you have done in this lesson.
List all the different mathematical skills you have used.

Explore

Reflect

11 Check up

Unknown sides

1 What is

  a the opposite side to angle θ

  b the adjacent side to angle θ

  c the hypotenuse?

2 Write each of these as a fraction.

  a $\sin\theta$

  b $\cos\theta$

  c $\tan\theta$

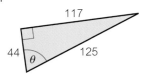

3 Work out the value of x for each right-angled triangle.
The trigonometric function that you need to use is given.

a

sine

b

cosine

c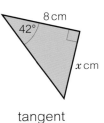

tangent

4 Work out the value of y for each right-angled triangle.
You need to decide which function to use.

a

b

c

Unknown angles

5 Work out the value of θ for each right-angled triangle.
The trigonometric function that you need to use is given.

a

tangent

b

sine

c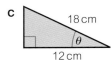

cosine

6 Work out the size of angle θ in each triangle.

a

8 cm
5 cm

b 2 cm

7 cm

Solving problems

7 The length of the diagonal in this rectangle is 12 cm.
The diagonal makes an angle of 28° with the horizontal.
  a Calculate the height of the rectangle.
  b Calculate the width of the rectangle.

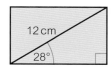

12 cm
28°

8 Work out the length of the base of this isosceles triangle.

18 cm
32°

9 A ship sails 20 km north and then 15 km east.
What is the bearing of the ship from its original position?

15 km
20 km

10 **How sure are you of your answers? Were you mostly**
  😟 **Just guessing**   😐 **Feeling doubtful**   🙂 **Confident**
  **What next? Use your results to decide whether to strengthen or
  extend your learning.**

Challenge

11 Draw a square of side 4 cm.

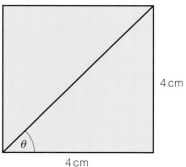

4 cm
4 cm

Draw the diagonal.
Calculate tan θ.
Explain why tan θ = 1 for any square.

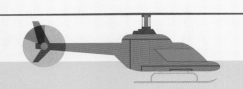

11 Strengthen

You will:
• Strengthen your understanding with practice.

Unknown sides

1 Sketch each triangle and label it with
  a 'opp' on the side opposite to angle θ
  b 'adj' on the adjacent side
  c 'hyp' on the hypotenuse.

  i   **ii**   **iii**

Q1 hint

opposite ⟵ hypotenuse

θ

adjacent

2 For each triangle
  a write the tangent ratio.
  b write the sine ratio
  c write the cosine ratio.

  i 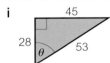   **ii** 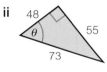   **iii**

Key point

The three trigonometric ratios can be remembered using the phrase **SOH CAH TOA**.

3 Copy and complete to work out x, correct to 1 d.p.

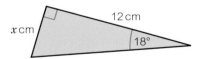

  a Write the tangent ratio.
   $\tan\square = \dfrac{x}{\square}$
  b Rearrange.
   $x = \square \times \tan\square$
  c Use a calculator to work out x.

4 Copy and complete to work out x, correct to 1 d.p.

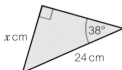

  a Write the sine ratio.
   $\sin\square = \dfrac{x}{\square}$
  b Rearrange.
   $x = \square \times \sin\square$
  c Use a calculator to work out x.

5 Copy and complete to work out x, correct to 1 d.p.

x cm 53° 37 cm

a Write the cosine ratio.

$\cos\square = \dfrac{x}{\square}$

b Rearrange.

$x = \square \times \cos\square$

c Use a calculator to work out x.

6 Follow these steps to work out the value of x.

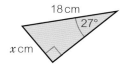

18 cm 27° x cm

Q6 Strategy hint

Sketch the triangle.
Label the sides opp, adj and hyp.
Which ones are you using?

a Choose the trigonometric ratio you are going to use.

b Write the ratio.

c Rearrange to find x.

d Use your calculator to work out the missing side.

7 Work out the length of each side marked with a letter.

a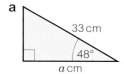

33 cm 48° a cm

b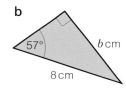

57° b cm 8 cm

c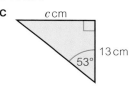

c cm 13 cm 53°

Q7 hint

Follow the same method as in Q6.

Unknown angles

1 Use the $\sin^{-1}$ function on your calculator to work out θ.

a $\sin\theta = \dfrac{2}{5}$

b $\sin\theta = 0.2$

Q1 hint

Rearrange to make θ the subject.
The inverse of sin is $\sin^{-1}$.
$\theta = \sin^{-1} 0.2$

[SHIFT] [sin] [0] [.] [2] [=]

2 Use the $\cos^{-1}$ function on your calculator to work out θ.

a $\cos\theta = \dfrac{3}{8}$

b $\cos\theta = 0.9$

3 Use the $\tan^{-1}$ function on your calculator to work out θ.

a $\tan\theta = \dfrac{3}{5}$

b $\tan\theta = 0.3$

4 Copy and complete to work out the missing angle, correct to 1 d.p.

a Write the tangent ratio.

$\tan\theta = \dfrac{\square}{\square}$

6 7 θ

b Rearrange.

$\theta = \tan^{-1}\dfrac{\square}{\square}$

Q4c hint

Press [SHIFT] [tan]

c Use your calculator to work out θ.

5 Copy and complete to work out the missing angle, correct to 1 d.p.

  a Write the sine ratio.

  $$\sin \theta = \frac{\square}{\square}$$

  b Rearrange.

  $$\theta = \sin^{-1} \frac{\square}{\square}$$

  c Use your calculator to work out θ.

6 Copy and complete to work out the missing angle, correct to 1 d.p.

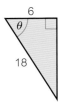

  a Write the cosine ratio.

  $$\cos \theta = \frac{\square}{\square}$$

  b Rearrange.

  $$\theta = \cos^{-1} \frac{\square}{\square}$$

  c Use your calculator to work out θ.

7 Follow these steps to work out the size of angle θ.

  a Copy the triangle and label the sides that you have been given or
    need to find.
  b Choose the trigonometric ratio you are going to use.
  c Write the ratio.
  d Rearrange to make θ the subject.
  e Use your calculator to work out the missing angle.

8 Work out the missing angle in each triangle. You need to decide which
  ratio to use.

Q8 hint

Follow the same method as in Q7.

  a 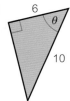   **b**   **c**

Solving problems

1 **Modelling / Problem-solving** A girl is flying her kite and wants to find out how high it is off the ground.

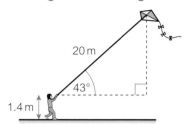

The length of the kite string is 20 m and the angle the string makes with the horizontal is 43°.
The girl is 1.4 metres tall.
a Which trigonometric ratio does she need to use?
b How high is the kite off the ground?

2 **Real / Problem-solving** A ship sails 40 km east and then 60 km north.
What is the bearing of the ship from its original position?

Q2 hint
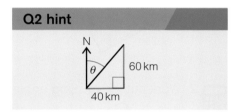

3 **Problem-solving** Work out the height of this isosceles triangle.

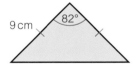

Q3 hint
Split the triangle in half to make a right-angled triangle.

Enrichment

1 **a** Calculate the value of x and y when

   i $\sin x = 0.3$ $\cos y = 0.3$
  ii $\sin x = 0.6$ $\cos y = 0.6$
 iii $\sin x = 0.8$ $\cos y = 0.8$
  v $\sin x = 0.9$ $\cos y = 0.9$
b Write down any patterns that you notice.
  Explain.

2 **Reflect** Look back at some of the questions in this strengthen section. What mathematical skills did you need when solving trigonometry problems?

11 Extend

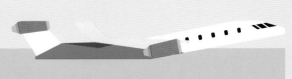

You will:
- Extend your understanding with problem-solving.

1 Work out the length of the sides marked with letters.

a
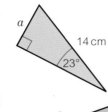
14 cm
23°
a

b
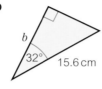
b
32°
15.6 cm

c
9.7 cm
52°
c

d
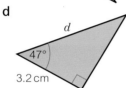
d
47°
3.2 cm

e
8.2 cm
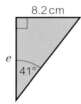
e
41°

f
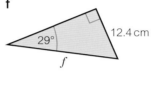
29°
f
12.4 cm

2 Work out the missing angle for each right-angled triangle.

a

7.2
θ
9.6

b
8.5
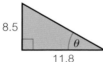
θ
11.8

c
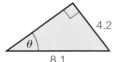
4.2
θ
8.1

3 Real / Problem-solving A children's slide in a park is 5.5 metres long.
It makes an angle of 30° with the ground.

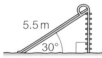
5.5 m
30°

What is the vertical height of the top of the slide?

4 Real / Problem-solving A wheelchair ramp is 2 metres long.
It needs to reach a height of 30 cm.

2 m
30 cm

What angle must the ramp make with the ground?

Q4 hint

You must have all measurements in the same units.

5 Real / Problem-solving A ladder is 6 m long and is leaning against a vertical wall.
In order for it to be safe, the ladder must be placed between 1.8 m and 2.4 m from the base of the wall.
a What is the largest angle the ladder can make with the wall?
b What is the smallest angle the ladder can make with the wall?

6 **Modelling / Problem-solving** A hiker walks 5.4 km north and then turns and walks another 8.9 km east.

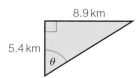

Calculate the hiker's bearing from his original position.

7 **Modelling / Problem-solving** A plane travels 120.2 km east and then 50.7 km north.
Calculate the bearing of the plane from its original position.

Q7 Strategy hint

Sketch a diagram to help.

8 **Modelling / Problem-solving** A ship leaves port and travels on a bearing of 245° for 40.6 km.
a How far west has it travelled?
b How far south has it travelled?

9 **Problem-solving** A right-angled triangle has sides 8 cm, 10 cm and 6 cm. Work out the size of all the angles in the triangle.

10 **Real / Modelling** Peter wants to find the height of a tree.
He is 2 m tall and 12 metres away from the tree.
The angle between his eyeline to the top of the tree and a line parallel to the ground is 64°.
Calculate the height of the tree.

11 **Problem-solving** In this triangle BD is perpendicular to AC.

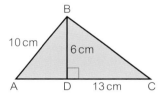

a Calculate the size of angle BCD.
b Calculate the size of angle BAD.
c Using your answers to parts **a** and **b**, calculate the size of angle ABC.

12 **Problem-solving** Work out the size of angle θ.

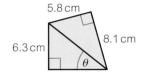

13 In this basketball court the basketball hoop is at the midpoint of AB.

a Work out the distance from D to the basketball hoop.
The hoop is 3.1 m off the ground.
b Work out the angle between D and the top of the hoop.

14 The diagram shows a cube of side length 7 cm.

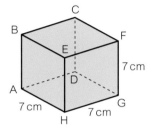

Calculate
a the length AG
b the angle between AG and AF
c the length of the diagonal AF.

15 The diagram shows a square-based pyramid.
The vertex E of the pyramid is directly above the centre of the square base and is 5 cm above the base.

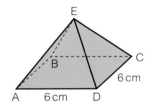

Calculate
a the length AC
b the angle EAC
c the length of AE.

16 **Modelling / Problem-solving** A balloon is hovering (remaining in the air) 100 m above the ground.
The balloon is observed by some people in a car as they look upwards at an angle of 15°.
30 seconds later, the people in the car had to look up at an angle of 70° to see the balloon.
How fast was the car moving?
Give your answer in m/s and km/h.

> **Q15c hint**
>
>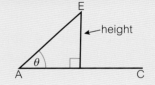

> **Q16 hint**
>
> Calculate the horizontal distances between the balloon and the car to find out how far the car has travelled.
>
>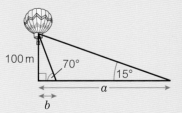
>
> Remember: speed = $\dfrac{\text{distance}}{\text{time}}$

Investigation

Problem-solving

1 Here is an equilateral triangle split into two right-angled triangles.

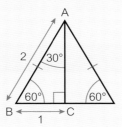

a Work out the length AC. Leave your answer in **surd** form.

b Copy and complete the trigonometric ratios.

i $\sin 30° = \dfrac{\square}{\square}$ **ii** $\sin 60° = \dfrac{\sqrt{\square}}{\square}$ **iii** $\cos 30° = \dfrac{\sqrt{\square}}{\square}$

iv $\cos 60° = \dfrac{\square}{\square}$ **v** $\tan 30° = \dfrac{\square}{\sqrt{\square}}$ **vi** $\tan 60° = \dfrac{\sqrt{\square}}{\square} = \sqrt{\square}$

2 Here is a right-angled triangle.

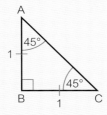

a Find the length of the hypotenuse. Leave your answer in surd form.

b Copy and complete the trigonometric ratios.

i $\sin 45° = \dfrac{\square}{\sqrt{\square}}$ **ii** $\cos 45° = \dfrac{\square}{\sqrt{\square}}$ **iii** $\tan 45° = \square$

 17 A plane travels for 1.5 hours at 120 mph on a bearing of 050°. It turns and continues for another hour at the same speed on a bearing of 140°.
At the end of this time, how far away is the plane from its starting point?

18 Reflect Most of the questions in the Extend section included diagrams. How useful is it to have a diagram? Did you sketch diagrams for the questions that didn't already have them?

> **Key point**
>
> Expressions with square roots like $\sqrt{2}$ are in **surd** form. An answer in surd form is exact.

> **Q17 hint**
>
> Draw a diagram to help.

Reflect

11 Unit test

1 Write these ratios as fractions for this right-angled triangle.
   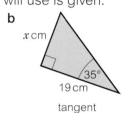
   a sin θ
   b cos θ
   c tan θ

2 Work out the value of x.
   The trigonometric function that you will use is given.

   a
   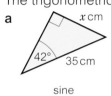
   sine

   b
   x cm
   19 cm 35°
   tangent

3 Work out the value of x. You need to decide which function to use.

   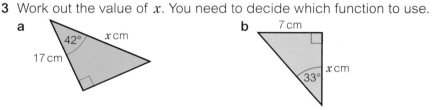
   a   42° x cm   17 cm
   b 7 cm   33° x cm

4 Use cosine to work out the size of angle θ.
   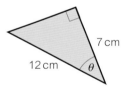
   7 cm
   12 cm θ

5 Find the missing angle for each triangle.
   a
   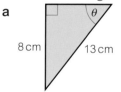
   θ
   8 cm 13 cm
   b
   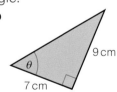
   9 cm
   θ
   7 cm

6 A 5 m ladder leans against a wall at an angle of 56° with the ground.
   How far up the wall does the ladder reach?
   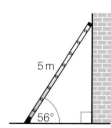
   5 m
   56°

7 A ship sails 30 km north and then 20 km east.
   What is the ship's bearing from its original position?

8 A ramp of length 5 m makes an angle of 40° with the ground. How high is the ramp from the ground?

9 **a** Work out the height of this isosceles triangle.
b Work out the length of the base.
c Work out the area of the triangle.

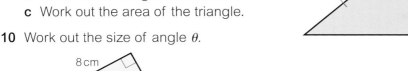

10 Work out the size of angle θ.

11 The diagram shows a circle with centre O and radius 5 cm. Find the length of the chord AB.

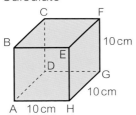

12 The diagram shows a cube with side length 10 cm. Calculate

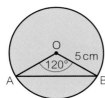

a the length AG
b the angle between AG and AF
c the length of the diagonal AF.

Challenge

13 The square and the isosceles triangle have the same area. Find $\tan \theta$.

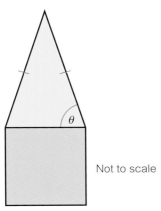

Not to scale

14 **Reflect** Write down five things you need to remember from your work in this unit.

12.1 Set notation and Venn diagrams

You will learn to:

- Use correct set language and notation.
- Sort and compare sets of data using Venn diagrams.

Confidence

Why learn this?
You can use set notation and diagrams to efficiently list groups of numbers and solve probability problems.

Fluency
- List the first four odd numbers.
- List the first six square numbers.

Explore
Why is there only one prime number that is also even?

Warm up

Exercise 12.1

1 From the numbers 1–10, list all the
   a even numbers   b prime numbers   c cube numbers.

2 From the set of numbers 10, 12, 15, 18, 24, 28 list the numbers that are multiples of
   a 4   b 6   c both 4 and 6.

> **Key point**
>
> Curly brackets { } are used to show a set of values.
> $\varnothing$ is the set with no elements, called the empty set.
> $\in$ means `is an element of' or a member of a set. Elements are usually numbers, but could also be letters, subjects or even animals.
> $\notin$ means is not an element of a set.
> ξ means the universal set.

Worked example

Set A is the set of days in the week.
a Write set A using set notation.
b Jamie has written: c Jasmine has written:
   Monday $\in$ A   January $\notin$ A
   Explain what this means.   Explain what this means.
a A = {Monday, Tuesday, Wednesday, Thursday, Friday, Saturday, Sunday}
b Monday $\in$ A means that Monday is a member of the set A.
c January $\notin$ A means that January is not a member of the set A.

> **Key point**
>
> The elements (members) of a set can be written in any order.

3 Set S contains the first five square numbers.
   a Write set S using set notation.
   b Is 36 $\in$ S? Explain your answer.

4 Which of these statements are true?
   a rabbit $\in$ {animals with two legs}   b square $\notin$ {rectangles}
   c 5 $\in$ {odd numbers}   d 8 $\in$ {factors of 35}

5 Which of these are examples of the empty set?
   a The set of days beginning with the letter A.
   b The set which has the common factors of 3 and 5.
   c The set with just the number zero as its only element.

6 **Reasoning** X = {1, 2, 3, 4, 5, 6} and Y = {prime numbers}
   Z is the set of elements that are in both X and Y.
   Write set Z using set notation.

Worked example

A = {3, 6, 9, 12, 15}, B = {4, 8, 12, 16} and ξ = {1, 2, 3, …, 16}
a Draw a Venn diagram to show this information.
b List the numbers in each set.
   i A ∩ B   **ii** A ∪ B   **iii** A'

a

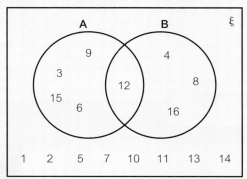

b **i** A ∩ B = {12}

   ii A ∪ B = {3, 4, 6, 8, 9, 12, 15}

   iii A' = {1, 2, 4, 5, 7, 8, 10, 11, 13, 14, 16}

> **Key point**
>
> A Venn diagram shows sets of data in circles inside a rectangle. You write data that is in both sets in the part where the circles overlap.
> A ∩ B represents the elements that are in both A and B.
> A ∪ B represents the elements that are A or B or both.
> A' represents the elements not in A.

7 Use this Venn diagram to complete these sets.
   a M ∩ S = { 4, ☐ }
   b M ∪ S = { 1, 2, ………..}
   c M' = { 1, 3, ………………}
   d S' = {……………………………..}

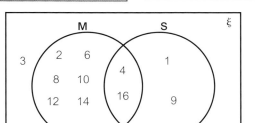

8 ξ = {1, 2, 3, ……………16}
   A = {Odd numbers}
   B = {Prime numbers}
   a Copy and complete the Venn diagram.
   b Write these sets using set notation.
      i A ∪ B   **ii** A ∩ B   **iii** A'

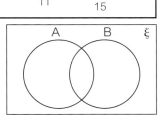

9 Given the sets, A = {1, 2, 3, 4, 5}, B = {6, 7, 8, 9, 10},
   C = {1, 4, 9} and D = {2, 3, 5, 7}
   Write down whether the following statements are true or false.
   a A ∩ B = { } = ∅   **b** A ∩ C = { } = ∅   **c** B ∩ C = ∅   **d** C ∩ D = ∅

10 **Explore** Why is there only one prime number that is also even?
   Is it easier to explore this question now that you have completed the lesson?
   What further information do you need to be able to answer this?

11 Look back at this lesson.
   Was there a question you found difficult? What made it difficult?
   Was there a question you found easy? What made it easy?

12.2 Probability diagrams

Confidence

You will learn to:
- Use correct set language and notation.
- Present the possible outcomes of single events, or two successive. events using lists, tables, Venn diagrams and sample space diagrams.
- Identify mutually exclusive outcomes and events.
- Find the probabilities of mutually exclusive outcomes and events.

Why learn this?
Manufacturers use probability to determine the reliability of a new product.

Fluency
You roll an ordinary fair dice.
What is
- P(5)
- P(even number)
- P(at least 3)?
In 30 rolls, how many 2s would you expect?

Explore
How likely are you to roll a double with two dice?

Exercise 12.2

Warm up

1 For this spinner, what is
  a P(red)   b P(blue)
  c P(red or blue)   d P(red and even)
  e P(blue and odd)?

2 A 5p and 10p coin are flipped at the same time.
  a Make a list of the possible outcomes.
  b How many possible outcomes are there altogether?
  c Work out
    i P(two heads)   ii P(a head or a tail).
  Discussion What assumptions do you need to make to answer part **c**?

> **Q2a hint**
> Organise the outcomes so that you don't miss any. For example:
> 5p 10p
> H H

3 Maria rolls a dice and flips a coin. Copy the **sample space diagram**.

	H	T
1	H, 1	
2		T, 2
3		
4		
5		
6		

> **Key point**
> A **sample space diagram** shows all the possible outcomes of two events.

  a Write in the possible outcomes. How many possible outcomes are there altogether?
  b Work out
    i P(an even number and a tail)
    ii P(3)
    iii P(a number greater than 4 and a head).

> **Q3b ii hint**
> With a head or a tail.

4 In a probability experiment, Khalid spun this fair spinner twice and added the results together.

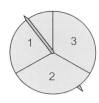

a Copy and complete the sample space diagram.

		First spin		
		1	**2**	**3**
Second spin	**1**	2		
	2			
	3			

b How many possible outcomes are there?

c Which total is most likely?

d Work out the probability that the total is

    i 2   **ii** 4   **iii** an even number   **iv** greater than 3.

e Khalid does 45 trials. How many times would he expect a total of 4?

5 An ordinary 6-sided dice is rolled once. The Venn diagram shows two sets A and B.

A = {square numbers} and

B = {multiples of 3}

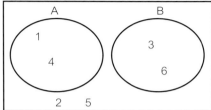

a Explain why the two events are **mutually exclusive**.

b Why are 2 and 5 outside the circles?

c What is P(A)?

d What is P(B)?

e What is P(A ∪ B)?

f True or false: P(A ∪ B) = P(A) + P(B). give reasons for you answer.

6 The Venn diagram shows two events when a 6-sided dice is rolled: square numbers and numbers less than 4.

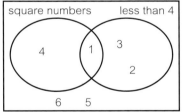

a Explain why the two events are *not* mutually exclusive.

b What is the probability of rolling a square number?

c What is the probability of rolling a number less than 4?

d What is the probability of rolling a square number or a number less than 4?

e True or false: P(rolling a square number or a number less than 4) = P(rolling a square number) + P(rolling a number less than 4). Explain.

Discussion How can you tell from a Venn diagram whether events are mutually exclusive or not?

7 Reasoning An ordinary 6-sided dice is rolled once. The Venn diagram shows three events: square number, prime number and biggest number.

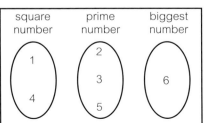

a Explain why the three events are mutually exclusive.

b What is the probability of each event?

c What is the sum of their probabilities?

d Copy and complete the rule:

The sum of the probabilities of all the mutually exclusive outcomes is ☐.

8 These beads from Danielle's broken bracelet were put into a bag.

She took one bead from the bag at random. Which of these pairs of events are mutually exclusive?

a The bead is E. The bead is square.

b The bead is red. The bead is diamond shaped.

c The bead is one of the letters D, I, N. The bead is round.

d The bead is a vowel. The bead is round.

9 In a class of 30 students, 24 study French and 11 study German. 5 students study both French and German.

a Draw a Venn diagram to show this information.

b What is the probability that a student chosen at random is

i studying French only

ii studying German and French

iii studying only one language?

Discussion 24 study French and 11 study German. Why aren't there 35 students in the class?

Q9a hint

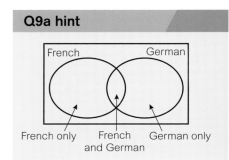

French only   French   German only
             and German

10 Jamilla always hits 5, 20 or 1 with a dart. She throws two darts and adds their scores.

a Draw a sample space diagram to show her possible scores.

b What is the probability that her total score will be

i 40   **ii** 6   **iii** less than 20

iv at least 20?

Q10b hint

Make a table like the one in Q4.

11 A fair coin is flipped three times.

a List the possible outcomes.

b What is the probability of getting

i all heads   **ii** exactly two tails   **iii** at least one head?

12 **Explore** How likely are you to roll a double with two dice? Is it easier to explore this question now that you have completed the lesson? What further information do you need to be able to answer this?

13 **Reflect** How likely is it that you will roll a double score with two dice? Naringa has just rolled a dice and got a 4. She rolls the dice again. Use what you have learned in this lesson to decide whether Naringa is less likely to roll a 4 on the second dice, given that she has already rolled a 4.

Explore

Reflect

12.3 Tree diagrams

You will learn to:
- Use tree diagrams to find the probabilities of two or more events.

Why learn this?
Probability models can help to predict the characteristics of a baby.

Fluency
What is the probability of this spinner landing on
- red
- yellow
- red or yellow
- not red?

Explore
What is the probability that a baby will be born left-handed and colour blind?

Exercise 12.3

1 Work out the probability of each event *not* happening.
   a The probability of a computer hard drive lasting 4 years is $\frac{4}{5}$.
   b There is a 42% chance that a UK marriage will end in divorce.
   c The probability of rain tomorrow is 0.7.

2 Work these out. Give each answer in its simplest form.
   a $\frac{1}{6} + \frac{2}{6}$ b $\frac{1}{12} + \frac{2}{12} + \frac{5}{12}$ c $\frac{1}{4} \times \frac{3}{4}$ d $\frac{7}{10} \times \frac{5}{9}$

Investigation
Reasoning

These three balls are put in a bag and one is taken out at random.
1 Work out P(R), P(Y) and P(B).
Joe takes out two balls, one at a time, like this:
take out a ball at random … put it back in the bag … take out a ball at random.
One possible outcome is R, B. This means that he takes a red ball, then a blue one.

2 Are the two events (take one ball, take the next ball) **independent**?

3 Draw a sample space diagram to show all the possible outcomes for taking two balls, one at a time.

4 Work out   a P(B, B)   b P(B) × P(B)   c What do you notice?

5 Work out   a P(R, Y)   b P(R) × P(Y)

6 Use P(R) and P(B) to work out the probability of P(R, B). Check your answer using your sample space diagram.

7 For a coin, how could you use P(head) to calculate P(head, head)?
   Check your answer, using a sample space diagram.

Discussion What is the rule for finding the probability of two independent events?

3 Which of these pairs of events are independent?
   A flipping a coin, then flipping it again
   B picking a black sock at random from a drawer, putting it on, then picking another black sock
   C rolling a 6 on a dice, then rolling another 6
   D getting 100% in a maths test, then getting 100% in the next maths test

Worked example

These YES/NO cards are shuffled (mixed up) and the top card is turned over.

The cards are shuffled again and the top card is turned over again.

a Draw a **tree diagram** to show the probabilities.

a

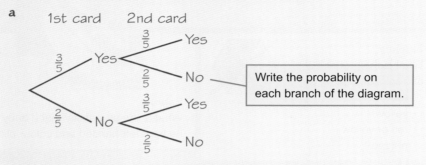

1st card   2nd card

Write the probability on each branch of the diagram.

b What is the probability of two YES cards?

b $\frac{3}{5} \times \frac{3}{5} = \frac{9}{25}$

Go along the branches for YES, YES. The 1st and 2nd cards are independent, so multiply the probabilities.

c What is the probability of one YES and one NO card?

c $\frac{3}{5} \times \frac{2}{5} = \frac{6}{25}$

$\frac{2}{5} \times \frac{3}{5} = \frac{6}{25}$

Go along the branch for YES, NO and NO, YES.

$\frac{6}{25} + \frac{6}{25} = \frac{12}{25}$

Add the probabilities of their outcomes.

4 A fair 6-sided dice is rolled twice. Work out
  a P(6 and 4)
  b P(5 and an even number)
  c P(6 and a number less than 4).

5 **Real / Modelling** A factory makes mugs. The factory owners have found that the probability of a mug being damaged at some point during production is 0.05.
  a What is the probability that a mug is not damaged?
  b Copy and complete this tree diagram to show the possible outcomes of picking two mugs from the production line.
  c Two mugs are picked.
    What is the probability that they are both damaged?
  Discussion How can the factory use this probability model to check that the mugs are being made properly day to day?

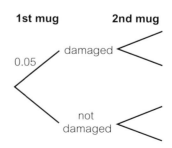

1st mug   2nd mug

0.05   damaged

not damaged

Topic links: Adding and multiplying fractions, decimals, percentages

6 Modelling The probability of being stopped at a set of traffic lights is 0.3.
  a What is the probability of not being stopped?
  b Giana goes through the traffic lights twice a day.
    Draw a tree diagram to show the possible outcomes.
  c What is the probability that Giana will be
    i stopped once   ii not stopped?
Discussion Is this a good model for working out the probabilities for traffic lights?

Q6b hint

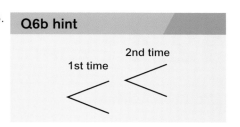

7 Real / Modelling A weather forecaster predicts that the chance of sunshine is 0.7 on Saturday and 0.6 on Sunday.
Draw a tree diagram for the two days, showing the two possible outcomes, 'sunny' and 'not sunny'.
What is the probability that there is sunshine on both days?

8 In a game of SCRABBLE®, these letters are left in the bag.

  a A player removes a letter E from the bag and doesn't replace it.
    What was the probability of picking an E?
  b How many letters are left in the bag?
  c The next player picks a letter from the bag. What is the probability of getting an E this time?
  d Copy and complete the tree diagram.
  e What is the probability that
    i both Es are picked
    ii one E and one I are picked
    iii a vowel is picked?

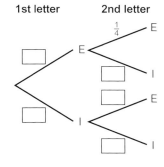

1st letter   2nd letter

Key point

If one event depends upon the outcome of another event, the two events are **dependent** events. For example, removing a red card from a pack of playing cards reduces the chance of choosing another red card. A tree diagram can be used to solve problems involving dependent events.

9 Problem-solving Kim's jewellery box contains 9 pairs of silver earrings and 3 pairs of gold earrings.
She always picks a pair of earrings at random. Once she's worn a pair she does not return the earrings to the box. What is the probability that the second pair of earrings she takes from the box are silver?

10 Explore What is the probability that a baby will be born left-handed and colour blind?
Is it easier to explore this question now that you have completed the lesson? What further information do you need to be able to answer this?

11 Reflect In this unit you have learned vocabulary to describe different types of events.
  a Write a definition, in your own words, for mutually exclusive events and independent events.
  b Write a mutually exclusive event that involves
    i a coin   ii a dice.
  c Describe how mutually exclusive events and independent events are different.
  d Write an independent event. Compare your events with those of others in your class.

Explore

Reflect

12.4 Experimental and theoretical probabilities

You will learn to:
- Compare experimental and theoretical probabilities.
- Compare probabilities.
- Solve problems involving probability.

Why learn this?
Scientists combine the results of repeated experiments to obtain (gain) more accurate probability estimates.

Fluency
1 Four out of one hundred batteries sampled are faulty.
What is the probability that a battery chosen at random is not faulty?
2 A fair dice is rolled once. What is the probability that the score obtained is a multiple of 3?

Explore
How many times would you need to flip a fair coin before you get 10 heads in a row?

Exercise 12.4

1 A fair 12-sided dice numbered 1–12 is rolled once.
What is the probability of getting
a a 7
b more than 6?

2 Work out

a $\frac{1}{6} \times \frac{1}{6}$

b $\frac{5}{12} \times \frac{4}{11}$

3 For which of these can you work out a theoretical probability?
A Getting a 6 when you roll a regular 6-sided dice.
B A bus being late.
C That it will rain tomorrow.

4 Artem flipped two fair coins lots of times. He recorded the results in a frequency table.

Outcome	Frequency
2 heads	46
1 head and 1 tail	101
2 tails	53

a What is the total frequency?
b Find the experimental probability of getting 2 tails.
c State the theoretical probability of getting 2 tails.
d Based on Artem's experiment do you think the coins are fair?
Explain your answer.
Discussion Why is there a difference between your answers to parts
b and **c**?

5 Two fair 6-sided dice are rolled once and the scores are added.
Which is more likely
  a a total of 6 or a total of 10?
  b a total of 2 or a total of 12?
Explain your answer.

6 Two sets of cards are numbered 1–5.
A card is chosen at random from each set and the numbers on them are added.
  a Complete the sample space diagram to show the possible outcomes.

		Set 2				
		1	2	3	4	5
Set 1	1					
	2					
	3					
	4					
	5					

Calculate the probability of
  b choosing a 3 and a 4   **c** getting a total of 7.

7 A box contains 6 blue and 4 green balls.
Two balls are chosen at random without replacement.
What is the probability that the two balls chosen are the same colour?

Investigation   Real / Reasoning

1 Roll two dice and add their scores.
Repeat this at least 50 times.
Record your results in a table like this.

Score			
Tally			
Frequency			

> **Part 1 hint**
>
> What scores are possible? Make sure that you include them all.

2 Which score occurred most often? What is the estimated probability of this score?
3 Which score occurred least often? How many times would you expect to get this score in 200 throws?
4 Combine your results with someone else's. Which is the least frequent score now? What is its estimated probability?
5 Which is most likely, a total score of 2 or 3 or a total score of 7? Use the results of your experiment to explain.
6 Draw a sample space diagram to display the results of rolling two 6-sided dice.
7 Compare the experimental probabilities with the theoretical probabilities in the game.
Discussion Why do you think some total scores are more likely than others?

8 Explore How many times would you need to flip a fair coin before you get 10 heads in a row?
Is it easier to explore this question now that you have completed the lesson?
What further information do you need to be able to answer this?

9 Reflect Look back at this lesson.
Which question did you find the most difficult?
Discuss the question with a classmate.

12 Check up

Set notation and Venn diagrams

1 Set E contains the first five even numbers.
   a Write set E using set notation.
   b Is 2 ∈ E? Explain your answer.

2 Which of these statements are true?
   a spider ∈ {animals with four legs}
   b triangle ∈ {quadrilaterals}
   c 2 ∈ {prime numbers}

3 ξ = {1, 2, 3, 4, 5, 6 ,7 ,8, 9, 10}
   a Copy and complete the Venn diagram.
   Calculate
   b P(prime)
   c P(prime ∪ multiple of 2).

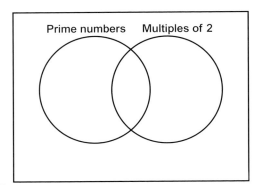

4 34 students play a sport. 24 students play an instrument.
   8 students play sport and an instrument.
   a Draw a Venn diagram to show this information.
   b What is the probability that a student picked at random plays
   an instrument but not a sport?

Probability diagrams

5 The arrow on this fair spinner is spun twice.
   The results are added to get the score.
   a Copy and complete the sample space diagram
   of possible scores.
   b Work out the probability that the score is
      i 3
      ii an even number.
   c Are the two spins independent? Explain.

		1st spin		
		1	2	3
2nd spin	1			
	2			
	3			

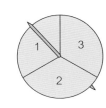

6 The two-way table shows the membership of a tennis club.
   A member of the club is picked at random.
   a What is the probability that this member is
      i female
      ii aged over 50
      iii a male aged under 25
      iv a female aged 25–50?

	Under 25	25–50	Over 50	Total
Male	21	16	5	42
Female	18	13	7	38
Total	39	29	12	80

   b Which type of member is more likely to be picked: a male aged
   25 or over or a female aged under 25?
   c All the female members' names are put into a hat and one is
   picked. What is the probability that the person picked is over 50?

Tree diagrams

7 Lucy has a mobile phone and a landline.
The probability that the next call she receives is to her mobile phone is 0.7.

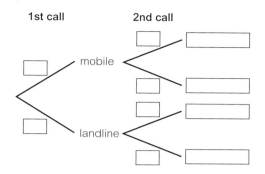

1st call   **2nd call**

mobile

landline

   a What is the probability that the next call is to her landline?
   b Lucy receives two calls. Copy and complete the tree diagram.
   c Work out the probability that
      i both calls were to her mobile phone
     ii only one call was to her mobile phone.

Experimental and theoretical probabilities

8 The theoretical probability of drawing a 4 from a pack of numbered cards is 0.2.
   a Timo thinks there are 16 cards in the pack. Explain why he cannot be correct.
   When he counts them, he finds there are 20 cards in the pack.
   b Timo selects two cards at random without replacement. Calculate the probability that neither is a 4.

9 **How sure are you of your answers? Were you mostly**
   😞 **Just guessing**   😐 **Feeling doubtful**   🙂 **Confident**
   What next? Use your results to decide whether to strengthen or extend your learning.

Challenge

10 a Use the numbers 2 and 3 to fill in the sectors of these two spinners.

    Spinner 1   Spinner 2

   b The two spinners are spun and their results added.
     Make a table to show the totals.
   c Work out the probability of getting a total of 4.
   d Draw a tree diagram to show the results of the two spinners.
   e Use your tree diagram to find the probability of spinning two 3s.

12 Strengthen

You will:
• Strengthen your understanding with practice.

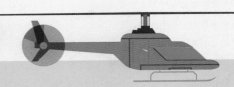

Venn diagrams and mutually exclusive events

1 In an athletics club
   15 members train on Wednesdays
   12 members train on Fridays
   10 members train on Wednesdays and Fridays.
   a Copy the Venn diagram.
      i Write the number for Wednesdays
         and Fridays in the section where
         the circles overlap.
      ii How many people need to go in
          the rest of the Wednesday circle,
          so that the total in the whole Wednesday circle is 15?
      iii How many people train on Fridays?
           Write the number of people in the rest of the Friday circle.
   b How many members are there altogether?
   c What is the probability that a member chosen at random trains on
      i Wednesdays and Fridays   ii Wednesdays only?

2 16 people go to a knitting group.
   13 people go to a sewing group.
   9 people go to a knitting and sewing group.
   a Copy the Venn diagram.
      i Write the number for knitting and
         sewing in the section where the circles overlap.
      ii How many people need to go in the rest of the knitting circle?
      iii How many people need to go in the rest of the sewing circle?
   b What is the probability that a person chosen at random goes to a
      i knitting and sewing group   ii knitting group only?

3 **Reasoning** Here is a set of cards.

1	2	3	4	5	6	7	8	9	10

   Jamie picks one card at random.
   Which of these pairs of events are mutually exclusive?
   A the card has a circle; the card has a 6
   B the card has an odd number; the card has a triangle
   C the card has a square number; the card has a square
   D the card has a factor of 10; the card has a circle

Q1a hint

Q1b hint

Add the numbers from every section.

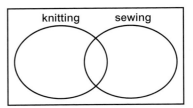

Q2a ii hint

The total in the whole knitting circle needs to be 16.

Q3 hint

If there is a card that fits both descriptions at once, the events are not mutually exclusive.

Topic links: Adding, subtracting, multiplying and comparing fractions, Venn diagrams

Probability diagrams

1 The table shows information about the birth months of Year 8 students.

Birth month					
	Jan–Mar	Apr–June	Jul–Sept	Oct–Dec	Total
Girls	24	16	31	17	88
Boys	18	29	20	25	92
Total	42	45	51	42	180

a How many girls were born in the months October to December?

b What is the probability that a student chosen at random is
  i a girl born in the months October to December?
  ii a boy born in the months April to September?

c A boy is chosen at random. What is the probability that he was born in July, August or September?

d A girl is chosen at random. What is the probability that she was born in the first half of the year?

Q1b i hint

Use your answer to part **a** and the total number of students.

Q1c hint

Use only the values for boys.

2 Adam plays two racing games where he can finish 1st, 2nd or 3rd.

a Copy and complete this sample space diagram to show all the possible outcomes for both races.

b How many possible outcomes are there?

c What is the probability that Adam finishes 2nd in both races?

d Write down the outcomes that give Adam at least one win.

e What is the probability of getting at least one win?

Race 1 (vertical axis): 3rd, 2nd, 1st. Race 2 (horizontal axis): 1st, 2nd, 3rd. Cell at (2nd, 3rd): 2, 3. Cell at (1st, 1st): 1, 1.

Q2b Strategy hint

Look carefully at what each cell in the sample space tells you.

Q2d Strategy hint

'At least one win' means one win or more than one win.

3 Brianne spins these two spinners.

a Draw a sample space diagram to show all the possible outcomes. How many are there?

b Work out the probability of
  i a 3
  ii one number being half the other
  iii both numbers being at least 2.

c Which is more likely: two even numbers or two odd numbers?

d Brianne spins the two spinners and adds the two numbers together. Draw a new sample space diagram to show the scores.

e Which score is most likely?

f What is the probability of scoring at least 4?

Spinner 1: 1, 3, 2, 1, 3, 2. Spinner 2: 2, 2, 6, 4, 6, 4.

Q3a hint

Put spinner 1 on the horizontal axis and spinner 2 on the vertical axis.

Q3d hint

Use the same axes. For the result 1, 2, the score is 1 + 2 = 3.

Tree diagrams

1 The tree diagram shows probabilities of picking red and yellow counters from a bag.
  a Work out the probability of picking two yellow counters.
  b Work out the probability of picking
   i yellow then red (Y, R)
   ii red then yellow (R, Y)
   iii red or yellow in any order.

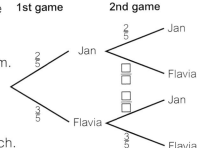

2 Jan and Flavia play draughts.
They play two games. The result of the first game does not affect the result of the second game.
  a Copy and complete the tree diagram.
  b Work out the probability that
   i Jan wins both games
   ii Flavia wins both games
   iii Jan and Flavia win one game each.

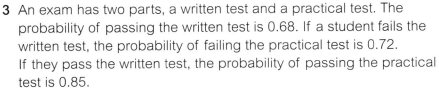

3 An exam has two parts, a written test and a practical test. The probability of passing the written test is 0.68. If a student fails the written test, the probability of failing the practical test is 0.72.
If they pass the written test, the probability of passing the practical test is 0.85.
Yinka takes the exam. What is the probability that he passes only one of the tests?

4 4 red and 2 blue counters are placed inside a bag.
One of the counters is removed from the bag.

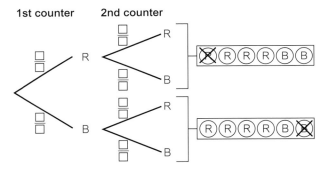

  a What is the probability that the counter is
   i red
   ii blue?
  b The first counter is not replaced.
   How many counters are left in the bag?
  c Copy and complete the tree diagram.
  d Work out the probability that
   i both counters are red
   ii both counters are blue
   iii the counters are different colours.

Q1a hint

Move your finger along the branches for yellow, then yellow. Do you add or multiply the probabilities?

Q1b iii hint

This means (R, Y) or (Y, R). Is the probability of these two outcomes greater than the probability of just one of them? Do you add or multiply?

Q2a hint

The second game results are independent of the first game results. So each pair of branches for the second game is the same as for the first game.

5 The probability that Megan will be late for school is 0.1.
What is the probability that she will be late one day but not the next?

Experimental and theoretical probabilities

1 Abi makes an 8-sided spinner numbered 1–8.
She rolls it 800 times and gets the number 1 a total of 173 times.
  a How many 1s would you expect to get in 800 spins of a fair spinner?
  b Do you think Abi's spinner is fair? Explain your answer.

2 An electrical appliance retailer knows that 5 of every 100 dishwashers she sells will be faulty. She replaces any faulty dishwashers and gives the customer a £25 voucher.
She sells 35 dishwashers per month.
  a What is the total value of the vouchers that she gives to customers every year?
  b If a customer gets two faulty dishwashers, she gives them a free dishwasher.
  How often will she expect to give a customer a free dishwasher.

Enrichment

1 a Sketch five 8-sided fair spinners like this.
  b Fill in the sectors with any numbers between 1 and 8, so that:

Spinner 1 $P(5) = \frac{1}{2}$

Spinner 2 $P(\text{less than } 3) = \frac{1}{4}$

Spinner 3 $P(\text{not a } 6) = \frac{3}{8}$

Spinner 4 $P(2 \text{ or } 7) = \frac{5}{8}$

Spinner 5 $P(\text{at least } 4) = \frac{3}{4}$

2 There are 7 milk chocolates and 8 dark chocolate in a box.
Sunni thinks that the probability of choosing two chocolates of the same type is less than 0.5.
Is he correct? Explain your reasoning.

3 Reflect In these strengthen lessons you have answered probability questions that use
  • Venn diagrams
  • sample space diagrams
  • two-way tables
  • tree diagrams.
Which types of question were easiest? Why?
Which types of question were hardest? Why?
Write down one thing about probability that you think you need more practice on.

12 Extend

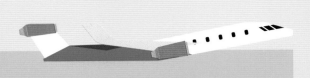

You will:
• Extend your understanding with problem-solving.

1 A is the set of the first 10 square numbers.
  B is the set of the first 5 cube numbers.
  C is the set of the elements in A that are also in B.
  Use set notation to list the elements of
  a A
  b B
  c C.

2 **Problem-solving** Lily spins these two spinners
  and then adds the scores together.
  Is the total score more likely to be over 5
  or under 5?
  Explain how you found your answer.

Spinner 1   **Spinner 2**

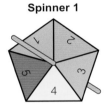 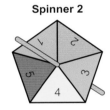

3 **Reasoning** Imagine you roll a 4-sided dice (numbered 1 to 4) and a
  6-sided dice (numbered 1 to 6) and add the scores together.
  Are you more likely to get a score of less than 6, or of 6 or more?
  Explain how you found your answer.

4 **Modelling** A coin and a 4-sided dice are used in an experiment.
  The coin is flipped and the dice is rolled at the same time.
  This is done 200 times. Here are the results of the experiment.

	1	2	3	4
H	26	20	19	27
T	28	25	28	27

  a Calculate the experimental probability of getting a 3 and tails from
    these results. Give your answer as a percentage.
  b Calculate the theoretical probability of getting a 3 and tails.
    Give your answer as a percentage.
  c How many times would you expect to get a 3 and tails from 200
    trials?
  d Do you think that either the coin or the dice were biased?
    Explain your answer.

5 In a class of 50 students, 25 students study French,
  15 students study Spanish and 8 students study both.
  a Copy and complete the Venn diagram.

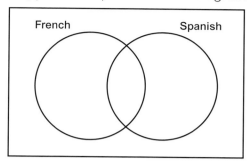

  b What is the probability that a student chosen at random studies
    neither French nor Spanish?

6 Work out the probability of getting three heads when you flip a coin
  three times.

Q6 hint

Are the outcomes independent?

7 The Venn diagram shows people's choice of pepperoni (P), ham (H)
  and mushrooms (M) as pizza toppings in a restaurant.

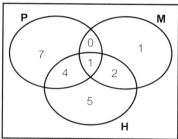

  a How many people had
    i three toppings
    ii only one topping?
  b How many people had pizza?
  c What is the probability that one of these people, picked at
    random, had two toppings?

8 **Problem-solving** A bag contains euro coins and £ coins.
  Bhavna takes out a coin, records it and replaces it.
  She records her results for 100 trials in total.

Number of trials	10	50	80	100
Number of £ coins	4	15	25	34

  a Work out the best estimate of the probability of picking a £ coin
    from the bag.
  b Bhavna weighs the bag and works out that there are 60 coins in it.
    How many are likely to be £ coins?

9 Darnel makes an 8-sided spinner.
The sides are coloured red, green, blue and yellow.
He spins the spinner 1000 times and records his results.

Colour	Red	Green	Blue	Yellow
Frequency	135	487	266	112

Draw a diagram of how the spinner might look.

10 A group of 50 students are interviewed about the
sports they participate in.
All of them participate in at least one of football (F),
rugby (R) or cricket (C).
The results are shown in the Venn diagram.
What is the probability that a student chosen at
random plays all three sports?

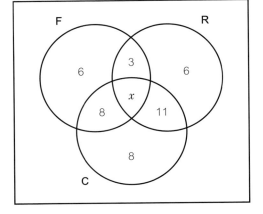

11 The tree diagram shows the probabilities of picking
coloured counters from two bags.
Work out the probability of picking

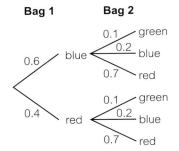

a red then green
b blue then red
c two colours the same.

12 This tree diagram shows the possible outcomes when a 6-sided
dice is rolled three times.

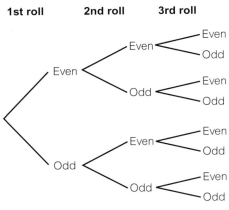

What is the probability of getting an even number
a every time
b in none of the rolls
c in both the first and last rolls
d in at least one of the three rolls?

13 Draw a tree diagram to show the probability of picking a milk, dark or white chocolate at random from this box, eating it, then picking another chocolate at random.

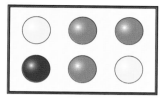

Work out the probability of picking
a two white chocolates
b at least one milk chocolate.

14 Reasoning Umeka placed some red and blue counters in a bag. She drew this tree diagram to show the probabilities of taking two counters from the bag at random, one at a time.

1st pick   2nd pick

$\frac{5}{9}$ Red   Red

$\frac{1}{2}$ Blue

Blue   Red

Blue

a Was the first counter replaced in the bag before the second counter was taken? Explain your answer.
b Copy and complete the tree diagram.

15 Last season, a football club won 20 games, drew 8 games and lost 10 games.
Use a tree diagram to estimate the probability that the club will
a win the next three games
b win two of the next three games.

16 Reflect Write a probability question where the answer is 0.6 for each of these types of probability:
- mutually exclusive events
- independent events
- experimental probability.

Compare your three questions with those of others in your class.

Q15 hint

1st game

win

draw

lose

Q16 hint

Look back at the lessons where you learned about these types of probability. You could use a game or a sports match as the context.

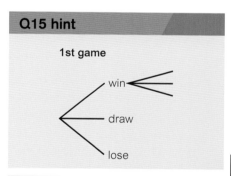

Reflect

12 Unit test

1 A is the set of the first 5 odd numbers.
  B is the set of the first 5 prime numbers.
  C is the set of the elements in A that are not in B.
  Use set notation to list the elements of
  a A
  b B
  c C.

2 In a probability experiment, this spinner was spun twice.
  a List all of the possible outcomes.
  b Work out the probability of each event.
     Event A: The spinner lands on red twice.
     Event B: The spinner lands on the same colour twice.
  c Are the events A and B mutually exclusive? Give a reason for your
     answer.

3 Jayden catches two buses to school.
  The probability that the first one is on time is 0.8.
  The probability that the second one is on time is 0.9.
  Work out the probability that
  a both buses are on time
  b the first one is on time but the second one is not.

4 A street vendor sells burgers and hot dogs.
  Each customer gets a hot or cold drink for free.
  The probability that a customer buys a burger is $\frac{2}{5}$.
  The probability that a customer chooses a hot drink is $\frac{1}{3}$.
  a Copy and complete the tree diagram.

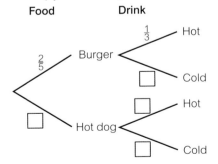

  b Work out the probability that a customer buys
     i a burger and a cold drink
     ii a hot dog and a cold drink.

5 80 students are surveyed about what they have for lunch.
64 have a main course (M), 34 have pudding (P), 28 have both and the rest have neither.

a Copy and complete the Venn diagram.

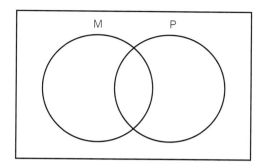

What is the probability that a student chosen at random has

b a main course only

c either a main course only or nothing?

6 The tree diagram shows the probabilities of winning or losing a game.
Work out the probability of

a losing both games   **b** winning at least one game.

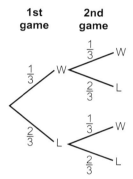

1st game   2nd game

7 Joe throws two darts at a dart board.
The probability that he gets a bull's-eye (centre target) is 0.4 for each throw.

a Draw a tree diagram to show the probabilities.

b Work out the probability that he gets exactly one bull's-eye.

Challenge

8 A pack of cards consists of 30 cards numbered either 1 or 2.
The probability that two cards chosen at random are both numbered 1 is $\frac{38}{87}$.
How many of the cards are numbered 1.
Explain your answer.

9 **Reflect** Look back at the questions you answered in this test.
Which one are you most confident that you have answered correctly?
What makes you feel confident?
Which one are you least confident that you have answered correctly?
What makes you least confident?
Discuss the question you feel least confident about with a classmate.
How does discussing it make you feel?

Q9 hint

Comment on your understanding of the question and your confidence.

Reflect

Index